THE ROMANS
IN SPAIN

217 B.C.— A.D. 117

by

C. H. V. SUTHERLAND

of the Ashmolean Museum, Oxford;
University Lecturer in Numismatics;
Lauréat de l'Institut Français

METHUEN & CO. LTD., LONDON
36 Essex Street, W.C.2

PREFACE

SPAIN was among the oldest, and long remained one of the most valuable, of the Roman provinces, and it is therefore all the more remarkable that English historians have not hitherto set themselves the task of describing the development of Roman Spain in continuous narrative. In the following short and, for the most part, general survey I have attempted to make good the deficiency, being convinced that the time is ripe (if not overdue) for the interpretation and re-exposition of the many profound studies of Roman Spain which have lately been made by scholars in other countries—and particularly by Professor Adolf Schulten and Professor Pedro Bosch Gimpera. To their publications, cited so frequently in the pages which follow, I have been constantly indebted ; and to them my gratitude must be expressed. It was a matter of regret to me that Vol. IV of their invaluable *Fontes Hispaniæ Antiquæ* reached me only after my manuscript had been completed.

The notes to the book, which are occasionally of a full and critical character, have been collected together at the end, thus leaving the main body of the book tidy and compact for the more general reader who is concerned rather with clear outlines than with detailed criticism.

My sincere thanks are due to Mr. Russell Meiggs, Fellow and Tutor of Balliol College, Oxford, for his great kindness in reading and criticising my whole manuscript, and helping me to remove errors of fact or method; to my colleague, Mr. D. B. Harden, for doing me a like favour in connection with the first chapter; to Mr. A. R. Burn, of Uppingham School, for allowing me to see the text of the late Mr. R. L. Beaumont's paper, on the first Rome-Carthage treaty, before publication; to the late Professor Tenney Frank, for permission to quote (p. 198 f.) from Vol III of *An Economic Survey of Ancient Rome*; to Mr. W. P. Burden for his skilful preparation of Maps II and III; and finally to my wife, for her most welcome assistance in the work of compiling the index.

The coin of which a cut appears on the title-page is a *denarius*, struck at Rome by A. Postumius Albinus in the earlier part of the first century B.C., and commemorating the Spanish successes gained by his ancestor, L. Postumius Albinus, in 179 B.C.

C. H. V. S.

CUMNOR, OXFORD.
August, 1939.

CONTENTS

PLATES AT END

MAPS

* Drawings by W. P. Burden

ABBREVIATIONS

C.A.H. = *Cambridge Ancient History.*

C.I.L. = *Corpus Inscriptionum Latinarum.*

E.S.A.R. = *Economic Survey of Ancient Rome* (ed. T. Frank).

F.H.A. = *Fontes Hispaniae Antiquae* (ed. A. Schulten, P. Bosch Gimpera).

I.L.S. = H. Dessau, *Inscriptiones Latinae Selectae.*

J.R.S. = *Journal of Roman Studies.*

M.L.I. = E. Hübner, *Monumenta Linguae Ibericae.*

CHAPTER I

INTRODUCTION: PRE-ROMAN SPAIN

THE geographical position of Spain is of striking peculiarity. This great peninsula, set at the western extremity of the European continent (to which it is joined by a mountainous ridge of land less than 300 miles wide), washed on two sides of its immense seaboard by the wide Atlantic and on its third by the Mediterranean, has but a single point of natural relationship with any other country, namely, where it approaches northern Africa at the Straits of Gibraltar. It may appear strange that Spain, to which nature has given such unusual geographical independence, should always have been, from the earliest period of pre-history, an area characterized by differentiation of peoples and cultures. This process of differentiation, however, was itself the result of other natural causes.

Foremost among these is the physical configuration of the country.[1] Round the coasts runs a belt of relatively low-lying land, varying in width but nowhere very extensive, which constitutes the only truly fertile soil in Spain. The rest of the peninsula is composed of a vast upland plateau, rising in many places to mountain ranges of considerable height: in the southern half of this plateau the soil is mainly poor and dry, and further north it is even worse. Such sharply differing zones of fertility were bound to cause diverse levels of population and culture; and this diversity was further accentuated by climatic variations. The coastal belt running along the north and west coasts, humid and densely wooded, was not suitable for the general pursuit of agriculture: in early times these districts were but sparsely populated, and were not ever destined to rival the south and east coasts in density. In the highest ground of the central plateau, extremes of temperature, combined with poverty of soil and intermittent forest, were not likely to produce a level of culture above that of the hardy mountaineer who tends his herds when he is not engaged in warfare; and the population of upland pastoral areas, however regularly distributed, is normally low. The extreme south of Spain, however, corresponding to much of the modern province of Andalusia, and the coastal strip running upwards along Murcia, Valencia, and Catalonia, show a strong contrast to all the regions mentioned above. Here the climate is sunny and more temperate: the fertility of the soil in the lower valley of the Guadalquivir has always been proverbial, and, though along the rest of the south and east coasts the fertile tracts are interspersed with occasional arid patches, the general productivity of the soil is such as to encourage a high and fruitful level of agriculture by a settled population, with a consequently swift progress in the arts of civilization and peace. To many of the ancient writers Spain appeared to be a paradise of agricultural wealth and prosperity.[2] Had they been less enthusiastic and more critical, they would not have applied to Spain, as a whole, a conception which is true only of a small part of the country. Even to-day, after centuries spent in labour and development of the land, it has been reckoned that 40 per cent of the total area of Spain is covered by forest and pasturage and that over 20 per cent is sterile, only a little over a third of the country being given up to cultivation.[3]

The physical geography of Spain, then, and marked climatic variations must always have been strong factors in the differentiation of the Spanish peoples. Geography, indeed, is involved also in another factor of importance. If we turn to the consideration of the principal rivers of Spain, as possible corridors along which communication to or from the central plateau might be made and the process of extreme differentiation thereby moderated, we shall at once notice that they comprise two most dissimilar classes. Of the five largest rivers which are fed from the plateau—Douro (Durius), Tajo (Tagus), Guadiana (Anas), Guadalquivir (Baetis), and Ebro (Hiberus)—the latter alone, flowing between the central massif and the Pyrenees, pursues an eastward course. All four others are westward-flowing rivers, their courses being roughly at right angles to that of the Ebro : the Durius and the Tagus meet the inhospitable Atlantic on the west coast : the Anas, after a sharp southward turn, debouches on the south coast some hundred miles outside the Straits of Gibraltar ; and the Baetis, after a similar turn, flows into the sea nearer the straits by half that distance. This predominantly western aspect of Spain's river system was to assume importance, for, when the age of maritime communication began to link the lands of the east and west Mediterranean in a closer relationship, a great part of the peoples of central Spain, lacking an eastward-looking outlet from their plateau, were bound to remain untouched by external influences, and themselves incapable of expansion in a wider world. To the early navigators of the Mediterranean, who were often reluctant to put their seamanship to tests much sterner than those afforded by the open stretches of the ' inland sea ' itself, and who came to regard the ' Pillars of Hercules ' (or Straits of

Gibraltar) as the natural western limit of their voyages, the only easy corridor into the Spanish interior was the valley of the Ebro. With the increasing fame of the remarkable mineral wealth of the watershed of the Baetis, there was indeed special inducement to proceed past the straits as far as that river ; further, however, there was no great need to go. Accordingly, the Anas, Tagus, and Durius played but a small part in opening up those parts of the central highlands through which they flowed, and external influences were naturally most attracted to the south and east coasts, thus helping to differentiate still more an area already marked by a fertile soil and a good climate.

These general remarks may be illustrated by a brief survey of the history of Spain down to the time of the Roman invasion. With the question of the indigenous stock in Spain in the Palaeolithic Age we are not here concerned : it is enough to say that the ancient historians gave to it the general name Ligurian, probably understanding by this an early racial affinity between the peoples of Spain and those of western Europe as a whole.[4] That some such affinity existed, and that in the earliest periods of pre-history Spain formed something like an ethnographical unity, is probably true enough. But cultural unity, if such a thing ever existed at all, had disappeared in Palaeolithic Spain. Already there was becoming apparent a contrast between the northern peoples, on the one hand, and those of the south and east on the other : this contrast is shown chiefly by the rock-paintings which decorated the walls of the numerous caves which frequently served as human habitations in a pre-architectural age. The so-called ' Franco-Cantabrian ' art of the north, well represented by the paintings of the hand-silhouettes from the Castillo cave and by the magnificent poly-

chromatic bison-figures from the neighbouring Altamira cave, excelled in the naturalistic reproduction of
objects not composed into set scenes.[5]   But the
' Capsian ' style which produced the paintings of south
and eastern Spain has a different idiom ; here we find
fewer animals,—a loss compensated by the introduction of the human figure, which is represented, often
in composite scenes, in a lively, impressionist manner
suggesting acute perception and an increase in ideology:
good examples of this style are shown by the Cogul,
Saltadora, and Alpera paintings.[6]

The difference between these two styles was to be
accentuated still further. Whereas, in the late Palaeolithic period, the civilization of the north appears to
have become subject to impoverishment and consequent conservatism, the south and east continued their
development on the lines of a kindred culture in
northern Africa. In the Neolithic Age (which we may
regard as having lasted, in Spain, down to about the
middle of the third millennium B.C.) these divergent
tendencies become clearer. This was an age of consolidation, in which the desire of small communities
to maintain their places of residence unchanged (as is
shown by the ' kitchen-middens ' of the Portuguese
coast,—great heaps of mollusc-shells, fish-bones, and
implements, which in time became burial-mounds)
encouraged the peaceful pursuit of agriculture. Pottery and architecture were two of the achievements of
Neolithic Spain, and in both these arts the southern
area showed the swifter progress : its pottery, with its
bands of roughly incised decoration, is found fairly
widely distributed, and its architecture, which produced
the *cupula*, or ' domed ' community-grave, was an
advance upon the simpler geometric *dolmen* of the
north.[7]

Towards the end of the Neolithic period, change and disturbance in many parts of Spain interrupted the comparative tranquillity of the previous centuries. In the south, this change is to be recognized in the so-called culture of Almeria,—the site which provides the clearest indications of the sudden and intense intrusion of new influences.[8]   That these influences accompanied immigration from northern Africa, and formed the prelude to what is known later as the Iberian culture of south and east Spain, is not generally doubted.[9] Nor is it difficult to determine the characteristics of this intrusive culture ; they are essentially practical and warlike, and are shown by the construction of strongly fortified towns on hill-tops, and by the use, at first, of undecorated pottery.   It is much less easy to decide where this extraneous culture first took root in Spain. The fact that the name ' Iberia ' is given to the region between the rivers Baetis and Anas in the early Greek geographical tradition embodied in Avienus' *Ora Maritima* (a work to which fuller reference will be made later) has encouraged the view that this was the earliest focus of the Almerian culture.[10]   On the other hand, the region most generally conceived of as Iberian by the ancients was the east coast ; and from this it might be concluded that the new immigrants, after crossing by the straits, for the most part turned eastward.   Whatever the solution of the problem may be, it is sufficient for our present purposes to say that during the Bronze Age (*c.* 2500–1000 B.C.) the original Almerian culture extended itself over much of southern Spain, up the east coast as far as the Pyrenees, and inland up the valley of the Ebro—perhaps even to the head-waters of the Tagus and the Durius.[11]   In the course of this period of expansion, considerable differentiation took place even within the Iberian area itself.   The

swiftest progress was for a time confined to the southern coastal district, as the finds at Los Millares indicate. Here, indeed, architecture was of the same massive and ' cyclopean ' type as was found (e.g. at Tarraco) fully developed in the east and northern areas also ; but the pottery was subject to marked decorative improvement and, more important, the prevalence of precious metals induced the steady production of metal objects, chiefly of copper, but also of gold and silver to a lesser extent.[12] The same region also supplies evidence of the first tentative efforts at maritime communication between Spain and the eastern Mediterranean, in the form of beads, dated about the fourteenth or thirteenth century B.C., similar to those of Egyptian provenance. But, granted both the birth of the age of maritime expansion and also the recognition of precious metals as such, the centre of gravity in southern Spain was bound to be shifted, to a point favourable no less as a convenient approach for sea-borne traffic than as an efficient control-centre of the mineral routes of the interior of Spain itself. Both these advantages were offered by lower Andalusia, in the south of the valley of the Baetis ; and thus, when a westward expansion of the Almerian culture led settlers to this district.   ey were destined, under the later distinguishing name of Tartessians, to outstrip the civilization of all other parts of Spain.[13]

This intrusion of new and vigorous elements in the south and east was not without its effect upon the rest of the country ; but this effect was, in general, one of unwilling impact. The working and use of metal implements, indeed, spread steadily over the west-centre, west, and north. Yet the widespread construction of elaborately fortified hill-top camps—the *citanias* —in these areas is evidence of a state of fear and sus-

picion, in which communities withdrew each into their
regional stronghold.[14] Such a change in the conditions
of life was bound to retard cultural progress, and,
although the arts of sculpture, pottery, and architecture
were not here lacking, the sculpture was of the most
primitive type, architecture was controlled by considerations of durability and strength, and pottery scarcely
advanced beyond a stage of simple geometric decoration, which continued almost without modification
even through the Iron Age, and of which Numantia,
destroyed in 133 B.C., has produced examples. This
conservatism was not lessened by the two Celtic
irruptions into Spain during the Iron Age ; of these,
more will be said later.

Towards the end of the second millennium B.C. the
stage of proto-history begins in southern Spain. We
must suppose that by this time a highly differentiated
culture, induced by agriculture, mining, and (to a
lesser degree) commerce, had appeared among those
peoples of the lower Baetis valley who have been previously referred to as Tartessians. This name is
derived from that of Tartessos, the legendary town
(and still legendary, for no trace of it has ever been
revealed by the archaeologist's spade) which is thought
to have stood some twenty miles north-west of Gades
(Cadiz), at the mouth of the Baetis on the shore now
known as the Coto de Doña Ana. Of Tartessos the
ancients wrote with wonder, as of the fabulous ; and
the stimulus of fable and legend has not been lost upon
those modern historians who have made researches
into a most difficult and complex problem.[15] On the
one hand we have the assurance that contacts between
Spain and the Cretan and Mycenaean cultures of the
second millennium were negligible.[16] On the other
hand, numerous Biblical sources (the earliest of them

referring to a period about 1000 B.C.) testify to a constant maritime relationship between Phoenicia (represented by Sidon and Tyre) and a remote source of precious metals, called Tarshish, and now usually held to be the same as Tartessos.[17] Against the legendary wealth of Tartessos, and the volume of its trade, must be set the facts that it has left behind no vestige of its site, and that archaeological evidence for foreign commerce with Andalusia at this early date is almost non-existent. Gades itself supplies further complications : the traditional date of its foundation by Phoenician colonists is about 1100 B.C., and, if tradition is accepted, Gades was therefore in existence during the first florescence of Tartessos ; but the sixth-century Massiliote sailor whose description of the Spanish coast is embodied in Avienus' *Ora Maritima*, and whose natural hatred of the Phoenicians did not prevent his mention of the 'Libyphoenikes' on the Malaga-Almeria coast,[18] makes no mention of the place, though his description of Tartessos is full and vivid. Nor, according to the experts, is the Gades necropolis marked by Phoenician characteristics of a date earlier than the end of the sixth century.[19]

Out of this welter of inconsistencies only one stable conclusion can emerge. Whatever the date at which the Tartessian culture first became strongly differentiated in southern Spain (and this was probably well within the second millennium), Tartessos as an element in international commerce was a phenomenon which has been ante-dated. Before the eighth century B.C., Tartessos was perhaps too much concerned with her own affairs to realize the advantage to which the already growing reports of her wealth might be turned. It is even possible that a people blessed with fertile soil, a good climate, and access to remarkable mineral wealth were for a time subject to enervation and lack of enterprise. This would at least explain the Biblical tradition of a Tarshish semi-dependent on Phoenicia about the time of the seventh century.[20] Of the close relationship between Phoenicia and Tartessos at this time there is indeed no doubt: this was the zenith of Phoenician colonization, and the foundation of Ebusus (Iviza), about 660, serves to remind us of Phoenician overseas enterprise. But the Phoenician monopoly of the Tartessian metal-market was not destined to last much more than two centuries. The subjection of Tyre by Nebuchadnezzar early in the sixth century resulted in the end of the Phoenician phase in southern Spain. That the importance of this phase has been exaggerated is due chiefly to the Phoenician bias of the bulk of the historical sources. Apart from their connection with Tartessos, the Phoenicians left but few traces in southern Spain, their stations at Gades, Malaca (Malaga), Sexi, and Abdera (Adra) being probably little more than ports of call; even the intensity of their trade may be questioned, for almost the only finds of definitely Phoenician date in Spain are the scarab of Psammetichus I of Egypt (615–609 B.C.) at Alcacer do Sal (Portugal) and the gold treasure of La Aliseda.[21] Nor does the sphere of Tartessian influence seem to have been sensibly diminished, for the light which sixth-century Greek sources and enterprises throw upon Spain shows that, with the exception of the small and unimportant Phoenician nuclei on the south coast, the whole of southern Spain from the Anas up to the modern Cape Palos was dominated either by the Tartessians themselves— including the neighbouring Tartessic groups of Elbisini, Ileates, Oretani, and Cilbiceni—or by the powerful group of kindred Mastieni, whose capital, Mastia, was

later to make way for the building of Carthago Nova.[22]

The decay of Phoenician contacts with Spain was succeeded by the era of Greek colonization.[23] Already, about 630 B.C., a Samian, Kolaios by name, had chanced to sail as far as Tartessos, where he had put in; but the rich cargo which he had thence brought home did not tempt the Samians to exploit the wealth of the far west.[24] Yet stories of the wealth of Tartessos, and of the activities of the Tartessians as middle-men in the trading of tin shipped from Brittany, were by now sufficiently common to earn for themselves a place in Greek literature.[25] When, therefore, the sixth century ushered in the great thalassocracy of Phocaea, it was not surprising that a Phocaean colony should be planted at Massilia, for, apart from the control thus acquired over the Rhone trade-route of the Gallic interior, the new foundation was but nine days' sail from Tartessos itself.[26] From about 600 B.C. (the approximate date of the founding of Massilia) Greek enterprise along the coasts of Spain was supreme for two generations. For the Massiliotes themselves the chief necessity at first was to ingratiate themselves with the Iberians of the east, along whose shores their coasting vessels must pass; and thus arose the 'Old Town' at 'The Mart', Emporion (the modern Ampurias), and Hemeroskopeion.[27] The merchants of Phocaea itself were no less energetic, and their sea-route, jumping westwards from island to island, is traceable in the '–ussa' termination of place-names; it approached Spain by Ophiussa in the Pityussa islands (Ebusus), and did not terminate before it reached a second Ophiussa at the mouth of the Tagus.

It was probably through Phocaean rather than Massiliote enterprise that intimate mercantile relations were

established with Tartessos proper ; and, if Herodotus'
account of the welcome given to the Phocaeans by
King Arganthonius of Tartessos, the 'Silver Man'
who reigned 80 years and lived 120, and of his desire
that they should settle in Tartessia, is most naturally
interpreted, we might conclude that these relations
were established late in the sixth century, and not
earlier. The 80 years of Arganthonius' rule must
stand for a revival of Tartessos, freed from Phoenician
influences, under a successful dynasty ; and Herodotus
himself records that the Phocaeans, threatened with
extermination by Cyrus of Persia, and unwilling to
colonize Tartessia, proceeded to settle at Alalia in
Corsica. Thus the Arganthonius episode is the climax,
and not the prelude, to the period of intensive Greek
activity in Spain.[28]   But, though abruptly frustrated,
this episode may have been connected with one step of
importance : the foundation of Mainake (the site of
which is uncertain, though it probably lay a little east
of Malaca) seems to represent the zenith of large-scale
colonization by the Greeks in Spain. This town,
planted boldly on a partly Phoenician section of the
coast, and near enough to Tartessos to encourage
the later development of a land-route thither across the
high ground which divided them, was the supreme
challenge of the western Greeks against all other
comers.[29]

At some date within the second half of the sixth
century B.C. a Greek author, most probably a sailor
or merchant of Massilia, wrote a fairly detailed description of a voyage round the coasts of Spain, and this
'Periplus', later embodied in the *Ora Maritima* of
Rufus Festus Avienus, a Roman of the fourth century
A.D., gives us the clearest available picture of the
extent of Greek influence in Spain.[30]   Although its

author had compiled notes (conceivably from Tartessian sources) of the sea-route as far north as Brittany, and even the British Isles, his real interest lay in the voyage from Ophiussa, at the mouth of the Tagus, up to Massilia, with which he was personally familiar. His description, though summary, is vivid and suggestive : he notes the varying character of the shore, as rocky, sandy, bare, etc. : he records the time taken in sailing between the principal points : he alludes to the flourishing state of Tartessos and, in contrast to the paucity of Phoenician communities then surviving, refers by name to the Greek colonies of the south and east, with the curious exception of Emporion. It may well be that the steady Greek expansion down the east coast and along the south temporarily diminished the original importance of Emporion, where the bulk of archaeological evidence points to a date at the end of the sixth century as the period of chief development. But much of this evidence consists of works of pure Greek craftsmanship ; and the real index of Greek influence in Spain is to be found in the essentially hybrid art which characterized the tract dominated by the Mastieni, from Cape Nao down to Cape Gata. The most famous example of this art is the ' Lady of Elche ' (=Ilici), a fine and mature statue which reflects this influence all the more because it belongs probably to the post-Greek era of Spain (Pl. V) ; but the sculptures and bronzes which have been found in such numbers at Cerro de los Santos, some fifty miles inland from Alicante, and at Despeñaperros (at the head of the Baetis valley) and many other sites, combined with the prevalence of pottery imitated from Greek types, are certain proof of the intensive spread of Greek ideas. These influences can be traced in Andalusia as well, but, though widely distributed in this area too, they were not so strong nor so lasting.[31]

There is no reason to doubt that Greek activities in Spain were due chiefly to the desire to acquire the precious metals : this conclusion is suggested not only by the intimacy of the Greeks with Tartessos, which controlled the distribution of copper from the Rio Tinto mines and of the gold from the Sierra Morena, but also by the Greek concentration upon the Mastieni, to whom the working of the rich silver-mines around Cartagena must have been a most important and remunerative occupation. But the Greek foot-hold in Murcia and Andalusia was suddenly lost after the virtual defeat of the Phocaeans at Alalia by the joint forces of the Carthaginians and Etruscans in 535 B.C. The collapse of Phocaean maritime supremacy in the western Mediterranean was followed quickly by the maritime expansion of Carthage. Originally a Phoenician colony, this city had been pursuing an increasingly independent existence since the decay of Tyrian prosperity, and was greatly assisted in its competition with Greek commerce by its close relationship with Etruria. From the time of Alalia onward, the Carthaginians steadily transferred into their own hands the commercial advantages formerly enjoyed by the Phocaeans and Massiliotes. At first, indeed, Punic policy may have been satisfied with the sea-control of the straits of Gibraltar ; and this may have caused the temporary development of that land route between Mainake and Tartessos of which even the author of the *Periplus* knew. Later, however, with the increase of Punic strength and the reinforcement or re-colonization of the old Phoenician posts on the south coast of Spain, Carthage was able to remove both Tartessos and Mainake literally off the map ;

and she did this so well that the site of each is now problematic. It has been conjectured that the addition to Emporion of the ' New Town ' (dated by archaeological evidence to the last years of the sixth century) was due partly to an influx of refugees from Alalia, partly to the later migration of the survivors of Mainake.[32]

Some idea of the degree of Punic power attained by the end of the sixth century is afforded by Polybius' details of the first treaty between Rome and Carthage, which he assigns to 508 B.C.[33] Although Sardinia was now held by Carthage (Etruria had taken Corsica) and Sicily was partly under Punic influence, the Romans and their allies (i.e., the Massiliotes ?) were not debarred by the treaty from trading with these islands. Further west, however, the scope of Roman commerce was expressly restricted, being forbidden (in Polybius' words) to extend ' beyond the Fair Promontory ', i.e. the site of the later Carthago Nova. Much controversy has beset the interpretation of this phrase : it has been argued that, if it means ' west of the Fair Promontory ', Carthage now closed southern Spain to Greek and Roman traders, whereas the meaning ' south of the Fair Promontory ' would keep the traders who coasted down the east of Spain from crossing to the trading-stations of north Africa.[33a] It would probably be wrong to press Polybius' rather ambiguous words too far. The treaty does not, indeed, make specific reference to trade with Spain ; but Greek (and Roman) traders would most naturally approach the western Mediterranean by way of the east coast of Spain, and a limit to navigation ' beyond ' the Fair Promontory, stipulated by international treaty, would by its very ambiguity discourage further advance (whether to south or west), especially after sedulous Punic propaganda had turned the Straits of Gibraltar into an international bogy by its reports of the dangers there awaiting even the wariest mariner. Beyond the Cartagena cape, therefore, Punic influence now probably developed, though this is not to say that Greek merchants did not sometimes run the gauntlet in forbidden waters.

Official Massiliote retaliation took the form of the foundation of two new colonies just north of the Cartagena cape,—Akra Leuke (Alicante) and Alonae (Benidorm).[34] Possibly these colonies were no great commercial success, for when Carthage, in 348 B.C., reaffirmed her refusal to allow Roman commerce with southern Spain, the boundary still remained the same.[35] The temporary check which Carthage suffered by the defeat at Himera in 480 B.C. in no way endangered her new Spanish empire, which was not intrinsically impaired even by the Massiliote naval victory over Carthage in 340 B.C. This empire now consisted of the territory of the Mastieni, the Tartessii, and the dependants of the latter. Although the expulsion of the Greeks from these areas has robbed us of historical records of the Punic domination, archaeological evidence for its extent and intensity is extremely eloquent.[36] Along the coastal strip especially, it shows a wealthy and mature Punic culture, with sculpture, pottery, and jewellery of types current at Carthage itself: Gades, Astapa (Estepa), Malaca, and the cemetery at Villaricos (north-east of the modern Almeria) have supplied some of the richest material; and this culture may safely be predicated, in greater or less degree, of the whole chain of coastal towns, which now became busy industrial centres, many of them engaged in pickling *garum*, or salted fish (as at Gades, Baesippo, Carteia, Malaca, Sexi), and some in

mining (as in the lead mines of Abdera) or the manufacture of the esparto grass, which grew by the modern
Cartagena, into ships' tackle and domestic commodities. But the chief source of Punic wealth lay in
the mines of the interior, distributed along the watershed of the Baetis ; hence came the gold, silver, iron,
and copper, of which such graves as those at Villaricos
were to receive their portion. The archaeological finds
from Urso (Osuna) northwards, stretching through
the agricultural settlements at Acébuchal, Gandul,
Bencarron, and Carmona up to Despeñaperros and
Castellar de Santisteban in the mining country of the
Oretani, leave no doubt that these districts, though
not settled with a Punic population, were in constant
touch with Punic influences and Punic merchants.[37]
These influences touched even the essentially Greek
sphere north of Cartagena : Emporion (the third-
century coinage of which betrays Punic affinities)[38]
has produced Carthaginian jewellery and pottery in
considerable amounts, as well as a Carthaginian
inscription, and Massilia itself has yielded similar
evidence.

So far as is known, the Punic domination in southern
Spain continued without interruption from the end
of the sixth century until the middle of the third ;
according to Polybius,[39] Carthage still had her Spanish
interests when she engaged in her first war against
Rome. We should exercise care in attempting to
define the character of this domination. There is
nothing to justify the view that the Carthaginians
replaced the semi-political federation which seems to
have existed previously in Tartessia by any system of
political subjection to Carthage itself; and such a
system is still less likely among the Mastieni. Tribute,
according to Polybius,[40] was first exacted for Carthage

by Hannibal. Spanish mercenaries had, indeed, fought in Carthaginian armies as early as the time of Himera, but these were Iberians of the centre, and not the more highly civilized men of the south. It is probably correct to conclude that the Punic domination was almost wholly commercial, having as its object the monopoly of Spanish minerals and of the tin brought round by sea from Brittany, as well as the profitable control by Carthaginians, as middle-men, of the eastern trade with Spain. The absence of any political suzerainty would help to explain why southern Spain, in the short interval between 264 and 237 B.C., fell away so easily and so quietly from Punic control that, when Hamilcar Barca began the task of recovery in the latter year, he found Gades to be the only substantial Punic base left in Spain (below, p. 24).

He and his successors, Hasdrubal and Hannibal, were the first in historical times to extend foreign power systematically into the interior of Spain, and something must now be said of the developments which had there taken place. We have already seen (p. 6) how, during the Bronze Age, the Iberian culture extended itself up the east coast and up the valley of the Ebro. Between Cartagena and the Ebro this culture remained comparatively unchanged; its representatives, differentiated in the course of time into the three main groups, Contestani, Edetani, and Ilergetes, were destined to become the recipients of vigorous Greek influences in the sixth and following centuries.[41] North of the Ebro there was a partial fusion of the Iberian with a native stock, represented by such later historical tribes as the Cessetani, Ausetani, and Indigetes; these last, even in the era of Emporion, were sufficiently uncivilized to be assigned a separate part of that city.[42] At the top of the valley of the

Ebro, Iberians established themselves on the north coast,—the Cantabri of historic times. The rest of Spain, at the end of the Bronze Age, had probably witnessed no disturbance of its indigenous peoples. The early Iron Age was perhaps accompanied by a moderate influx of Celts from across the Pyrenees, about or a little before 1000 B.C. ; but the effect of this influx was confined to the diffusion of Celtic influences north of the Ebro.[43] A second Celtic influx, some four hundred years later, was much more intense, and profoundly modified the previous ethnographical scheme in Spain, especially in the central plateau, henceforth characterized by a fused race known to ancient historians as Celtiberians. Of the problem raised by this name—whether it implies Celts absorbed by a later infusion of Iberians, as Schulten supposes, or Iberians on to whom a proportion of Celts was later grafted, as Bosch Gimpera has argued—no discussion can be given here.[44] It must suffice to say that the irruption of these sixth-century Celts, perhaps accompanied by an advance-guard of those very Germans who displaced them in central Europe,[45] produced in the centre and north-east of Spain a culture of mixed Iberian and Celtic characteristics, exemplified in historical tribes such as the Arevaci, Vettones, and Olcades. The comparative isolation of this central culture from external influences kept it free from substantial change ; and the Celtiberians of the third century onwards, well known to Roman soldiers and historians for their hardy and sober habits, their small clans living almost devoid of political cohesion in their strong mountain forts, their magnificent horsemanship, their indifference to all precious metals save iron (from which they forged their superb weapons), and their poor and often sordid

manner of life, with few of the comforts born of
agriculture,—these may be taken as typical of the
fused race from the start.[46]   Besides this fusion, the
Celtic influx of the sixth century had one other result
of importance.   Hard pressed by the immigrants, part
of the Lusones,—probably a pre-Celtic and semi-
Iberized tribe,—who dwelt on the mountains south-
west of the Ebro, seem to have moved westward,
and by the third century they appear, under the name
of Lusitani, widely spread over what is now Estremadura and southern Portugal, i.e. between the courses
of the Anas and the Tagus.   In their level of culture
they were comparable to the Celtiberi.   Their westward thrust was balanced by that of a smaller body of
Celts who, known to the ancients as Celtici, penetrated
to the middle reaches of the Anas, and subsequently
intermingled with the more northern elements of the
Tartessian area, known to the Romans as Turdetani or
Turduli.   By the third century B.C. only the Asturian
corner of Spain remained virtually unaffected by
racial disturbances, its culture being proportionately
backward.

A summary survey has now been given of the processes of differentiation to which Spain was subject
down to the time of the first Roman enterprises in
that country.   These processes had produced (see
Map I) ethnical groups of widely varying culture
and experience,—the Turdetani (or Tartessians) of
Andalusia, civilized, boasting a past age of literature
and art,[47] and now partially soaked in Punic influences ;
the Mastieni, less civilized and more independent ;
the Iberians of the east coast, long familiar with Greek
traders and Greek ideas ; the rougher tribes of the
coast north of the Ebro ; the hardy Celtiberi of the
centre and north-east, strong yet undeveloped like

the Lusitani of the west; and in the extreme north the Cantabri and Astures, furthest removed from civilizing influences. These were the peoples for whom Rome was called upon to devise a system of government and a plan of administration.

Finally, a word must be said about the Balearic Islands. Here a peculiar and primitive culture, combining Bronze Age with Iron Age characteristics, was still surviving when they were first opened up by Phoenician merchants about the eighth century B.C.; before this, external contacts had been slight, and the much-vaunted archaeological evidence of Mycenaean connections appears to be capable of widely different interpretation. Carthaginian expansion from the late sixth century onwards resulted in an accelerated progress in Balearic culture, but, compared with the island of Ebusus, which is rich in Punic remains, the Baleares remained comparatively untouched, and even savage and uncivilized, until their conquest by Metellus in 122 B.C.[48]

CHAPTER II

THE EXPULSION OF THE CARTHAGINIANS

IT has already been remarked (above, p. 17 f.) that both the extent and the nature of the first Carthaginian empire in Spain are incapable of exact definition, although the diminution of Carthaginian influence in Spain during the First Punic War may suggest that the empire aimed rather at the monopoly of Spanish minerals than at any form of political subjugation. This diminution of influence must have been viewed with all the greater anxiety after the result of the First Punic War had deprived Carthage of Sicily and saddled her with a large war-indemnity.[1] It was now vitally necessary to draw upon new resources of men and money. The tradition of the early Roman annalists, preoccupied as it is with the theme of the rising imperial aspirations of Rome, will not concede similar aspirations to Carthage, and ascribes the activities of Hamilcar and his successors in Spain to motives of personal ambition which the government of Carthage was unable to check. Thus Fabius sees in Hasdrubal's exploits an effort to dispel personal unpopularity at Carthage, and holds that Hannibal's Spanish policy, including his attack on Saguntum, was carried through in the face of Carthaginian displeasure.[2] Polybius, indeed, perceived the absurdity of this tradition, and, in the course of a detailed refutation of it, he points out that the events

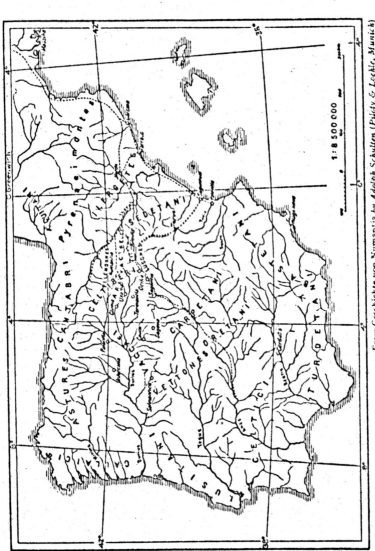

From *Geschichte von Numantia* by *Adolph Schulten (Piloty & Loehle, Munich)*

THE TRIBES OF THE IBERIAN PENINSULA, 150 B.C.

at Saguntum and on the Ebro were no more than the occasions of a war which was actually caused by general Carthaginian desire to raise resources in Spain for a renewed war against Rome.[3] Spain could scarcely have been more swiftly or more systematically exploited than by the series of able generals whom Carthage sent out for the purpose. The consequent use of Spain as a Punic base and storehouse against Rome and Italy, and the resultant Second Punic War, thus justify Mommsen's view of the Roman penetration and capture of Punic Spain as due to 'the accidents of external policy'—an expansion forced upon Rome by the hostile policy of Carthage.[4]

Hamilcar landed at Gades in 237 B.C., and for nine years he successfully pursued the policy of conquest and exploitation, the result of which was described by Polybius as the subjugation of the greater part of Iberia. This, like most generalizations, is an exaggeration. Hamilcar certainly extended Punic domination over a large area, but neither he nor Hannibal ever subdued the greater part of the peninsula.[5] Our fullest account of Hamilcar's activities is that of Diodorus,[6] from whom it is evident that the conquest of the Tartessians of Andalusia (Pl. VI) was followed by offensives against the Iberians, i.e. the peoples of the lower east coast, and large bands of mercenary 'Celts', i.e. highlanders of the southern part of the central plateau, under their leaders Istolatius and Indortes. These offensives were successful, and it is clear that, from a basic position which originally comprised little more than the support of Gades and probably some others of the string of Phoenician sea-towns in the south, Hamilcar quickly extended Punic power to the east and north-east. By 231 B.C. he had presumably reached Cape Palos—the promontory on

which Cartagena was soon to be founded, for in that year a Roman embassy was sent to investigate his activities : [7] ever since the treaty of 348 B.C. this promontory had marked the eastward limit to Punic expansion in Spain (see above, p. 15 f.). Hamilcar's reply was adroit and unanswerable ; the hostilities were necessary if the war-indemnity was to be paid to Rome. And thus he was able quietly to push on beyond Cape Palos. According to Diodorus he founded (in fact, he must have re-founded) the strategically important Akra Leuke—a town of Massiliote origin[8]—and at the time of his death in the winter of 229–228 B.C. he was engaged in the siege of 'Helice', perhaps to be identified with Ilici (the modern Elche), close to Akra Leuke. He had by then secured what was probably the equivalent of the later Roman *Provincia Hispania Ulterior* in its early form (see below ,p. 46 ff.), with the addition of the coastal strip (including Carthago Nova and her silver-mines) northward to Cape Nao.

His successor, Hasdrubal, chose conciliation rather than force as a means of winning over the numerous small communities which, ruled by petty kings or tribal leaders, remained to be absorbed north of Cape Nao : and he married the daughter of an Iberian king.[9] But the tribes between Cape Palos and Akra Leuke called for sterner measures, the necessity of which is seen in the foundation by Hasdrubal of Carthago Nova, the modern Cartagena,—a citadel of great natural strength, with a magnificent harbour lying at an easy distance from Africa, to act as a suitable military base in East Spain and as a storehouse for the silver from the adjacent mines, 'most opportune' (as Polybius remarks) 'in its relation to both Spain and Africa.' This notable increase in Punic strength, and a virtual extension of domination over the coastal Iberians as far north as the Ebro, led Rome in 226 B.C. to ask for Carthaginian assurances that this river should be regarded as a boundary between them, beyond which the Carthaginians should not make armed passage ; and this was the basis of the notorious Ebro treaty of that year. Its terms have been variously disputed, particularly in regard to the position and subsequent fate of Saguntum, for, although Livy, Appian, and Dio's epitomator agree in regarding Saguntum (and perhaps even other communities) as having been expressly excepted in the treaty, as constituting a legally defined sphere of Roman influence, yet it is hardly possible to accept this account in the face of Polybius' more trustworthy tradition.[10] According to the latter, no specific exceptions were made south of the Ebro, and it is reasonable to regard his reference to a Saguntine treaty with Rome ' some years before Hannibal's time ' as evidence that, between 226 and 221 B.C., Rome perpetrated an almost deliberate diplomatic blunder by contracting an alliance with a community known to lie within the Punic boundary. It is, indeed, possible that Rome was merely trying to save her face, after Carthaginian absorption of Akra Leuke, Alonae, and Hemeroskopeion,[11] all of which were colonies of Massilia. Menaced as she was by the Gauls in the north of Italy, Rome must have hoped that her Saguntine bluff would not be called ; but called it soon was, by Hannibal's unerring instinct, and the ineffectual foolishness of the alliance palpably exposed.[12]

On Hasdrubal's death in 221 B.C. the command in Spain devolved upon Hannibal, now twenty-five years old. Sixteen years before he had been sworn by his father Hamilcar to perpetual hatred of Rome ; and

it was to his father's active and warlike policy that he now reverted.[13] He moved at once against the Olcades—a tribe probably to be assigned, as Schulten has suggested, to the uplands in which the Anas rises ; and it is after their subjugation that Polybius and Livy first mention the imposition of tribute in Punic Spain. After wintering at Carthago Nova, he turned in 220 to the far-off basin of the Durius, where he attacked the Vaccaei and captured their towns Salmantica (Salamanca) and Arbocala,—the latter only after a stubborn siege. But he was dangerously far from his base. The Carpetani, in the upper valley of the Tagus, were roused by refugees from both the Vaccaei and the Olcades, and Hannibal was obliged to fall back on to the line of the Tagus, where he defeated the opposition and subsequently devastated Carpetania.[14] If he had not soon exchanged Spain for Italy as a theatre of war, he would possibly have realized how superficial were the effects of these swift and brief campaigns, and how great were the forces which were later to wear out army after army of Romans in guerilla warfare on the Spanish highlands. But as it was, he had for the moment intimidated and weakened the tribes of the interior, and might claim that Punic Spain reached, past the Anas, to the lower waters of the Tagus, and that eastward it comprised the Sierra Morena, together with a strip narrowing northward to the Ebro.[15]

In 219 B.C. Hannibal turned his attention to Saguntum (Murviedro), which (as Polybius remarks) he had hitherto deliberately neglected through his reluctance to afford Rome a cause for open war until his preparations in the rest of Spain were sufficiently complete. Now, however, his plans for the invasion of Italy must have been ready, and the time for their execution was at hand. The activities of the Saguntines themselves dictated an obvious course for immediate action. Their city,[16] a strongly fortified acropolis of typical Iberian character, lying not a mile from the sea, and surrounded by fertile land, constituted a strong sphere of independent influence in an otherwise predominantly Punic area; and it appears that Saguntine interests had come into conflict with those of the Turduli, or Turbuletes,[17] inland. The latter alleged harsh treatment at the hands of Saguntum, and Carthaginian intervention (even if the feud owed nothing to Carthaginian instigation) was thus a logical result in view of the political domination now exerted by Carthage over the territories of the Turdetani, Turduli, and Iberians alike,—a domination conceded by Rome under the terms of the Ebro treaty, from which there is no reason to think that Saguntum was excluded. It is true that this treaty probably guaranteed the security of all allies, existing and future, of both Carthage and Rome,[18] and that Saguntum had probably become an ally of Rome soon after the treaty was made: in this sense Hannibal was technically in the wrong when he attacked Saguntum. But Carthage might well consider that a Sagunto-Roman alliance made after the treaty was an absurdity, for the treaty gave Rome no justification for interfering in what was an indisputably Punic sphere. Hannibal's technical error was indeed the result of something very like infringement of a treaty on the part of Rome.

Rome herself had already perceived the probable result of her own diplomatic blunder, for in the previous year the Punic menace to her ally had been a matter under discussion.[19] Wholly unable to avert this menace, Rome was equally powerless to take positive action when Hannibal's attack materialized.

Having first consulted the Carthaginian Government, Hannibal delivered his onslaught upon Saguntum, which then settled down to a siege of some nine months; and a Roman embassy sent to Hannibal returned to Rome without having obtained the slightest satisfaction. The fall of Saguntum was merely a matter of time: Hannibal himself had sufficient time and confidence to leave the scene of siege and march north-west against the Oretani and Carpetani, who had risen in revolt and captured Punic recruiting-officers. At length, towards the close of 219, the walls of Saguntum were breached and the city was stormed, though not before many lives and valuables had been given voluntarily to the flames.

The news came as a profound shock and mortification to public opinion at Rome, where, for the first time, the extent of Carthaginian influence in Spain and the quality of Carthaginian leadership were now clearly understood.[20] But there was no hesitation in accepting the challenge. Plenipotentiaries sailed at once to Carthage with an ultimatum: the Carthaginian Government refused to admit a ground for Roman protest, and the Second Punic War thus began.[21]

Hannibal retired for the winter of 219-218 to Carthago Nova, and there prepared his dispositions before leaving Spain for Italy. Foremost among his obligations was that of collecting the force with which he intended to invade Italy. But this must not involve denuding Punic Spain of adequate defence forces, for it was clear that Roman policy would, sooner or later, attempt to cripple this powerful and wealthy limb of the Carthaginian empire. Moreover, he could not long presume on the quiescence of the tribes of the interior—Oretani, Carpetani, Olcades, and Vaccaei— with whom he had fought in 220 and 219.

Accordingly, Spanish troops amounting to over 20,000 (including drafts from the Olcades and Iberians of the east coast) were shipped to Africa, and, to take their place in Spain, Hannibal assigned to his brother Hasdrubal an army of 15,000 men (mainly African), as well as elephants and a fleet.[22]   He himself, in the spring of 218 B.C., marched northward to the Pyrenees with an army of some sixty or seventy thousand men, from which 11,000 under Hanno were detached *en route* for service in Spain north of the Ebro.   It may be noted that Hannibal took the opportunity afforded by his march to subdue the Ebro-Pyrenees littoral, with parts of the interior besides : the Ilergetes of Ilerda (Lérida) contributed 300 cavalry to Hasdrubal's army, and there is little doubt that Roman influence in Spain scarcely extended beyond Emporion.[23]   Such was the position when Hannibal left Spain in 218 B.C.

Much has been written of the confusion and inter-play of policies in Rome at this period—sometimes, perhaps, with exaggerated emphasis, for intelligent opinion had only to consider the situation caused by an imminent invasion of Italy by Hannibal, backed as he was by the strength and resources of a Spain which was now in great part held by Carthage.   The success of the rôles played in 218 B.C. by Publius Cornelius Scipio, one of the two consuls, and his brother and *legatus* Cnaeus, lay not so much in diagno-sis as in decisive and comprehensive action, and this action was (as has been well said)[24] designed ' to make Spain not so much Roman as non-Carthaginian ', in order that its value to a Punic army in Italy might be cancelled or at least diminished.   There was at first an intention to match a Spanish offensive by one in Africa, led by the other consul, Ti. Sempronius Longus ; but the swift course of events, and the great accumula-

tion of war in Italy itself, made such a plan impossible for the next fourteen years. Publius Scipio, commanding northern Italy, sailed first to Massilia in an attempt to intercept Hannibal. He was, however, too late, and was obliged for the moment to return to Italy. But, lest any time should be lost, he sent on to Spain an army of two legions under the command of his brother Cnaeus, to whom (as Velleius says) it thus fell to be the first to lead a Roman army into Spain.

The army of Cnaeus was not, indeed, large in comparison with the total enemy forces of 26,000 men in Spain. But there was a significantly strong naval arm of sixty ships, which made it clear that, though the expedition was to land at Emporium (as we may now call it), the Romans were not to be limited to a base which, even twenty-three years later, was to be hostile to Cato. From the first, Cnaeus pursued a joint land and sea strategy, and soon his operations had extended Roman influence as far down the coast as the Ebro, near which he inflicted a decisive defeat upon Hanno's army, capturing Hanno himself, and gaining possession of Cesse—the future Roman Tarraco (Tarragona)—which had probably become a temporary Punic base.[25] Hasdrubal's swift march northward from Carthago Nova was of no real avail: Cn. Scipio, strongly based at Tarraco, now held the line of the Ebro, virtually restoring the *status quo* of 226 B.C. Moreover, the rumours of his just diplomacy had been spreading inland to such good effect that he might hope soon to augment his legions with native auxiliaries.

The following year (217 B.C.) saw the Carthaginian position thrust even further back. Hasdrubal had advanced with his army and his fleet to the mouth of the Ebro, but the Roman ships under Cn. Scipio routed the Punic navy,[26] and Scipio, with the opportunism of a good general, sailed south as far as Carthago Nova, where he ravaged the country and destroyed an esparto-store, after which he crossed to Ebusus—a purely Punic island—doing further damage there, and received peace petitions from the Balearic Isles. It is not too much to say that the superiority of the Roman naval arm in these early years had a decisive influence upon subsequent Romano-Punic hostilities in Spain. Already Cn. Scipio had learned that advance by land alone was impossible, owing to the difficulties of the country and their effect on commissariat, and to the uncertain loyalty of the Iberian tribes. Therefore, his base and coastal strip north of the Ebro safely secured, he delivered these subsequent blows from the sea ; and this was a strategy which his nephew was later to employ with the most complete and brilliant success.

Cnaeus now returned to his base to receive the submission or allegiance of the neighbouring small communities.[27] There he was joined later in the year by his brother Publius, now proconsul, with 8000 men and 20 ships ; and together the two generals advanced across the Ebro—Polybius emphasizes this first historic occasion—and encamped five miles from Saguntum, whence, by the duplicity of an Iberian chieftain, they contrived to evacuate a number of Spanish hostages, lodged there previously by Hannibal, and repatriate them, to the consequent credit of the Roman policy.[28] This, with other actions of clemency and conciliation, now began to form that Scipionic reputation for equity which was still a byword over three-quarters of a century later.

After a winter spent at their base north of the Ebro, the brothers further consolidated the surrounding

territories, while Hasdrubal was engaged with a revolt of the Turdetani in the Baetis valley. The Carthaginian position in Spain at this time (216 B.C.) was unsatisfactory, if not disquieting. For the third successive year Spain had failed to transmit any reinforcements to Hannibal in Italy: moreover, the Roman hold on north-eastern Spain was gradually increasing, Roman domination having thus far proved acceptable in comparison with that of Carthage. But the Roman successes must not be exaggerated. Although the Scipios had indeed reached Saguntum, the Ebro was still their real frontier, beyond which operations were possible only because they were masters of the sea. For Hasdrubal, the passage of the Ebro would still win a path from Spain to Italy, and, reinforced by an army from Africa under Himilco, as well as by other troops, he now determined to force that passage, and moved up to the Ebro. There he found the Scipios besieging Hibera, opposite Dertosa (Tortosa),—a position of great strategic importance. His use of the tactics victorious at Cannae—the receding centre designed to draw the enemy into the enveloping wings—placed too great a strain on the Spaniards to whom he had assigned the centre. By their great triumph of arms, the Scipios finally closed the road from Punic Spain to Italy, and won over to the Roman cause considerable Spanish enthusiasm. Even the disaster of Cannae itself was the less dreadful now that Spain was safely isolated.[29]

In 215 B.C., therefore, the next move lay with the Scipios. But their plans could not be free from anxiety. Reinforcements were necessary in the face of the new army sent under Mago (brother of Hannibal) to join Hasdrubal; and Rome, temporarily

3

crippled by Cannae, and further distracted by the
threat of war with Macedon, was scarcely in a position
to think primarily of the needs of her army in Spain.
Moreover, heavy Roman expenditure in Sicily and
Sardinia made the shortage of pay and military food-
rations (*frumentum*) in Spain all the more difficult to
meet, so that in the end recourse was made to private
loans in order to supply the Scipios with money—not
before they had considered the possibility of contributions from the Spaniards themselves.[30]   And there
was still no Roman base south of the Ebro line.
Against this, Carthage was embarrassed in Spain by
possibility of revolt in the upper valley of the Baetis,
and in Africa by the attitude of Syphax. All these
considerations help to explain why the three years
215–213 B.C. were comparatively uneventful, with the
Romans perhaps the more successful owing to defec-
tions from the Punic cause. The tradition of the
Roman annalists fills these years with stirring accounts
of a Roman advance to the upper Baetis.[31]   How
absurd this tradition is may be seen from the fact that
the Scipios did not actually capture Saguntum until
the close of this period. This achievement, coupled
with the desertion of Castulo (Cazlona) to the Roman
side, ultimately tempted them to decisive action on the
upper Baetis.[32]   In 212 B.C. both the Romans and the
Carthaginians received additions to their strength,
the former having raised large levies of mercenary
Celtiberians, while the latter were reinforced from
Africa (now free from fear of Syphax) by a fresh
army under Hasdrubal, son of Gisgo. There is some
reason for supposing that the Roman forces—or at
least part of them, under Publius—spent the winter of
212–211 at the head of the Baetis valley—perhaps at
Castulo.[33]   The campaigning season of 211 thus

found the Scipios projecting their forces, well beyond their new base at Saguntum, in the face of three Punic armies, with Carthago Nova threatening their flank. Having divided their forces they prepared for an offensive. Separately, they were attacked, defeated and killed. First Cnaeus, stationed in the neighbourhood of Carthago Nova to safeguard communications with Saguntum, was deserted by his Celtiberians and destroyed; and, just a month later, Publius suffered similar disaster in the Baetis watershed.[34] In a moment the whole fabric of power which, for eight years,[35] the Romans had been building south of the Ebro, utterly collapsed. Towns changed their allegiance, Punic influence was now strongly in the ascendant, and even Saguntum probably lapsed once more, for the next regular Roman base of which we hear is to the north of the Ebro. That the Ebro remained still an adequate frontier was due chiefly to the presence of mind shown by L. Marcius, a Roman knight, who contrived to unite the broken remnants of the brothers' armies and to lead them northward for garrison service on the line of that river, now vitally important;[36] there they were presently reinforced by detachments sent out from Italy under Claudius Nero. Even so, they were powerless to prevent the adherence of the Ilergetes to Carthage.

In Rome assemblies were held for the election of a proconsul to succeed P. Scipio; and it was now that the Senate showed, in the highest degree, that sagacity, acumen, and boldness to which the wars of the third century had trained its members. Publius Cornelius Scipio, son of the dead general Publius, was no more than twenty-five years of age when he suddenly announced his intention to stand as a candidate for election. Public experience, in the strict sense, he had little—his only office so far was that of curule aedile in 213 B.C. ; but he was the gifted son of a noted member of one of the most famous families of the day, born into a circle where men forestalled experience by logical experiment. The Senate could argue that the Spanish policy of the two dead Scipios was unfortunate only in the manner of its ending, for it had achieved its object, namely, to nullify or diminish the value of Spain to Hannibal in Italy. Its continuation was therefore necessary ; and, accordingly, senatorial support successfully resulted in the election of the man most likely to carry on his father's plans. By that one action, as it turned out, was assured ultimate victory in the whole war.[37]

Towards the end of 210 B.C. Scipio, accompanied by M. Junius Silanus—an able propraetor and *adiutor ad res gerendas*—and commanding a new army of 10,000 foot and 1000 horse, landed at Emporium, and marched thence to Tarraco.[38] His first duty was to refresh and inspire the spirit of the Roman troops in Spain, now amounting to four legions ; his second, to revive the friendly loyalty of the tribes which had previously reacted so willingly to the equity of his father and his uncle. In both tasks he was successful, and, although the influence of his combined personality, charm, and genius was so far exaggerated as to induce the rationalist Polybius to discount or explain away its consequences, a later age of rationalists cannot deny to this young general the shining gifts of persuasion and reconciliation, of accurate planning and resolute execution, of spiritual fervour and worldly wisdom, of personal modesty and godlike dignity. The growth of the Scipionic legend is easy to explain, for it is easily understood.[39]

Having thus quickly consolidated the coastal area

north of the Ebro, Scipio could plan his first offensive. The twin disasters of 211 had shown clearly that between Roman Spain, north of the Ebro, and Punic Spain, mainly west of Carthago Nova, existed a kind of no-man's-land, through which either side could march in safety, though neither could use it as a base. From 218 to 212 the Roman generals had done little more than increase Roman influence in this intervening territory: their first attempt to use it as a base for further advance caused their defeat and death. Put briefly, the matter was one of communications: for operations in Murcia or Andalusia a base even at Saguntum was far too remote. Scipio intended to carry the war into Punic Spain. As a base, therefore, he decided to win the nearer of the two Punic bases: with Carthago Nova safely in his hands as a strategic position (quite apart from the value of its mines, its stores of money and arms, its hostages and its harbour), he could force Carthage to fight not for eastern but for southern Spain. His daring plan was favoured by the disposition of the three Carthaginian armies in the winter of 210–209. The nearest, under Hasdrubal Barca, was in Carpetania; Hasdrubal, son of Gisgo, was near the mouth of the Tagus, in the far west; while Mago was in the extreme south near Gibraltar. Not only their forces, but their counsels too were divided; and, finally, their harsh treatment of the Spaniards had alienated from them considerable local enthusiasm. As for Carthago Nova itself, it contained a garrison of no more than a thousand men.[40]

These were the arguments which Scipio himself addressed, in the spring of 209, to the troops—Romans and Italian allies (*socii*)—whom he mustered at the mouth of the Ebro. Then, leaving Silanus with 3500 men to guard the ever-important Ebro, he made for

Carthago Nova with all the possible speed of forced marches; Laelius, his friend and intimate, was ordered to sail down the coast, making his arrival coincide with that of Scipio by land. Such was Scipio's swiftness that no Punic army, even had his plans been known, could have intercepted him. Nevertheless, the presence of Hasdrubal Barca in Carpetania necessitated equally swift action once Scipio had reached his objective: a siege of even a few days would involve the greatest risk. But the manner in which Scipio beset and stormed this strong and famous arsenal within the compass of a single day leaves no doubt that he had already planned this most brilliant of tactical achievements, and that the topography was well known to him in advance. Carthago Nova is situated, within a deep inlet of the sea, upon a rocky projection which, joined to the mainland on the east by no more than an isthmus, is thus surrounded on three sides by water. To the north, however, the water was a mere lagoon, with an apparently regular rise and fall in level which made it fordable at known periods: elsewhere, the water was fully navigable.[41] Scipio at once encamped on the isthmus, thus cutting off the citadel from the mainland, and set up fortifications in case of the early arrival of Punic relief-forces from the interior. On the following day, after the customary exhortations, the action was begun: the fleet surrounded the citadel on the two navigable sides, south and west, and the army attacked sufficiently to encourage the Punic commander to attempt a sally of armed citizens which, rashly undertaken and easily beaten back, very nearly ended in the admission of Roman troops. Meanwhile, the garrison proper had been withdrawn from the walls to reinforce the safety of the gates: and it was now that the Roman fleet

launched its attacks of missiles and storming-parties on those parts of the walls which it surrounded. Evening was drawing on, and still the citadel held out. Suddenly the waters of the northern lagoon began to recede, not (it must be concluded) at the regular tidal period—for the Carthaginian commander would have foreseen that danger—but as the result of a stiff breeze from the land blowing out to sea.[42] Scipio may have known of the rare possibility of the phenomenon : in any case, he sent 500 men with ladders running round to the northern wall, now approachable, though still deserted. Their swift ascent found the garrison assailed on all sides, and actually attacked from behind. Quickly the Carthaginian defenders were cut down, and the gates opened to Scipio's main forces, who massacred the remaining combatants, and occupied the citadel.

One day's bitter struggle thus gave Scipio the key to south-east Spain, with all its wealth (a treasure of 600 talents, apart from the constant produce of the adjacent mines), its munitions and apparatus of war, and its thousands of prisoners : equally valuable was the immense admiration and personal prestige which his daring success had won for him. This was, indeed, enhanced by his very clemency in victory, of which the ancient authorities record numerous instances with a romantic fervour not necessarily exclusive of underlying truth.[43]

The remainder of the season was spent by Scipio in the drilling and reorganization of his army, and in the strengthening of the defences of the city ; and it is possible that a limited amount of reconnaissance was undertaken in the surrounding territory.[44] For the winter he returned to Tarraco, where he reaped the harvest of his equity and diplomacy in the allegiance

offered to him by native communities, and notably
by the Edetani, who occupied the strategically important area south of the Ebro : their example was
presently followed by Indibilis, chief of the Ilergetes.
Scipio's energies were now directed to the collection
of the largest possible army, preparatory to a resolute
advance from the newly won base, and we are told
that he even enlisted his marines, doubtless owing to
the disappearance of an effective Punic fleet from the
east coast after the fall of Carthago Nova. In the spring
of 208 he moved southwards, seeking an objective in
one of the Carthaginian armies. This was furnished
when Hasdrubal Barca, now cut off from Carthago
Nova, and unwilling to chance the passage of the
Ebro and withdrawal to Italy before he had engaged
the Roman army, retired from Carpetania to the upper
valley of the Baetis, taking up his position at Baecula,
in the neighbourhood of Castulo.[45]   There he was
attacked by Scipio's army, which, probably superior
in numbers, used the new enveloping tactics with
such success that Hasdrubal was defeated. But he was
not routed, and, collecting his forces, he swiftly
withdrew to the Tagus valley, whence he marched to
the northern Pyrenees *en route* for Italy, unchecked by
the Roman forces on the Ebro. Scipio had but one
army, and further comment on the battle of Baecula
(which reduced the opposing armies to two) is
therefore superfluous : to leave two armies in his
rear while he risked the difficult feat of overtaking and
defeating Hasdrubal was not the part of the general
sent to hold Spain for Rome.

In the following year (207 B.C.) the Carthaginian
commanders, Hasdrubal, son of Gisgo, and Mago,
showed signs that they realized the growing menace of
Roman penetration. New reinforcements arrived from

Africa under Hanno, who was deputed also to recruit among the Celtiberians,—an activity which nearly ended in complete disaster when Scipio sent Silanus with a force of 10,500 men to attack him by surprise. As it was, the defeat, though it was crushing, and resulted in the capture of Hanno, was only partial, and survivors were able to escape, presumably along the highlands between the Anas and the Baetis (since the upper Baetis valley was now in Roman hands), to Gades, where Hasdrubal (son of Gisgo) now had his base. The latter, to avoid the decisive engagement for which Scipio was now striving, divided up his forces to act as garrisons in a number of local towns, whose strength and tenacity was to test Roman exertions in years to come : temporarily checked, Scipio sent his brother Lucius with a strong force of 11,000 men to capture a certain Orongis, a wealthy town of the interior, the exact position of which cannot be determined,[46] and this enterprise was successful, giving Rome yet another hold upon the upper waters of the Baetis. Meanwhile, Roman recruiting was proceeding apace : Culchas, the ruler of twenty-eight Turdetanian towns, had collected 3500 men, and, by the spring of 206 B.C.,[47] Scipio's forces amounted to nearly fifty thousand men, as against the fifty-five or sixty thousand of the Carthaginians.

For good or ill, Hasdrubal now had to fight a decisive battle. The Scipionic tide of victory was irresistible : the Ebro, Carthago Nova, Baecula, the Baetis valley—these brilliant successes had not been invalidated by any conclusive achievement of Hannibal in Italy. A single engagement might result in the complete expulsion of the Carthaginians from Spain ; but it might also nullify the greater part of Scipio's record, if he himself (like his father and his uncle) were defeated and killed: such was the influence of victorious prestige on the natives of Spain, ground as they were between the two millstones of Rome and Carthage. Hasdrubal therefore collected his army and advanced northward from Gades as far as Ilipa, a site probably to be identified with the modern village of Alcala del Rio, a little to the north of Italica (Santiponce).[48] Here he was opposed by Scipio, the regular daily routine of whose army lulled Hasdrubal into a sense of false security, which was rudely shattered when Scipio delivered a surprise attack. He again employed the enveloping tactics which he had tried before: again they were successful, though he had not sufficient troops to surround the enemy. Nevertheless, the number of those who escaped with Hasdrubal and Mago was no more than 6000: the rest of the great Punic army were killed or captured or dispersed. The Carthaginians were now pushed back to that very base from which Hamilcar had undertaken the reconquest of Spain thirty years previously. At this juncture Scipio made a daring crossing to Africa to negotiate with Syphax: to the man of genius Ilipa marked, not the end of the Spanish war, but the transference of the Punic war to Africa.

Fortune, however, was still to teach Rome, in the remaining events of this crowded season of whirlwind enterprise, that, while each of two foreign powers might command considerable native allegiance, varying with their success or failure, the victorious survival of one of the two at once changed the relationships from that of leaders and allies to that of conquerors and subjects. Forces of nationalism existed in Spain (and especially among the Turdetani, who boasted a glorious past) which Scipio, like many another and inferior general, perhaps underestimated. Ilurgia

(Lorqui) and Castax (an unidentif.d site)[49] had perhaps too willingly joined the Punic cause after the
double Roman tragedy of 211, though it is more
likely that, with the collapse of Punic power in 206,
they attempted to resume their old independent
position. Ilurgia was stormed and its inhabitants
massacred—an example which induced Castax to surrender: but Astapa (Estepa) required violent measures
for its capture. Similar difficulties arose in the extreme
north-east of Spain, though there the provocation
was different. Scipio, returned from Africa, fell ill at
Carthago Nova, and this news was followed by mutiny
among the Roman troops stationed on the Sucro to
act as a liaison between Carthago Nova and Tarraco:
we are told that the rising was due to arrears of pay,
a motive which was doubtless backed by discontent
caused by patrol-duty at a time when the main Roman
army was distinguishing itself in Andalusia. The
mutiny, not in itself difficult to overcome, became
highly dangerous when Mandonius and Indibilis, the
ever-fickle princes of the Ilergetes, took the opportunity to revolt north of the Ebro, with Celtiberian
support. A mixture of tact and severity on Scipio's
part put down the mutiny, but the native rebellion
was not quelled until a set battle had been fought on
the Ebro and the defeated princes encouraged by
clemency to fresh allegiance.

Meanwhile, Mago still held out in Gades, momentarily encouraged by these Roman difficulties to
collect money and prolong resistance. But his
exactions stood him in ill stead: having attempted to
emulate Scipio's exploit by a surprise attack on
Carthago Nova, he was repulsed and found on his
return that Gades (which some months before had
been in contact with Scipio) would no longer receive

him. Soon Gades went over voluntarily to the
Roman cause—commerce would still be commerce
whether under Carthage or Rome—and the Carthaginian abandonment of Spain was complete. Mago
might still hope for support from the islands, but,
although the Pithyusae were friendly, the Balearis
Major was strongly pro-Roman. Thus the theatre of
war moved from Spain, which was now destined to
undergo the longer and even more difficult process of
organization on Roman provincial lines. Scipio, his
work in Spain accomplished, returned to Rome in
time to stand as a candidate for the consular elections
for 205 B.C. His election, and the triumph which he
celebrated, were richly deserved, for in six years he
had won a third of the Iberian peninsula; and the
14,000 odd pounds of silver which he proudly displayed (doubtless for the greater part Carthaginian
treasure) afforded a comforting economic solace—
perhaps also promise—to a state which for twelve
years had faced incessant warfare on two widely
separated fronts. Livy, with the instinct of the
dramatist, ends this story of Spanish conquest with a
reference[50] to the gratitude of the Saguntines, who
were now to receive their dues from the neighbours
whose original recalcitrance had led Carthage into
war.

CHAPTER III

EARLY ROMAN ADMINISTRATION

THE provincial era in Spain may be regarded as having begun in 205 B.C., for, upon his departure, Scipio entrusted the government of the newly won territories to L. Cornelius Lentulus and L. Manlius Acidinus.[1] These two generals—Lentulus in the 'farther' part of Spain, and Acidinus in the 'nearer' —were subsequently prolonged in their dual command until 200 B.C., when Lentulus was replaced by C. Cornelius Cethegus ; and they, together with all other generals sent to administer Spain up to and including the year 198, enjoyed specially conferred proconsular *imperium*. Not until 197 B.C. was the annual number of praetors at Rome raised by two :[2] this innovation, which henceforth supplied Spain with regularly elected proconsular governors, was one part of the official plan of reorganization drawn up for the Spanish provinces in that year.

For nearly ten years, therefore, an *ad hoc* system of government was thought to be sufficient for the needs of Spanish administration. Nevertheless this system paved the way for the later and permanent scheme in and after 197 : the principle of dual command stood unchanged, and in this arrangement it is impossible not to discern the influence of Scipio, who, more than any other living man, knew how greatly the problem of military control in the peninsula was affected by its physical geography. The Punic War in Spain had been governed almost wholly by the courses of the two rivers Ebro and Baetis. In the first phase of the war, when Publius and Cnaeus Cornelius Scipio were in command, the line of the Ebro marked the farthest extremity of consolidated Roman territory; and it was their desire to extend their power in the direction of the Baetis valley which led to their undoing. For they neglected two vital necessities which their successor was quick to appreciate: first, the great distance between Ebro and Baetis must somewhere contain an outpost, or kind of advanced base (and the capture of Carthago Nova gave Rome what was almost the only such position available); and secondly, any projected base of this nature must rely upon undisputed naval supremacy along the east coast of Spain (and here, too, Africanus' instinct did not err). From this strong outpost the conquest of the Baetis valley was, though difficult, a matter which would need only time, skill, and patience, without waste of lives and money; and this was the second phase of the war. But, even though the war was now won, geographical factors could by no means be disregarded in the administration of Spain. The total area of Roman dominion was limited, but uncomfortably elongated as well (Map II). From the Pyrenees to the Ebro it consisted of a wedge, which tapered dangerously between the Ebro and Carthago Nova, whence communications to Castulo and the Baetis valley ran through difficult and mountainous country. The obstacles which hindered a widening of this attenuated 'province' were various. Its northern limit verged on the higher ground of the interior, where the peoples (if not actively hostile) were unstable or treacherous. Along the coast there were surprisingly few settlements friendly enough and strong enough to uphold the

Roman cause. In the extreme south-west, the Baetis valley contained loose confederations of towns under petty kings, whose policy developed an increasingly anti-Roman tone.

Clearly the operation of a single Roman army in this area, along such an interminable and hazardous route, was impossible. If attempted, it would invite the employment of Celtiberian mercenaries—a risky step which had already cost one Scipio his life, and had been expressly avoided by Africanus when he drafted them to Italy as ' auxiliary ' troops.[3] It was true that Roman expansion might be facilitated by a deliberate policy of conciliation : Cnaeus Scipio had won considerable native support, and even affection, by such methods ; and Africanus was never behind-hand in this respect. But it was easy to underestimate the forces and tendencies of Spanish nationalism, as the revolts of Castax and Ilurgia had already shown, and as the behaviour of the Ilergetes was yet again to prove.

Such were the lessons of past experience ; and it cannot be doubted that the tentative system of dual command which was in force between the years 205 and 197 was in fact an experiment (deliberately undertaken in order that the two-province system might be tested) for which Africanus was chiefly responsible. If there was any initial doubt of its success, it might have been on the ground that co-operation between two governors in these particular provinces was an urgent necessity, and that the very reasons which recommended a two-province system made co-operation very difficult. Difficult it may have been, but it was frequently achieved, especially in the experimental years before 197 B.C. ; and it continued after that date, being assisted by the wisdom of the two first regular proconsuls, acting as Provincial Commissioners, when they came to demarcate the inter-provincial boundary.[4] Disregarding the hallowed tradition of the Ebro frontier, the Commissioners concentrated on the security of the farther province—or Hispania Ulterior, as it now came to be known: the governor of Ulterior was chiefly dependent on coastal positions for his safety, and the shortest possible littoral would therefore save his strength and automatically curtail the amount of hinterland for which he bore responsibility. Accordingly the nearer province (Citerior) was extended westwards so as to include Carthago Nova: exactly how far west of this city the boundary was fixed cannot be said with certainty, though it was probably east of Baria (Vera).[5]   Inland, it appears to have run to the east of the Saltus Tugiensis and Castulo; and in its main bearing it remained without serious modification until Augustus carried out his great Spanish reconstruction (below, p. 132 ff.), being only extended as the series of wars in the second century B.C. called for the co-operation of the two governors ever farther into the interior,—successively to the Anas, the Tagus, and the Durius.   In the same way the northern frontier of each province remained vague, being defined only by the limit of Roman armed penetration at any given time, though for Ulterior the course of the Baetis served at first as a natural boundary.

In neither province was there any true homogeneity, either as a whole, or within the several elements which composed them.[6]   Citerior was little more than a coastal strip (deepening at one point in a salient) which extended for some four hundred miles and was primarily dependent for its safety on the two strong Roman positions at Tarraco and Carthago Nova.

Each of these towns was a nucleus of military power, which only later came to possess commercial importance once the economic development of Spain was begun. But they were widely separated, and to some extent were compelled to rely on the support of other towns and settlements, both Iberian and Greek. Of the Iberians on the coast Saguntum and Dertosa represented the chief centres. Roman relations with Saguntum have already been outlined: whatever the nature of the tie,[7] it had been strong enough to survive through the disastrous years of the Punic hostilities. Dertosa was not a coastal town in the strict sense, but it lay not far inland, where the Ebro was navigable—an important guardian of the river-crossing, destined to become quickly romanized: its prosperity was due to something of the same combination of geographical factors which assisted Massilia. The Greek settlements of the coast were more numerous,—Rhode (Rosas), Emporium, Dianium (Denia), Alonae, and Lucentum (as Akra Leuke was now known). In contrast to the Iberian coastal towns, whose inhabitants, being indigenous, must have possessed a surrounding *territorium*,[8] the Greek towns consisted of foreigners whose sole livelihood was in trade and commerce, the importance of which is to be seen in the coinages of Rhode and Emporium (Pl. I, 1, 2): Rhode began to mint money early in the fourth century, and Emporium in the late fourth or early third, the coins of both towns circulating widely enough to be made the subject of barbarous imitation directly inland.[9] It is true that no mints existed at Dianium, Alonae, or Lucentum; but it must be remembered that these were mere outposts of a Greek commercial orbit which centred around Emporium and Massilia; their importance had dwindled during the Carthaginian domination over Spain (see above, p. 16), and it is probable that the coming of the Romans may even have appeared to them as a means of future self-improvement. Rhode and Emporium, on the other hand, had previously combined in a trading monopoly of much of the east coast, and the increasingly commercial tone of Roman policy in Spain could only be regarded as a threat to their prosperity: Emporium, in particular, took advantage of the initial unrest among the Ilergetes to adopt a less friendly attitude towards Rome.[10]

North of the Ebro came the salient to which reference has been made; and here the Romans were faced with the problem of dealing with genuinely tribal areas, which centred chiefly in Ilerda and Osca (Huesca). Here there was but little indigenous culture (in comparison with the Iberians of the coast) on which Roman civilization could be built, for external influences did not readily penetrate inland. But the chief importance of this region was its mineral wealth which, as will be seen below (p. 55 f.), resulted in a swift extension of Roman power. This extension may have been welcome enough to those Iberians to whom the resumption of mining (probably interrupted during the Punic war) was likely to bring profit:[11] but even they were soon to be disillusioned, while the rest of the Iberians of this district as a whole long continued to be hostile and untrustworthy. South of the Ebro the province narrowed abruptly, where the central plateau frowns closely upon the coast; and nearly twenty years were to pass before any effective Roman penetration took place.[12]

The problems of Ulterior were different. This was the area in which Punic influence had been strongest.

Although the period of the Barcid generals had conferred no political system on the communities of the Baetis valley, the Carthaginian desire for Spanish mineral wealth had nevertheless made not unwilling middle-men out of the Turdetanians and their neighbours, who, familiar with the tradition of foreign intervention and sufficiently cultured to take advantage of it, had doubtless kept on good enough terms with Carthage. The coast itself, from Baria to the mouth of the Baetis, was studded with a series of trading and fishing stations of Phoenician or Carthaginian origin —Abdera, Sexi (Almuñécar), Malaca, Suel (Fuengirola), Mellaria (Fuente Ovejuna), and Gades : here there was frequent use of Punic coin, and the Punic character of the settlements themselves persisted down to, and even during, the Empire (cf. Pl. III, 4). These settlements, though peaceful and capable of self-government on Punic lines (Gades, for instance, was administered by suffetes), exerted little political influence around them. The lower courses of the Baetis enclosed a large number of agricultural communities, both prosperous and capable of a certain coherence under petty regional kings of the type represented by Culchas and Luxinius.[13] Higher up the valley, between the Sierra Morena and the Sierra Nevada, lay the towns of the famous mining district which centred in Castulo. East of this extended a mountainous tract of country (for long the haunt of brigands) which must be traversed by those wishing to go by land to Carthago Nova. In all the province there was not a single town of any mature Roman character. Scipio Africanus' sure instinct had led him to found his veteran colony at Italica (Santiponce)—a highly advantageous site in the lower Baetis valley, where the river was fully navigable.[14] But Italica was yet in its infancy ; and on the coast there was no Roman nucleus at all, until the foundation of Carteia (see below, p. 76) in 171 B.C.

Such were the diverse elements for whom Rome was now to devise an administrative scheme. Hitherto the Roman policy of aggression in Spain had been in fact a tactical defence against Carthage : fighting what has been called a war of propaganda, the Romans had contracted formal alliances with various of the native groups, doubtless posing as the champions against Carthage ; and any natural infidelity on the part of the Iberians was to some extent offset by the equally characteristic Iberian indifference to all foreigners, whether Punic or otherwise, and by the perpetual inability of Iberian communities to achieve any solid or permanent federal spirit. The Spaniards were now left alone with the Romans, and the liberators now became the conquerors, not only of Carthage, but of Spain as well. In framing an administrative system for the new provinces, the Romans had but little experience to guide them : imperialist philosophy in the true sense was the creation of Caesar and Augustus. Sicily, Sardinia, and Corsica had all become provinces of the Republic, but their incorporation was recent, and had occurred in circumstances of stress and anxiety comparable to those in which Spain had been won. Of material advantage the Romans had perhaps thought little at first ; but even the least familiarity with Spain would have soon shown them the rich possibilities of economic exploitation and the vast resources in manpower—which, indeed, had already been tapped. Labour and expense in acquisition could therefore be counterbalanced by exploitation of Spanish wealth and man-power ; and this, in brief, was the philosophy which underlay the administrative system applied

during the Republic to backward and (by Roman standards) uncivilized communities.[15]

By this system the newly won provinces became, in the technical phrase, *ager publicus populi Romani*, ' the common property of the Roman state.' Communities which were actually subjugated, or which yielded voluntarily to Rome, ceased to own the land upon which they were settled, and paid instead for a tenancy which was theoretically revocable.[16]   For equality in independence was now substituted equality in subjection : to all alike Rome was to be the sole source of change, amelioration, or profit. Exceptions were nevertheless made, for (as W. T. Arnold has truly remarked) Rome was not cursed with a passion for uniformity when latitude and variation were likely to benefit her or assist her in her heavy work of administration.   Certainly Gades, and probably others of the Punic coastal towns, gained the speedy friendship of Rome in this manner, being rewarded by the grant of status as *ager privatus ex iure peregrino*, by which they became either *civitates liberae*, i.e. autonomous, and with their own code of laws, or *liberae et foederatae*, when this autonomy depended not merely on Roman goodwill, but on a formal treaty as between equals. But such favoured cases were few at first in comparison with the overwhelming number of *civitates stipendiariae*, or tenant communities, which even two centuries later formed by far the largest proportion of Spanish towns (below, p. 147).[17]   These were compelled to pay *stipendium*, i.e. tribute in money and kind, to furnish *auxilia* for service in the Roman army, and (to some extent) to observe Roman law.[18]

To deal first with *stipendium* : the communities of Spain were fortunate in that they paid a fixed sum in tribute,[19] assessed by a census of the rateable value of their buildings, land, and produce : they thus avoided the evil of tithes, i.e. compulsory payment of a proportion of their harvest varying with the yield, with the attendant scourge of the *publicani*, or tax-farmers. The Spanish *tributum* was a direct tax, for the collection of which the provincial quaestors (as the governors' chief financial officers) were responsible. In the early years of the Roman administration the precise nature and rate of the tribute-payments was not clearly defined, and at no time is the total revenue recorded. Thus in 205 B.C. the fresh subjection of the Iberians north of the Ebro was followed by the imposition of a double *stipendium*, as well as six months' supply of grain, and cloaks and togas for the army.[20] But this may probably be regarded as a war-indemnity, and it would probably be correct to say that the *stipendium* normally payable was a duly assessed sum in money, which in the case of poorer communities was commuted to an equivalent amount in corn or other commodities, and to which richer communities might sometimes be obliged to add contributions in kind : possibly Cato systematized the method of payments in 195 B.C.[21] It may be noted that *stipendium* probably became (in later years at any rate) a dual tax, on property (*tributum soli*) and persons (*tributum capitis*) : the latter impost was presumably a poll-tax in origin, but it seems ultimately to have developed the character of an income-tax, under which allowance was made for differences in earnings or trades.[22]

This system of a fixed *stipendium* was obviously one which encouraged payment in coin, and, in Citerior at least, seems to have resulted in a regular tribute-coinage. Whatever be the correct date to be assigned to the first Roman X-*denarius*,[23] it is reasonably certain that comparatively few Roman silver coins could have

penetrated into the Iberian districts by *c.* 205–200 B.C., for, though Roman troops were the chief means by which coinage was disseminated, the armies were seldom long settled in any one district, and the Iberians were not rich in commodities which they were at liberty to sell. Tribute-payment in Roman-distributed Roman coins was therefore a poor means of benefiting the Roman treasury: and it cannot have been long before orders were given that the *stipendium* imposed on any one suitable district should be paid in coins struck locally from local silver. Such regional silver coinages[24] were an innovation for the peoples of the interior, though, as we have noted, there was a variety of well-established coastal coinages. The origin of the new issues can be approximately dated by Livy's lists of the bullion and specie brought back to Rome by the earlier governors of Spain.[25] Before 197–196 B.C., when Cn. Cornelius Blasio returned from Spain with 34,500 *denarii*, there is no record in Livy of the acquisition of coin by the governors of Spain, other than that which Scipio brought home in 206, and which (as Schulten has observed) was doubtless Punic money from Carthago Nova and elsewhere. Blasio's *denarii* are not distinguished by Livy[26] as anything but Roman silver coins: and these must represent a proportion of the Roman coinage which had entered Spain in the preceding twenty years. In 195 B.C. Helvius, a former governor of Ulterior, and Minucius, a former governor of Citerior, brought home (besides very large quantities of bar-silver) 119,439 and 278,000 respectively of what Livy calls 'Oscan silver' (sc. coins):[27] these coins appear later in the lists for 194, 191, 180, and 168 B.C. The use of the term *argentum Oscense* is of much interest. Clearly it should indicate that the mint of Osca was the earliest of a series of newly established native mints; and from the application of this term to *denarii* brought back from Ulterior it may be deduced that the Oscan coins, by a greater frequency in their circulation, resulted in a generic name applicable to all native Iberian issues. This deduction is confirmed by modern study of the coins in question (cf. Pl. I, 4–7): the coins attributable to Osca (Pl. I, 4; cf. 3) are extremely common.[28] But other mints were active too—that of Secaisa in particular,[29] of which the coins have been found very widely distributed, at Corduba, Numantia, the Ebro valley, and even southern France: this dispersion helps to explain how Helvius in 195 B.C. was able to collect over 119,000 Iberian *denarii* from a chiefly non-Iberian area. The extension of Roman power in subsequent years is reflected in the steady expansion of the coinage area:[30] mints sprang up further and further inland, all striking coins of similar types—a bearded (Iberian) head on the obverse, and a horseman on the reverse, bearing a palm when the coins were struck in the area of the original conquests (as at Ausa, Ieso, Ilerda, Laietania, Tarraco, Alavona, Celsa, Salduba, Lagne, Gili, Lauro, Agreda), and a lance in the districts which needed greater efforts for their subjection.[31]

All coins of this type bore legends in Iberian characters, which have been read as tribal names, and not as town names—a fact which may be interpreted as a sign of Roman readiness to acknowledge, and deal with, the Iberians on a tribal basis rather than to pursue a *divide et impera* policy. The coins themselves were carefully struck, from dies which were usually adjusted in a fixed relationship, with strict uniformity of types and weight—this latter being that of the Roman *denarius*: and from this it may be deduced that there was strict Roman supervision of their production. The

silver coins were accompanied by issues of bronze, which became increasingly common as the days of internal barter gave way to an era of safer communications and regular buying and selling as between community and community.

In the *argentum Oscense* we therefore see the means by which the Iberian communities of Citerior in particular paid their *stipendium*, in silver mined and coined at their own expense and afterwards melted down at Rome for re-coinage as *denarii*. We must imagine that the communities of Ulterior, Turdetanians and others, paid partly in native coins ' imported ' from Citerior, and partly in raw metals and grain, for which the district was famous. It would have been chiefly from Ulterior that extraordinary requisitions of grain were made in the earliest years of the administration : Ulterior, again, was most likely to feel the burden of the *vicesimae* (the gradually increasing system by which Spaniards were forced to buy twentieths of their harvest at slump-prices arbitrarily fixed by Roman control),[32] and of the arbitrary pricing of all corn by Roman officials, until these pernicious practices were stopped in the ' petition year ' of 171 B.C. Schulten has suggested that a similar levy existed on oil within the area of its production : and this, too, would primarily affect Ulterior.

Schulten, indeed, has concluded that, of the two provinces, Ulterior was the richer.[33] Potentially, this may have been true ; and in an era of peace which encouraged the fullest economic development it certainly was true. In the early years, however, Citerior produced an amount of raw metal and hard cash greater than that of Ulterior, as analysis of Livy's lists will show. Nor is this surprising in view of the distribution-areas of the precious metals :[34] the rich gold

deposits of the north-west, of the Tagus, and of the
Durius, were as yet untapped, but there was gold in
Murcia and in the Sierra Morena (enough to counterbalance what came from Ulterior), while silver was
being mined in the immensely prolific deposits at
Baebelo and Carthago Nova,[35] to say nothing of what
the Ebro valley yielded—sufficient for the name ' Oscan
silver ' to be applied to it all indiscriminately. Not yet
were the richest mineral sources of Ulterior equally
well developed. It was, of course, from the mines of
both provinces that the great quantities of uncoined
gold and silver appearing in Livy's lists were derived.
If it is asked why the amounts vary so widely from
year to year (and this applies also to the requisitions in
corn), then it may be answered, first, that the tribute-
lists even of the highly organized Athenian Empire had
fluctuated similarly, as the fortunes or scope of that
Empire varied ; and secondly, that until the mines and
mining system had been thoroughly organized there
was bound to be a considerable fluctuation in output.
It is likely that such organization was begun by Cato
in 195 B.C., at least in Citerior, as a means of increasing
the yield.[36]   The precise system of working and ownership in the early Republican period cannot be stated,
though more is known of the later years (see below,
p. 107) ; but it is perhaps correct to say that, while the
ownership of certain gold and silver mines was vested
directly in the State, most mines of silver (e.g. Carthago
Nova in later years) and of lead, copper, and iron were
leased to individuals or companies who paid a royalty
on the yield. Labour in the State-owned mines might
be supplied by slaves, and sometimes perhaps by free
and wage-earning Spaniards : the other mines soon
attracted a large influx of Romans and Italians—the
πλῆθος Ἰταλῶν of Diodorus[37]—whose activities would

naturally tend to reduce the employment, and therefore
financial benefit, of the Spaniards themselves.

Mines therefore were responsible for two entries in
the Roman credit-account of Spain : they supplied the
tribute-coinage, and also vast quantities of bullion
worked and exported under the direct supervision or
lease of the Roman state. Of the various commodities
imported from Spain, such as mineral salts, esparto
grass, stock, horses, timber, textiles, fish, oil, and wine,
more will be said in a later chapter.

The second of the obligations laid upon the subject
communities of Spain was that of compulsory military
service in the auxiliary regiments of the Roman army.
Even before the organization of the two provinces,
Spaniards had been conscripted for this purpose,[38] as
well as serving as mercenaries. From 205 B.C., however, mercenary service must have disappeared for all
effective purposes, though it is of interest to note that
Cato employed Celtiberians as mercenaries to produce
national disruption in 195 B.C.[39]

Thirdly, there was the necessity (in part at least)
of observing Roman law. The scope of this obligation increased with the years : bureaucracy was
clearly beyond the powers of the Roman governors,
either to expect or to introduce, in the earliest years ;
and knowledge of Roman law had to wait, for its
extension, until sufficient centres of Roman life and
customs existed for its dissemination. A wise
governor would not therefore always interfere in
every detail of local government. Nevertheless,
either he or his deputies could, if moral scruple were
absent, take such a thorough interest in local affairs
that only money would procure deliverance, for it
must be remembered that the governor was not only
commander-in-chief of the provincial army, but the

chief judicial officer as well. Some conception of the abuses to which the early provincial system was open can be gained from the petition of Gades—a privileged town—in 199 B.C. against the imposition of *praefecti*. Two years later the defection of other and doubtless similarly privileged Punic towns to the rebel cause of Culchas and Luxinius may have been due to the same causes. The whole question was raised prominently in 171 B.C., together with the wheat-quota abuse already mentioned, and suppression of these odious practices was then promised.[40]

Such, in very brief outline, was the administrative system applied to the Spanish provinces from about 200 B.C. onwards. Within this framework were many details of policy and organization, to which only passing allusion can be made here. The object of the Roman system was profit with security: the provincials must contribute their share to the burdens of the Roman state, and contribution was possible only if they were living in peace. Consequently the administration was primarily dependent on standing armies within the provinces, the presence of which was perhaps a psychological obstacle to the extension of an urban civilization based on Roman models. Indeed, it is doubtful whether, in the earliest years, the Romans attached more than occasional importance to urbanization. Amalgamation was another matter: it is more difficult to control a country made up of innumerable distinct and disunited communities— mostly quite small (the τείχη, *castella*, and *turres* of the ancient authorities)—than to direct and influence an organic and federated assemblage. For the moment, however, the notorious lack of unity among the Iberians prevented their fusion in times of peace, though they were ready enough to combine, in heroic

and desperate resistance, against the common in-vader.[41]   The invader's success too often brought only one result—the extermination of the opposition : and this was to be the great problem of Citerior.   In Ulterior amalgamation was perhaps secured more easily, through its generally superior civilization ; and to this may be due the persistent decrease in the territory ruled by Culchas, as the communities split away from him and formed into new groups.   Apart from the peaceful conditions which resulted from readiness to amalgamate, there was little economic or material advantage offered to the Spaniards.   Mines, where not the source of tribute-coinage, were either monopolies of the Roman state or leased to foreign companies or individuals who might (but probably did not) employ native labour.   There was indeed a trade to be carried on in textiles, timber, livestock, and the like ; but shipping ports tended to come under the control of Roman companies, thus reducing native profit, already perhaps cut down owing to lack of co-ordination in a naturally disunited country.   Accept-ance of Roman law and Roman customs, even if readily undertaken, brought no benefit to a province like Citerior, whatever the case in Ulterior, where acceptance of foreign cultures was no new thing. Amalgamation is worthless unless it is to lead to a new version of provincial autonomy.   All that it implied in Republican Spain was that the governor going round on Assizes found it easier to visit five centralized communities than ten which were distinct and isolated, and that his agents could the more conveniently assess and exact their tribute.[42]

Many of these disadvantages were inherent in the Roman system of theoretically annual, or biennial, governors : this system prevented a governor from becoming really familiar with the true conditions and problems of his province. In the twenty-seven years after 205 B.C., twenty-eight governors can be numbered: in five (or possibly six) cases there was an extension of both for an extra year: twice one of a pair was prorogued after his first year: and for one period of four years fresh governors were sent out each year—from 197–194 B.C. inclusive, when the provincial era was officially inaugurated.[43] From 193 to 189 there was no fixed system, the two provinces together receiving a total of five governors: from 188 to 179 the governors were all prorogued in pairs for an extra year. In exceptional circumstances a single governor might be sent to rule both provinces, as from 171 to 168, and again in the wars against Viriathus, the Numantines, and Sertorius; and his command was frequently prolonged. Not only was a short command an obstacle to a governor's familiarity with his province, but in the second century B.C., when the Roman conscience was becoming dulled by mounting successes from end to end of the Mediterranean, it actually encouraged extortion and self-enrichment, while time allowed. We have no reason to suppose that the burden of *stipendium* was, in general, unjustly assessed: but the whole tenour of ancient tradition suggests that illegal exactions were constantly made—a supposition best proved by Augustus' institution of regular salaries for provincial governors, and perhaps supported in part by the curiously divergent totals of Livy's lists of bullion and specie.[44] Augustus, as Feliciani has said, created a new conscience towards the provinces; but even so, extortion still continued after Augustus.[45]

Given a succession of just and enlightened governors, Spain might have viewed the new system

with resignation, for *stipendium* certainly could be paid, and the law observed, and even conscription tolerated, as long as a governor's efforts were directed not only to the benefit of the Roman treasury but to the organic improvement and political progress of his province. Good governors, indeed, there were— such as Cato and Tiberius Sempronius Gracchus; but ironically enough they were famous chiefly for their contrast with the rest. Thus it resulted that the Roman provincial system in Spain, expressly designed for the profit of the administration as an unfailing asset, was quickly turned into a heavy liability by over half a century of fierce rebellion and warfare. The gross profit derived from Spain was to be nullified by the terrible drain upon Roman and Italian soldiers and by a constant deterioration of Italian morale: as has been justly remarked,[46] 'the chief item imported from Spain to Rome between 200 and 133 was experience'.

CHAPTER IV

REBELLION AND WARFARE

WITH the departure of Scipio Africanus from Spain the two new governors, L. Cornelius Lentulus in Citerior and L. Manlius Acidinus in Ulterior, were left to face the task of initiating the provincial system sketched out in the previous chapter. They, and most of their successors, were to find that the process of romanizing the new provinces was constantly delayed by insurrection, and often by the fiercest of warfare; and only a small minority of intelligent and disinterested commanders appears to have realized that the causes of delay sprang from the inherently suspect nature of Roman policy. For a few years there existed a comparative tranquillity, disturbed only at the very beginning when the ever-fickle princes of the Ilergetes, Mandonius and Indibilis, raised their tribesmen in conjunction with the neighbouring Ausetani and Sedetani, and attempted to shake the Roman power north of the Ebro; the defeat and death of Indibilis was, however, followed by the surrender of Mandonius after Lentulus and Acidinus had joined forces, and the rebel tribes were systematically disarmed and heavily fined (see above, p. 54). These events fell in 205 B.C., and an echo of this unrest was heard in 200 when Cethegus, who had succeeded Lentulus, defeated a force of Sedetani.[1]

Suddenly, in 197 B.C., revolt blazed up from end to end of Roman Spain.[2] The movement originated in

Turdetania, being headed by two regional 'kings' —Culchas, whose dominion in twelve years of Roman rule had shrunk from twenty-eight to seventeen towns, and Luxinius, at whose instigation the towns Carmo (Carmona) and Bardo joined the rising.[3] Other support was quickly forthcoming: Baeturia— the district forming the northern basin of the Baetis— and the Phoenician towns of Malaca and Sexi on the coast threatened, by their support, to make the revolt a serious one, not only because the diversity of its elements suggested a common cause that was unusually fundamental, but also since, as Livy remarks,[4] the Spaniards were for the first time fighting a purely personal war against the Romans. The two governors, Helvius (Ulterior) and Sempronius (Citerior), were compelled to join forces; but Helvius' first dispatch to Rome (then implicated in the Gallic war, and but lately relieved through the waning of hostilities with Macedon) was followed by a second in 196, announcing the defeat and death of Sempronius in Citerior, whither the insurrection now began to spread. Although a joint success at 'Turba'[5] was reported by the new pair of governors in that year, they failed to check the growing unrest, which now extended north-wards along the coast of Citerior to the very region which had risen and been subdued in 205: Dio's epitomist can write that 'Spain was almost entirely alienated'.[6]

This grave crisis led to the appointment, for 195, of the consul M. Porcius Cato to the supreme Spanish command, with a full consular army of two legions and 15,000 Latin *socii* which he might add to the two legions and other troops already in Spain. Praetors were also assigned to the two provinces, Appius Claudius Nero to Ulterior and P. Manlius to Citerior;

and from Livy's description of Manlius as an *adiutor* to Cato it may be deduced that, supreme though Cato's command was, the nearer province was regarded as its primary focus.[7] Such a view was only too well justified : the arterial road joining Spain with Gaul and Italy, even though its importance was as yet limited, was dependent for its safety at its passage of the Pyrenees on the loyalty of the district between Pyrenees and Ebro ; but when Cato landed with his forces at Emporium—the traditional *pied-à-terre* of the Roman invader—he found this vital link momentarily broken, for his first task consisted in defeating an Iberian army massed against him in the neighbourhood of Emporium itself.[8] Having thus re-established Emporium afresh as a Roman base, he was able to relieve the Ilergetes, whom the memories of their punishment ten years previously had kept faithful, and to advance to Tarraco, whence he issued his famous order for the demolition of Iberian fortifications. In a trice the line of the Ebro was recovered for Rome, and Cato was free to consider the more distant problems of Ulterior where Nero, joined by Manlius with the troops specially assigned to him, was already proceeding with the subjugation of Turdetania. The peoples of this province, being themselves unwarlike, had enlisted Celtiberian mercenaries to assist them, and Cato found it necessary to come in person with his army in order to buy over the Celtiberians to the Roman side. Rebellion in Ulterior now subsided, and doubtless a prudent redistribution of Roman troops effectively discouraged any recrudescence of it. Cato turned to Citerior once more, and now initiated the conquest of that part of central Spain which threatened the security of the coastal tract south of the Ebro : he set out for the upper courses of that river by a

march through Celtiberia itself. He laid siege to
Segontia (Siguenza) without success, and possibly
spent some time at Numantia;[9] but his only achievement consisted in stirring up tribesmen whose subsequent hostility was to cost Rome dearly in men,
money, and prestige. On the lower Ebro more
profitable work awaited him, and he successfully
pacified the Sedetani, Ausetani, Suessetani, and
Lacetani—a step which was followed by the reorganization of the local mines mentioned in the preceding
chapter. A busy year of fighting was now over, and
the comparative quiet in the two provinces allowed
Cato to return to claim his triumph in Rome. For the
second time in twelve years Spanish resistance had
collapsed under Roman pressure: the special army
was disbanded, and the following year—194 B.C.—
saw two regular praetors in the Spanish command.[10]

There was, however, no cessation of guerilla
warfare in Citerior, with its constant drain upon
Roman troops: Livy can write that the new governor
lost nearly a half of his army in this manner during
his year of office.[11] In Ulterior more progress was
made—and probably much more easily—as Scipio
Nasica systematically 'mopped up' communities
which had presumably joined in the recent revolt.
To Nasica also belongs the credit (if the events of
subsequent years justify the term) of coming to grips
with the Lusitani, who, after making a raid into
Baeturia, were defeated in a regular engagement near
Ilipa. The new governors appointed for 193 B.C.
appear to have co-operated in a real advance, successes
being gained in this and the following year against a
muster of Carpetanian tribes at Toletum (Toledo) on
the upper Tagus, and also in Oretania, by the head-
waters of the Baetis. Thus the dangerous re-entrant

in the inland frontier of Citerior was slowly and laboriously being converted into a salient : in Ulterior, too, the inland frontier was being projected ever further north and west.[12]

The direction of these advances led the Romans into inevitable conflict with the Celtiberi and Lusitani. Already, in 190 B.C., L. Aemilius Paullus of Ulterior had suffered a crushing defeat by the Lusitani, the seriousness of which was not lessened by his victory in the following year, when the Lusitani had carried hostilities to the mouth of the Baetis itself.[13] In 187 the Lusitani and Celtiberi appear to have achieved some unity of plan and action—an ominous precedent ; once more a special army, this time of some 35,000 men, was requisitioned in Rome. For the moment, however, the Roman offensives were successful : in Citerior the advance extended as far north as Cala-gurris (Calahorra), where there was a signal victory over the Celtiberi ;[14] and north of Ulterior Roman troops penetrated to the Tagus and effectively stemmed the immediate Lusitanian danger. In 181 B.C. the Celtiberi made a fresh effort and gathered together a large army for an attack : it would seem also that general insufficiency of land had produced unrest among the Lusones, Belli, and Titthi to the south-east of Celtiberia.[15] The Roman retort was an immediate penetration into the affected highlands, where Fulvius Flaccus defeated the Celtiberi and crowned his campaign with the capture of Contrebia in the territory of the Lusones. Flaccus was now free to overrun the country, and what he left undone was effectively completed in 179, when Tiberius Sempronius Gracchus (father of the tribunes), ably supported on his left flank by L. Postumius Albinus of Ulterior, swept through Celtiberia, defeating all hostile forces and

capturing numerous towns and villages, of which the
most conspicuous and important strategic point was
Ercavica. Among the many communities with which
he was brought into contact was that of Numantia,
which experienced in an apparently marked degree
those qualities of equity and consideration that
Sempronius employed to crown his campaign with
success—qualities for which (see below, p. 74 f.) his
name long remained famous.[16] His work completed,
Sempronius returned to Rome with Postumius, each
to triumph deservedly: they were the sixth and
seventh commanders, respectively, to celebrate a
Spanish triumph in the short period which had elapsed
since 205 B.C.

Not for twenty-five years after their return was
there to be any serious trouble in Spain, and it is
therefore convenient at this stage to review briefly the
initial working of the administrative system already
described, and to mark both the actual progress
which was made and the cost at which it was achieved.
Anything in the nature of a connected narrative is
impossible: ancient historians were chiefly students
of military and political affairs, for whom social and
economic questions had but few attractions; with a
few exceptions, little is told us by epigraphy; the
dating of the Iberian coinages is notoriously difficult;
consequently, since analogy alone is a dangerous
method, our digression cannot furnish us with
anything but an imperfect picture of the progress of
romanization. Indeed, it is likely that the years of
incessant disquiet and revolt from 205 B.C. onwards
retarded considerably the normal processes of pro-
vincialization and reduced its visible effects to a
minimum. Certainly, to the contemporary historian
there was little that suggested a ready absorption of

Roman ideas by the Spanish communities. At no period had Rome been completely free from the bogy of Spanish rebellion; and the grim persistence of her efforts at conquest is well seen in the large numbers of the troops who were, according to Livy, sent out to Spain during this period from 205 to 179 B.C.

In all, over 70,000 legionaries and 80,000 Latin *socii* were drafted to Spain in the course of these twenty-seven years. The two crises of 195 and 187 B.C. were, of course, responsible for a proportionately large share of these soldiers. But each province appears to have received fairly regular reinforcements varying from a half-legion, as happened frequently, up to eight or ten thousand men, this incessant drain being caused partly by the ever-widening area of warfare and partly by the peculiarly wearing and expensive character of guerilla tactics, at which the Spaniards were so adept. So far as can be told, these reinforcements were not annual: from 205 to 196, indeed, we have no figures at all, and the forces sent for the campaign of 195 were, as has been pointed out, of special strength. Not until 191 is there further mention of reinforcements; but from then onwards until 179 there are only four years in which fresh troops were not sent out. The proportion assigned to Citerior as compared with that given to Ulterior is, very nearly, as 5 : 2,[17] though it must be remembered that Cato's army of 195, designed nominally for Citerior, operated in Ulterior as well. What Roman of the governing class, with this record before his eyes, could doubt that Spain was a *horrida et bellicosa provincia*,[18] unworthy of the civilization of Rome? For the Roman soldier in Spain hard experience took the place of arm-chair reasoning: in a land of perilous communications and frequently poor soil, where

'large armies starve and small armies get beaten', he might have to wait until not only his pay, but his *frumentum*, was long overdue; and the unrest in Fulvius Flaccus' army in 180 B.C. may be taken as a typical reaction to the burdens of the legionary in Spain.[19]

If this hypothesis of a very real strain on Roman strength and perseverance (suffered in a period of hard-fought wars elsewhere) be correct,[20] it can the more easily be understood why the Romans made such slight progress in administration during the first fifty years of their rule, especially if it is remembered that the essential characteristic of that rule was exploitation, not unmixed with extortion. From the point of view of Rome, obligation lay on the Spaniards alone; and, if the Spaniards fulfilled their tributary duties, administration justified its name. Nevertheless, even if Rome failed conspicuously to pursue a policy of reciprocal advantage, there was in this period a genuine extension of the area of Roman influence—a development which ensured at least that the Spaniards should become better acquainted with Roman political ideas. It is true that Cato's activities in the interior in 195 B.C. had amounted to little more than a punitive expedition. But subsequently the area of conquest had been enlarged: a line drawn from Iaca (Jaca, at the foot of the Pyrenees) to a point on the Ebro north of Calagurris, and thence south-west past Ercavica, Toletum, and perhaps Sisapo, to a point on the Baetis west of the future site of Corduba, would probably represent this extension with fair accuracy (see Map II).

Penetration up the valley of the Ebro is attested primarily by the great number of regional mints that began to work:[21] that of the Ilergetes (Pl. I, 9: probably at Ilerda) would have been one of the earliest, and we have seen already the arguments in favour of the institution of an Oscan mint in the 'nineties. The mint of Secaisa (assigned by Hill on grounds of style and distribution to the region of Salduba—the modern Saragossa)[22] should also fall in this early period of conquest, together with that of Iaca. Fulvius Flaccus is known to have operated as far north as Calagurris, and this extension of Roman influence is confirmed by Sempronius Gracchus' foundation, a few years later, of Graccurris,[23] not twenty miles south of Calagurris. And it may well be that the activities of Gracchus were not without influence even on the upper part of the valley of the Durius, if the very common occurrence of the name 'Sempronius' at Lara de los Infantes (some thirty miles north of Clunia—the modern Coruña del Conde) is allowed to be more than coincidence.[24] To the south-west, fixed points are supplied by the Roman victories at Ercavica and Toletum, and the conquest of the highlands of Murcia is confirmed by the operation of the mint of Segobriga (Pl. I, 7, 8). In contrast with the extension of Roman power up the Ebro and through southern Celtiberia, the advance in Ulterior is more difficult to trace. The hostilities against the Lusitani are not yet strictly localized, and there are no native mints from which deductions may be drawn. Roman progress to the Anas and then to the Tagus is certain enough; but, because of the growing danger of a Lusitanian flank-attack, this was a movement only to be undertaken in close co-operation with the governor of Citerior. The same danger must have cramped expansion between the mouths of the Baetis and the Anas, though it is difficult to believe that the Romans did not early turn their attention to the Rio Tinto copper-mines. In general we may define the Roman nuclei

of Ulterior as Gades, Italica-Hispalis, and Castulo, and we may say that the gap which divided them was slowly diminished until, in 151 B.C., Corduba (Cordova) was founded : meanwhile the chief development in this province lay along, and south of, the Baetis itself.

So much may be said regarding the main lines of advance in Roman Spain. Of actual details of early administration very little has come down to us, but, such as it is, it suffices to justify the essentially negative character of the general system sketched in the preceding chapter. Chance has preserved to us a document which throws some light on conditions in Ulterior in 189 B.C. This, the earliest Roman inscription found in Spain,[25] records an episode in the administration of L. Aemilius Paullus (see above, p. 68), being in fact a decree of Paullus 'actum in castreis a.d. xii k. Febr.', ordaining that those slaves of the men of Hasta who dwelt in the Turris Lascutana should be free, and that they should have and hold the land and town of which they were then possessed at the pleasure of the Senate and People of Rome. Paullus himself is styled 'Inpeirator' in this inscription—a reference to the victory by which he retrieved his initial defeat at the hands of the Lusitani ; and it is possible that the occupants of the Turris (or small village) of Lascuta had helped him, being perhaps oppressed by the neighbouring men of Hasta in a feudal dependency implied by the use of the word *servi*. Paullus' action can have been undertaken only with the object of reducing the power and authority of the Hastensians ; and this hypothesis agrees well with the subsequent assistance given by Hasta to the Lusitani, as a result of which the town was stormed by C. Atinius in 187 B.C.[26] It was to the advantage of

Rome to equalize her provincial subjects and to break up feudal ties, substituting for them, in the one case, fear of Rome, and, in the other, gratitude to Rome. Such seems to have been the policy of Paullus on this occasion, put into effect from the camp whither, perhaps, the oppressed had come with their petition.

But this is an isolated instance, from which no general deductions can be drawn. The only governor to whom anything in the nature of a clear and comprehensive policy can be assigned is Tiberius Sempronius Gracchus, whose swift and irresistible campaign in Celtiberia was followed by an administration revealing a personal greatness which fully deserved its enduring reputation. Briefly, his policy was to treat with the Spanish communities on a basis of friendship and equity in return for stipulated services. Appian[27] has preserved the details of his negotiations after the conquest of Contrebia : ' The poor he formed into a part of the community, making them a grant of land, and with all the tribesmen of this district he made clearly defined treaties, by which they were to be friends of Rome ; and he exchanged oaths with them to this effect, for which they often yearned in the subsequent wars.' Nor did Gracchus fail to exact the primary obligations which Roman provincial policy imposed : twenty-five years later, when the Senate forbade the rebuilding of the fortifications of the town of Segeda (below, p. 81), it was able at the same time to demand ' the tribute defined in the time of Gracchus, and ordered the furnishing of troops for the Roman armies : for this too was one of the provisions of the Gracchan treaty '.[28] It speaks much for the justice and diplomacy of this administrator that he was able to equate the burdens of the provincial system with a corresponding sense of the value and

benefit of Roman protection and friendship. Un-
happily the validity of all such individual treaties was
not great. It appears, for example, that the people of
Segeda were, at some time between 179 and 154 B.C.,
released by Rome from the obligation to furnish
money and men : but when Rome reimposed these
burdens in 154, the Senate affirmed its inveterate
policy (which underlies the much earlier decree of
Aemilius Paullus) that such exemptions ‘shall be
valid only during the pleasure of the Senate and People
of Rome’.[29] It was in the highest degree unfortunate
that the enlightened policy of Gracchus lacked any
moral guarantee in the Roman State, and that his
growing fame in later years was to be contrasted with
the opposite tale of bad faith, oppression, and extortion. For the moment, however, his achievement was
great ; and in crowning his work with the foundation
of Graccurris he perhaps introduced into the inland
part of Citerior the first town from which something
of Roman urban institutions might be observed and
imitated.

Elsewhere than in Celtiberia, the administration
seems to have deteriorated rather than improved, and
the climax was reached in 171 B.C., the ‘petition year’,
when complaints were made to the Senate about the
malpractices of its officers.[30] L. Canuleius Dives was
at the time sole praetor in Spain, and he was at once
commissioned to set up boards of inquiry into each
case of complaint and to appoint *patroni*, or legal
representatives, for the various plaintiff communities.
Four *patroni* were chosen : for Citerior, M. Porcius
Cato and P. Cornelius Scipio, and for Ulterior,
L. Aemilius Paullus and C. Sulpicius Gallus. This
important series of investigations was followed by the
exile of two former governors, and by the formulation

of regulations forbidding abuses in the sale and pricing of wheat (see above, p. 57), and abolishing the system by which *praefecti* had been assigned to towns, nominally to supervise their administration, but actually to fill their own pockets.[31]   It is a bitter reflection on Roman provincial theory that a generation had to elapse before such elementary rules could be publicly declared necessary.

Meanwhile, it should be noticed how, in at least one subtle though very important way, romanization was proceeding apace.   In the 'petition year' leave was asked, and obtained, to found at Carteia (El Rocadillo) a *colonia iuris Latini* for the sons of Roman fathers and Spanish mothers : this was the first of such colonies outside Cisalpine Gaul.   In seeking for concrete evidence, in the form of administrative measures, for the extension of Roman influences in Spain, we must by no means overlook such causes as the constant presence of Roman and Italian troops in Spain, and the gradual fusion, by familiarity and intermarriage, of the Spanish and Roman cultures.   The army of occupation did not conquer by its weapons alone : the original colonists of Carteia numbered over four thousand.[32]

In 154 B.C. the slow growth of the opportunist and inadequate system of Roman government was again interrupted by active Spanish resistance.[33]   The warfare which followed lasted, almost without pause, for twenty years ; and for Rome it was to result in a gloomy and disastrous chapter of history, both because it was generally adverse to her cause and damaging to her prestige, and because Lusitanians (Pl. VII) and Celtiberians co-operated in a joint and parallel effort.   The trouble began with a Lusitanian raid into Ulterior, in the course of which Punicus, the Lusitanian

leader, successfully repulsed the Roman forces sent
against him, and, encouraged by the active support of
the Vettones from the upper Tagus valley, carried his
marauding down to the south coast of the province, in
the neighbourhood of the mouth of the Baetis. A
fresh army from Rome under Mummius was defeated
with the loss of 9000 men, and Kaisaros (who had
succeeded Punicus on the latter's death) turned his
success to full advantage when he sent the captured
Roman standards into Celtiberia in order to invite
support. The situation in Celtiberia was indeed ripe
for rebellion: the fortification of Segeda and the
hardening resistance of the Arevaci provided problems
enough for the governor of Citerior. Fortunately,
however, the Romans were able to insulate the
Celtiberian danger and temporarily to end it (see
below, pp. 80 ff.); and for the time being the full
possibilities of concerted action by Lusitanians and
Celtiberians remained untested. Even so, the position
in Ulterior continued to be extremely dangerous: such
successes as Mummius gained were counterbalanced
by Lusitanian ravages along the whole coast west of
the Baetis; and Appian records that he was even
forced to transport an army to Africa, whither
tribesmen had crossed, to relieve the city of Ocilis.[34]
A new governor checked the Lusitanian inroads for a
moment in 152 B.C., and made peace with the Vettones;
but when Servius Sulpicius Galba assumed office in
151 rebellion was again rife, and he himself was
severely defeated, and with heavy loss, near Carmo.
When his colleague Lucullus, now free from the
immediate danger of Celtiberian attack, arrived with
help from Citerior, he was forced to fight near Gades
itself.

The joint efforts of the two generals seem to have

induced the Lusitanians to submit, and Galba received
a formal deputation asking for peace on Roman terms.
Peace was granted—the terms being a ruthless and
carefully organized massacre carried out by the orders
of Galba, a shameful incident which impressed itself
deeply on the minds of the ancient historians, who
record his subsequent trial (with Cato's bitter invec-
tive)[35] and his inexplicable acquittal with uniform
emphasis.

Ironically enough, Galba might have deserved
better of his country if his massacre had been quite
complete. As it was, a considerable number of
Lusitanians had escaped, and when C. Vetilius took up
office in 148 B.C. he found a force of some 10,000
rebels vexing the province. Among them was Viriathus, the most famous champion of Spanish independence, who now by his influence prevented the
formulation of a treaty between his countrymen and
Vetilius, and by his genius extricated his men from a
threatened defeat at the hands of Vetilius' troops. His
leadership was at once assured, and was soon seen to
good effect, for in the following year he ambushed the
Roman army in the southernmost part of the province
and killed Vetilius himself, ' old and fat '. By the end
of 146 B.C. he had moved north-east, defeating the
new governor, C. Plautius, and making himself master
of Carpetania (the upper basin of the Anas), and had
ensconced himself in a strong base—the ' mons
Veneris '—in the *iuga Carpetana*, on an outlying spur
of the main Guadarrama range, whence he dominated
the centre and south-west of the peninsula.

Viriathus' alarming and lengthening tale of success
called forth from Rome a consular army of two legions
under Fabius Maximus Aemilianus, who operated for
two years in Spain. Though he once defeated

Viriathus, and captured a few of his positions, he achieved no decisive result; and the dismal record was continued under Quintus Pompeius Aulus (143–142 B.C.), during whose command Viriathus, by winning over the active support of the Arevaci, Belli, and Titthi, now definitely implicated Celtiberia in the war. In 141 a consular army was again sent out, under Fabius Maximus Servilianus; but Viriathus soon had it in his power. Surprisingly enough he let it go in return for a treaty; and, equally surprisingly, this treaty was ratified at Rome, where his reputation evidently loomed large enough to make him a foe worthy of the Republic and thus, by treaty, a 'friend of the Romans'.[36] In neither province was the sanctity of treaties much more, by now, than a diplomatic method for extricating Roman soldiers from a strategic *impasse*. Servilianus' successor and brother, Servilius Caepio, at once set to work in 139 to violate the treaty, not without senatorial connivance: worse still, he found, in the treachery of friends of Viriathus, a means of assassinating a tried opponent of unblemished honour. Alive, Viriathus had represented all that was fine in the national character: a man who, 'considering that he was a barbarian, had the most eminent qualities as a commander',[37] typically brave, sober, hardy, and resourceful, he was the one leader whom Spain was ever to produce, being capable of keeping an army in the field for eight years without a hint of unrest or sedition. Dead, his name was a perpetual reproach to Roman arms and chivalry; and Spaniards assumed it in his honour for long years afterwards.[38]

Caepio's successor, D. Junius Brutus, founded the town of Valentia (Valencia), south of Saguntum, for the veterans released from the Lusitanian war, the end of which he signalized by a great northern offensive in which he penetrated to the verge of Callaecia, winning victories at Talabriga and among the Bracari.[39] His expedition had the desired effect of rehabilitating Roman self-esteem, and also of stamping out many fortified posts from which descent might be made upon Ulterior: but it would be wrong to suppose that his conquests enjoyed any permanence, or that they hastened the pacification of these backward and warlike tribes, which still awaited subjection over a century later. However, the Lusitanian menace was, for the time being, scotched effectively enough, and Brutus deserved his title ' Callaicus '.

The principal Roman problem in the Lusitanian war had been its elusive and shifting character, owing to which the hostilities had dragged along at such wearisome and costly length. The Celtiberian war offered sharply contrasting difficulties: in this the theatre of hostilities was for the most part constant and restricted, being confined chiefly to the high ridge which lies between the upper waters of the main stream of the Durius and the valley of the modern Jalon, a tributary which flows into the Ebro a little north of Saragossa; and the warfare was concerned with siege and counter-siege rather than with swift raids and long marches.[40] Roman progress up the valley of the Ebro has already been noticed, with its limits at Calagurris and Graccurris, and with a westward expansion (including such towns as Numantia, Nertobriga, Contrebia, and Ercavica) made possible by the energy and wisdom of Tiberius Sempronius Gracchus. In 153 B.C. events were announced at Rome which threatened not only the loss of this highland annexe, but also the fatal weakening of the Ebro line itself. The Belli had begun to synoecize

themselves and their neighbours the Titthi into the town of Segeda, which they proceeded to fortify. Excuse and occasion alike were good, for the Arevaci to the north-west appear to have been pursuing an increasingly aggressive policy, while Roman attention was already sufficiently distracted by the successes of the Lusitanian leaders Punicus and Kaisaros in Ulterior. Nevertheless, both the Belli and the Titthi must have known that their actions would be construed at Rome as a breach of the Gracchan treaties (see above, p. 74 f.); and orders soon came for the demolition of fortifications and for the resumption of tribute and auxiliaries, from the supply of which Rome had apparently excused them. Refusal to comply with these orders led to the appointment of the consul Quintus Fulvius Nobilior to the command against the rebel tribes: Nobilior himself was destined to be prorogued for a second year as proconsul in Citerior, and this system of two-year consular commands continued throughout the years of Celtiberian warfare.[41]

Nobilior advanced to Ocilis (Medinaceli) on the upper Jalon, and from there he prepared to march upon Segeda, to the south of Bilbilis (Calatayud). But its inhabitants forestalled his move and fled for safety to the Arevaci at Numantia, thus implicating a larger and yet more difficult area in the war. Nobilior now turned against Numantia: from his base at Ocilis he marched northward, probably constructing an intermediate camp at the modern Almazán on the Durius.[42] On August 23rd, as his army was passing along a densely wooded defile, it was ambushed by a much larger force of Arevaci commanded by Karos, a man of Segeda: 6000 legionaries were killed, and only the success of the Roman cavalry, combined with

6

Karos' death, enabled Nobilior to hold his remnants together.[43] Even so, his position was bad enough, for the news of the defeat (henceforth commemorated at Rome as a *dies ater*) resulted in the defection of Ocilis, and he was therefore compelled to employ aggression as the best means of defence. The Arevaci promptly assembled in Numantia after their victory : Nobilior therefore advanced to the modern Renieblas, some three and a half miles east of Numantia, where, on La Gran Atalaya, he constructed a legionary camp of full size, doubtless in the expectation of reinforcements.   An attack on Numantia failed signally—its size, position, and strength were to prove a match for much more than a half-strength Roman army—and after a similar failure at Uxama (Osma) Nobilior settled down in his camp at Renieblas for the winter, which he spent in conditions of terrible hardship.[44]

In the following year he was succeeded by Marcellus, who quickly reduced Ocilis : Nertobriga, which had apparently joined the rebel cause, also capitulated under the promise of an armistice made conditional upon the sending of joint embassies by the Arevaci, Belli, and Titthi to Rome. The response of the tribes was immediate, and a renewal of the Gracchan *status quo* was eagerly entreated. In Rome, however, in spite of a personal letter of advice from Marcellus, the Senate rejected the embassies and declined to negotiate, mainly owing to the aggressive behaviour of the Arevaci,[45] and at once appointed Lucullus to the command, with a fresh army specially enrolled by lot owing to the nervous state of public opinion : Lucullus was accompanied by a voluntary second-in-command, Scipio Aemilianus, in whom history was once more to see the double conqueror of Spain and Carthage.

But on his arrival in Spain Lucullus found that Marcellus, forewarned of the Senate's attitude, had acted on his own initiative, having received the unconditional surrender of all the rebel tribes after a threatened siege of Numantia, together with a vast war-indemnity. Lucullus thus saw that, with the end of the revolt achieved, his own presence was unnecessary. But personal disappointment, combined with a realization that the previous panic in Rome had been unjustified, worked on the desires of a normally unscrupulous provincial governor: it is possible, too, that Lucullus found in the society of Scipio—a true representative of his imperialist line— a stimulus rather than a sedative.[46] The year 151 B.C. therefore witnessed an entirely unforeseen campaign among the Vaccaei, further west along the Durius. After gaining Cauca (Coca) by treachery and massacre, Lucullus moved against Intercatia, which he conspicuously failed to capture, though Scipio, both by his personal prowess and by his skill in negotiating a treaty, won some private distinction. Worse awaited Lucullus at Pallantia (Pallencia), whence his army was put to flight : he subsequently withdrew into Ulterior, where he came to the support of Galba against the Lusitanians (see above, p. 77 f.). Here the shameful and gratuitous campaign ended : Rome was fortunate in that it caused no breach of the peace which lasted from Marcellus' treaty with the Celtiberians in 152 until 143 B.C.

If this first part of the Celtiberian war was (with the episode of Lucullus expected) a vindication of Sempronius Gracchus' policy of peaceful penetration by adjustment and treaty, the second part became the *locus classicus* for the repudiation of treaties. War broke out again in 143 B.C. among the Arevaci, at the instigation of Viriathus (then, as we have seen, piling success upon success). The consul Caecilius Metellus was sent to Citerior, and was faced with a task similar to that of Marcellus in 152: he subdued the Arevaci (i.e. the Jalon valley) and captured Contrebia and Centobriga; and it was not long before Numantia and Termantia were alone in resisting him. Unfortunately his successor, Quintus Aulus Pompeius (141–140 B.C.), was anything but a match for the task: with his well-trained army of 30,000 men he failed in his attempts upon each of these towns. For the moment he retired to his camp at Castillejo, immediately to the north of Numantia, whence he seems to have contemplated besieging the town. All the time he was losing troops, cut off by the Numantines while foraging or scouting; and neither the advisers sent out to direct him, nor the recruits who replaced his time-expired veterans, nor the rigours of winter at Castillejo,[47] helped matters to a favourable conclusion. The Numantines themselves suffered many privations, and therefore when, in 140 B.C., Pompeius negotiated secretly with them, they readily undertook to surrender and to pay 30 talents' weight of silver.

His successor, Popillius Laenas[48] (139–138 B.C.), brought senatorial instructions to disregard the pact; and Pompeius himself took the opportunity of disowning it. Popillius, for his own part, accomplished nothing: certainly his attack on the Lusones was not calculated to reduce Numantia. So the miserable business lengthened out. But much worse was to come. Hostilius Mancinus succeeded to the command in 137: after a series of defeats and alarms he was driven from Numantia in defeat and surrounded at the site of one of Nobilior's former camps—presumably Renieblas. Mancinus' numbers were far superior to

those of the Numantines, but he was powerless to
help himself, and was compelled to make a disgraceful
peace ' ἐπὶ ἴσῃ καὶ ὁμοίᾳ Ῥωμαίοις καὶ Νομαντίνοις '.[49] In-
dignation at Rome was not accompanied by any increase
of military acumen in high places : Aemilius Lepidus,
the consul sent to relieve Mancinus of his command,
could find nothing more useful to do than harry the
Vaccaei—an enterprise ending in his own discomfiture;
and Calpurnius Piso after him studiously neglected
Numantia in favour of the same district. Meanwhile
Mancinus' treaty had been repudiated at Rome, and
Mancinus himself had been delivered up to the
Numantines—a derisive and worthless act of compensation rightly rejected by a brave and independent
people.

Stung by this long and unworthy record, public
opinion forced the special election, for the year 134,
of Scipio Aemilianus to the command of Citerior.
Fresh from his conquest of Carthage, Scipio brought
to his task qualities which most of his predecessors
had lacked,—experience in training and strategy,
ability to frame a far-sighted policy, self-confidence,
and the weight of his name. Demoralization and
inefficiency among the Roman troops in Spain were
his first adversaries : these he reduced by intensive
exercises in manœuvres and field-engineering. Still
taking his time, he next proceeded towards Numantia,
destroying the standing crops in its vicinity and
interrupting the supplies of food sent to Numantia
by the Vaccaei. Only then did he turn to Numantia
itself (Pl. VIII)—a city which for close on nine years
had suffered intermittently from conditions of siege :
this circumstance doubless influenced his subsequent
policy. From two main base-camps,—Castillejo, half
a mile north of the town, and Peña Redonda, lying

even nearer to the south,—he undertook the construction of an embankment completely encircling the
town : this fortification, in its finished state, was
strengthened by the addition of five more permanent
camps, lying at intervals on its circumference, from
which any passage over the circumvallation could be
prevented.[50] Scipio by now had a force of 60,000
men under his command, and he could afford to wait
until famine had reduced the now weakened and
dwindling defenders : he even refused an offer of
conditional surrender. At length, during the course
of the year 133, starvation had reached the pitch at
which cannibalism begins, and the town surrendered :
of the almost bestialized survivors a number killed
themselves, fifty were chosen by Scipio to adorn his
triumph, and the remainder were sold ; the town
itself was razed to the ground, and its land divided
among its neighbours.

'Such was the passion for liberty and bravery in
a small barbarian town.'[51] The ancient historians,
indeed, were not slow in expressing admiration and
wonder at the heroism shown by the Numantines.
For there was little enough on the Roman side to be
set against it : the Celtiberian war did more to cheapen
the reputation of Roman policy and Roman arms than
almost any other. Incompetence, varied only by
treachery, had been the prelude to the siege. Even
Scipio's final success could not be counted an unquali-
fied one : it was the success of 60,000 men against
4000 ;[52] it was not gained in the field ; it possessed
no lustre of victory. Nevertheless he had put an end
to a black chapter of provincial history, in which the
drain on Italian man-power, together with incessant
expenditure and anxiety, had produced severe repercussions in Italy itself.[53] In Spain, however, it was

now necessary to disregard the labour and the loss, and to look ahead, secure in the knowledge that Celtiberian resistance had now collapsed for good and that Roman dominion in that country could never be seriously disputed again.

CHAPTER V

PROGRESS AND DEVELOPMENT UNDER THE LATER REPUBLIC

THE fall of Numantia ushered in a new provincial era for Spain, which was marked officially by the sending out of a full senatorial commission charged with the reorganization of the country. For twenty years each of the two provinces had been administered in conditions dictated by almost incessant warfare, the most serious and obvious effects of which were the reduction and displacement of rebel communities, and a widespread devastation of territory—facts which vitally affected the internal economy of the provinces. The work of the commissioners would therefore include the readjustment of tribute for many previously subject communities, whether they had revolted or not, as well as the drafting of individual treaties (presumably on the Gracchan model) defining the terms of their loyalty to Rome, and a redistribution of territory : this last measure was necessary if land-hunger, with its attendant danger of banditry and unrest, was to be avoided.[1] Conspicuous among the territories to be apportioned was that of Numantia itself : the city, completely destroyed and denuded of inhabitants, long remained unoccupied (except, per-haps, for occasional use as a base-camp) until it was rebuilt and again occupied as a purely Roman town at the beginning of the Imperial epoch.[2]

Much work, therefore, awaited the commission

within the previously defined area of Roman dominion
(above, p. 71 f.). The task was greatly increased by the
large extension of this area during the inevitable
course of the recent conquests (Map II). The
most remarkable feature of the old frontier line of
Citerior had been the wide re-entrant lying approximately between Calagurris and Toletum. With the
subjection of the Arevaci this was now removed, and
may even have been replaced by a salient : the effects
of the repeated Roman incursions into the territory
of the Vaccaei, without being yet stable or permanent,
were nevertheless soon to be consummated, and it is
reasonable to regard the quadrangle bounded by
Toletum, Intercatia, Calagurris, and Ercavica as an
accession to the sphere of regular Roman influence.
This accession gave Rome the control over the upper
parts of both the Tagus and the Durius valleys. In
Ulterior, too, there had been a distinct advance, owing
to the provocation offered by Viriathus ; and the
subsequent penetration of Brutus into Callaecia presupposes conditions of fair security, behind a natural
frontier provided by the lower half of the Tagus,
throughout an area which now came to include those
parts between the Anas and Tagus which Augustus
was later to incorporate in his province of Lusitania.
Concurrently with the projection of the two main
provincial frontiers, the inter-provincial boundary
had also to be extended. Its course was determined
by the previous wars. The generals in Citerior had
fought the Arevaci and Vaccaei : those of Ulterior,
the Lusitani and Vettones. The boundary thus ran
between the Arevaci and the Vettones, and, during the
following century, crept slowly northward : eventually its direction seems to have been recognized as
leaving the Anas where the river turns suddenly from

north-west to south-west, passing north between Caesarobriga and Toletum, turning north-west at the *iuga Carpetana* (so leaving the Vaccaei to Citerior), and joining the Durius somewhere west of Ocelodurum.[3] Its origin and purpose were purely administrative.

The wars had therefore nearly doubled the Roman possessions in Spain: the work of the commission was correspondingly heavy, and may possibly have continued over a term of years.[4] There was, indeed, no need for haste. The Spanish wars had cost Rome dear, and only a careful reconstruction could be expected to provide a dividend at all worthy of her expenditure. Rome herself was vexed by a generation of troubles elsewhere,—the Gracchi, Jugurtha, the Cimbri, and Mithridates: Spanish peace must be maintained at all costs. Roman preoccupation with other problems resulted in the temporary neglect of Spanish problems by Roman historians;[5] but this same preoccupation explains the ruthlessness with which the last flickering embers of Celtiberian resistance were stamped out. It appears that, after successfully repelling from Spain bands of the Cimbri fresh from their signal victory at Arausio, the Arevaci were stimulated to a final attempt to regain their lost independence—an attempt which they may have been preparing for some time.[6] When the danger to Italy had been averted, a consular army was sent to Spain in 98 B.C. under Titus Didius, who (according to Appian) destroyed some 20,000 of the tribesmen. The town of Termantia also claimed Didius' attention: never previously subdued, it was now captured and rebuilt on lower and more open ground. Other communities were more harshly treated: one, called by Appian 'Colenda', capitulated after an eight-

months' siege ; another, unnamed, fell into Didius'
hands by the time-honoured method of massacre ;
and similar slaughter attended yet another Celtiberian
rising when Caius Valerius Flaccus turned against its
centre, the town of Belgida (92 B.C.).

Any doubt that may remain concerning the latent
dissatisfaction and unrest among the Spanish communities at large is at once dispelled by the episode
of the Sertorian War.[7] Quintus Sertorius, a Sabine
by birth, had been forced by the political strife of the
late eighties to withdraw from the capital. Already he
had gained some experience of Spain while serving
under the general Didius ; and it was to Spain that he
now turned.[8] There, safe from the violence of
the Sullan faction, he appears to have originated the
plan of making himself master of Spain in order to
impose military control over his political opponents
in Rome—an adaptation of provincial administration
which was to recur, with modifications, during the
Principate. But the mastery of Spain could not be
won by the methods of Didius, as Sertorius well
knew, even if he had possessed an army of any size or
homogeneity. As it was, his miscellaneous forces—
Romans, Italians, and Spaniards—amounted to less
than 10,000 men : this fact was later an asset to him,
enabling him to move rapidly and easily about the
peninsula, but for the moment it compelled him to use
the arts of diplomacy, in the place of strength, in
winning the Spaniards over to his cause. This he
began to do during the year 82 B.C., but he had
insufficient time to perfect his organization : unable
to hold the line of the Pyrenees against the Roman
forces sent against him,[9] he withdrew to Mauretania,
perhaps intending to pursue a parallel policy there.
Late in 81 B.C., however, he received a deputation

from the Lusitani, inviting him to be their leader.
Sertorius did not refuse this paradoxical recognition
of the progress of romanization in Spain, and crossed
over from Africa to begin a war which was to tax the
skill and energy of his opponents to the fullest degree.
The years 80–78 B.C. saw warfare in upper Baetica
and in ' Lusitania ' : Sertorius with his small army was
faced by the far more numerous co-operating forces of
Ulterior and Citerior, but he eluded the pincers spread
out for him, and withdrew ever farther into the
interior of the country, employing just those tactics
which had made Viriathus so formidable an enemy.
Quintus Caecilius Metellus, the principal general
sent against him, followed him up without ever being
able to force a decisive engagement : his path northwards, which helped to blaze the trail for the future
Emerita–Bracara road, can be traced by a series of
places named after him,—Metellinum (Medellin),
founded as a military colony at his crossing of the
Anas, east of the future Emerita ; Castra Caecilia, a
camp excavated at a site lying immediately to the
north-east of Norba (Cáceres) ; and Vicus Caecilius,
north of the Tagus crossing at Turmuli.[10] By 77 B.C.
the scene of the war had shifted north and east : the
Celtiberians, and the Iberians north of the Ebro,
joined in supporting Sertorius, who now fixed his
headquarters at Osca. The Spanish situation was
indeed serious for Rome : Sertorius, who was by
now receiving extensive reinforcements from various
sources (and perhaps overtures from not a few
Roman politicians as well)[11] had successfully gained
control of the whole of the centre of Spain, and only
Saguntum and Lauro resisted him on the east coast
between Carthago Nova and the Ebro.[12]

Pompey's appointment to a consular command in

Spain—such reversions to second-century practice were now happily unusual—showed the measure of Roman anxiety. But the results of Pompey's campaign of 76 B.C. were not such as to lessen this anxiety. Forcing his way across the Ebro, he proceeded to march down the east coast as far as the plain extending round Saguntum, Lauro, and Valentia, intending to force a decisive engagement in an area at once vital for Sertorius' control of the centre of the peninsula and favourable for operations by legionaries unused to all the niceties of Spanish highland warfare.[13] Sertorius was once more too clever for his opponents: leaving his lieutenant Perperna to retire safely into Valentia, he himself besieged Lauro (thus drawing off Pompey's army) and afterwards cut up a legion sent by Pompey to its relief. Pompey was compelled to withdraw to the Ebro, the sole result of his campaign being the loss of Lauro: his own failures were, however, somewhat counterbalanced by Metellus' defeat of a Sertorian force under Hirtuleius at Italica, and by Metellus' unmolested march northward from Ulterior to the Pyrenees. This concentration of Pompeian forces north of the Ebro, and the close strategic co-operation which it allowed between Pompey and Metellus, foreboded Sertorius' ultimate defeat. The year 75 saw the capture of Segovia by Metellus,—the first step towards loosening Sertorius' hold on Celtiberia,—and Pompey's own capture of Valentia. In 74 Pompey carried the war into northern Celtiberia.[14] Still unable to compel Sertorius to fight the decisive battle that he wished for, Pompey spent this and the succeeding year in attacking and besieging highland towns, with Metellus at first in collaboration with him. His apparent success was strictly qualified, as his retreat from Pallantia and his defeat at Calagurris plainly suggested. But the real results of these campaigns were not to be measured in terms of military victories: history had often shown before that Celtiberian unity over a wide front was unable to endure for an unlimited period. Sertorius himself could not cover the whole front once Pompey had carried the war into the highlands, and gradually the Celtiberian communities fell away from his cause. Discontent and disappointment among his own followers increased, and in 72 he was treacherously assassinated by his own subordinate, Perperna. At once the Romano-Iberian movement collapsed. There appears, indeed, to have been less retribution exacted by Pompey than might have been expected. All but a few towns returned to their regular allegiance: those which still resisted—Calagurris in particular[15] —received scant mercy. His arduous work completed, Pompey set up a victorious trophy at the Pyrenees[16] and returned, with Metellus, to Italy in 71 B.C.

Such are the bare facts of the Sertorian war, the implications of which were so deeply important for Roman policy in Spain. Of Sertorius' brilliant qualities as a commander and an organizer, which enabled him to fight what was mainly a guerilla war of great length over a vast area, and to train Iberian troops to a pitch of almost Roman efficiency, this is not the place to speak. More important for our present purpose is the just emphasis which must be laid upon his administrative insight and his enlightened views, which point a fine contrast between him and the average Roman governor in Spain.[17] Sertorius lived in an age when the traditional leadership of an old-established Roman oligarchy, whether over Rome or over Italy at large, was being challenged by ideas involving wider repre-

sentation in political privilege and responsibility. The
claims of Italy to a due share in the Roman heritage
were but the prelude to an inevitable recognition that
the provinces also had, to some degree, contributed to
an extension of the Roman *imperium*. That Sertorius,
while acknowledging the truth of this assertion, turned
the position to his own ends in no way invalidates the
lesson which he tried to teach Rome. To say that he
attempted to use a partly romanized Spain as a political
weapon against Rome is to admit the progress of
romanization in Spain : and, even if this romanization
varied in its quality and intensity from area to area, it
was impossible to deny its general growth and occasional strength. Sertorius, in brief, dealt fairly with
the Spaniards, and showed confidence in them : in a
country where aggression, brutality, and cupidity had
made the foreigners hateful, he found little difficulty in
dealing with the chieftains, and in winning popularity
with the Iberians generally.[18] A man of magnetic
charm (as his personal band of ' war-devotees ', or
soldurii, showed), he nevertheless used positive methods
to gain goodwill, in remitting taxation and in exempt-
ing the communes from the compulsory billeting of
troops—the latter being a singularly popular measure.
This was no mere bribery. At Osca he even established a school where the better-born Iberian children
of the district might attend, wearing *togae praetextae*
and *bullae*, for their instruction in Latin and
Greek.[19]

It is, of course, easy to disparage his methods and to
exaggerate his personal motives. Like other and even
greater Roman commanders before him (Scipio Africanus among them), he seems consciously to have
hedged himself about with the air of the superman.
Plutarch aptly remarks that the pupils at his school at

Osca were in fact no more than so many hostages. His policy certainly turned on his fixed antipathy to the contemporary government in Rome. His creation of a ' Senate ' from among his friends in Spain, including the traditional officers of the Roman Republic, is evidence for his inability to break clean away from Roman tradition. And his contact with Mithridates shows his unwillingness to allow full national reconstruction in one country to preclude him from those wider world-relationships to which his birth and training had entitled him.[20] Nevertheless we must hold the balance fairly. His romanizing policy was too thorough and too successful to be no more than a cloak for other designs, and we must agree with Schulten in thinking that his venture, while primarily a political move affecting the future of the government in Rome, came to involve a romanization of the

tion in Rome rendered provincial appointments matter
for every kind of bribery and jobbery : the men who
secured the appointments not unnaturally looked on
the provinces as the obvious means of reimbursing
themselves for the sums spent in Rome in playing the
political game. Rapacity and extortion in the provinces
received little check. It is true that Extortion Courts
had been established as long ago as 149 B.C.—largely
owing to the infamous conduct of Lucullus and Galba
in Spain—and that the impeachment of an ex-governor
was the first and earliest step in the young advocate's
ladder to forensic success. But the venality of the
Roman courts nullified the few safeguards which
existed. The Senate might, perhaps, have pointed to
its ability to control provincial governors through its
control of finance and military forces, and through its

Osca were in fact no more than so many hostages. His policy certainly turned on his fixed antipathy to the contemporary government in Rome. His creation of a ' Senate ' from among his friends in Spain, including the traditional officers of the Roman Republic, is evidence for his inability to break clean away from Roman tradition. And his contact with Mithridates shows his unwillingness to allow full national reconstruction in one country to preclude him from those wider world-relationships to which his birth and training had entitled him.[20] Nevertheless we must hold the balance fairly. His romanizing policy was too thorough and too successful to be no more than a cloak for other designs, and we must agree with Schulten in thinking that his venture, while primarily a political move affecting the future of the government in Rome, came to involve a romanization of the Iberians which he then pursued willingly and whole-heartedly.[21] It is not surprising to find that later generations perpetuated his name by its common use, as that of Viriathus also was commemorated.[22]

After his death and the collapse of his movement, Sertorius' innovations doubtless perished, one and all : Pompey could be trusted to restore the old order, and his reconstruction, in the more romanized areas at least, proved popular enough (below, pp. 120 ff.).[23] Some account has already been given of the normal administrative system as applied to Spain. After a century and a quarter of Roman rule the old system still prevailed, with scarcely any changes in its essentials. Indeed, it had probably deteriorated through its inherent faults. The inability of the Senate to control the political situation at Rome was by now becoming a commonplace : the factors which later produced the Triumvirates were already forming. Political corrup-

tion in Rome rendered provincial appointments matter for every kind of bribery and jobbery : the men who secured the appointments not unnaturally looked on the provinces as the obvious means of reimbursing themselves for the sums spent in Rome in playing the political game. Rapacity and extortion in the provinces received little check. It is true that Extortion Courts had been established as long ago as 149 B.C.—largely owing to the infamous conduct of Lucullus and Galba in Spain—and that the impeachment of an ex-governor was the first and earliest step in the young advocate's ladder to forensic success. But the venality of the Roman courts nullified the few safeguards which existed. The Senate might, perhaps, have pointed to its ability to control provincial governors through its control of finance and military forces, and through its power of reversing policy. These safeguards too (if they were safeguards at all) were no more than nominal: a governor deprived of money or men would not scruple to exact what he required from the provincials, while reversal of policy, if carried beyond a certain point, might easily become a burden of inconvenience and wasteful expenditure. Continuity of policy was perhaps the greatest of the blessings conferred on the provinces by the Principate : provincial arrangements then acquired a permanency which had in great part been secured to the capital of the Republic by the system of *veto*.

In such a setting, it is not surprising to find the old provincial institutions unchanged : that was best, in the eyes of Rome, which paid best and (when there was no tedious war) cost least. So far as taxation was concerned, there is no evidence for any essential change in the original system, though we have noted occasions when, as at the end of a period of war, extension and adjustment would have been required. Means are lacking to decide whether any other, or regular, revisions were carried out, as was to happen under the Principate : the obtuse and effete nature of the Roman provincial system makes it improbable, indeed, that revision was frequent. If so, the better developed and richer parts of Spain would gain at the expense of the poorer : economic progress and the spread of coined money would lead to a cheapening of money in the former areas, not balanced by increase in the taxation-rate, while the declining fortunes of the old hill-towns of the centre and north, to which trade and traffic had never yet spread fully, were not upheld by proportionate decrease in the rate. It was, possibly, to the latter class of communities that Sertorius' remission of tribute[24] most properly applied.

Judicial arrangements, too, stood in urgent need of revision. Roman rule now extended over two-thirds of the Spanish peninsula—an area which thus depended for legal dispensation upon the efforts of two governors alone, unaided by the *legati iuridici*, or local commissioners, who were to become familiar under the Principate. In the more highly populated and closely knit areas, such as southern Ulterior, and the east coast, something like Assize circuits were possibly in existence : equivalent supervision of the centre and north was, however, a physical impossibility and, if attempted, burdened these areas with heavy expense consequent upon the official tour of the governor and his suite over long distances. Petty law might, of course, be dealt with in local courts ; and privileged communities, whether ' free ' or ' free and allied ', had the right of using their own legal code : but now, as before, it depended on a governor's policy or conscience whether he respected these provisions or not. Roman colonies

and *municipia*, of course, possessed their own charters defining the limits of their self-government, and in the nature of things were less liable than other communities to undue interference or oppression.[25]

Nor is there any evidence that any essential modifications had been made in the military arrangements affecting Spain. Indeed, the task of the army of occupation was scarcely lighter than it had been in the earlier period of conquest. It is true that—the Sertorian war excepted—long and costly campaigns were a thing of the past. But the total area of Roman domination was so vastly extended that garrison forces which had been adequate in a previous age could now scarcely hope to cover the whole of the ground successfully.[26] Many years were still to pass before brigandage and local unrest died down, and the areas which had achieved anything like the *Pax Romana* were few and small compared with those which stood in need of constant surveillance. Periodic movements of troops still laid local communities under the obligation of billeting—an obligation which Sertorius had been careful to avoid. And the furnishing of auxiliary troops was still compulsory: it is doubtful if a century and a half of habit had made the compulsion any pleasanter, though it is possible that the enfranchisement of a Spanish auxiliary unit in Italy in 89 B.C., as a reward for bravery,[27] was increasingly characteristic of the treatment given to a branch of the Roman army the importance of which was to grow steadily as the legions themselves gradually deteriorated.

Opinions may vary as to the extent of the failure of Republican Rome to govern in her provinces. Some may share the verdict of Schulten upon Spain, that ' the Iberians were treated little better than cattle'.[28] Others may reflect that the government from Rome failed

rather through lack of any true contact with Spain, or
of any elementary means of adequate Spanish representation, than through any deliberate policy of cruelty,
such as Schulten's words might be taken to suggest.
This is not to deny that Roman provincial administration was a one-way system : it was entirely so. Even
under the Principate it was to remain nearly so, but
with this great difference, that the provinces then came
to be regarded more clearly as organic members of a
single unit, not only economically, but politically as
well. For the Republic the separate provincial organ-
isms—little known, and often sources of trouble and
anxiety—were considered mainly as centres of economic
productivity, with strongly commercial motives quickly
supervening : an obvious parallel is to be found in the
early history of certain of the British territories overseas.
Yet the fact that Roman interests fostered economic
and commercial development in Spain did not prevent
the Romans from opening up the resources of the
country in a way which must inevitably, in the end,
benefit the native inhabitants as well. It will not be
out of place to review briefly the main aspects of this
development during the later period of the Republic.

The Republican picture is, indeed, partially obscured
by the lavish panegyrists of a later age, who were wont
to regard Spain as the land of unrivalled agricultural
and mineral wealth almost from time immemorial.
This view, false as it is, is not easily corrected, for anything in the nature of an economic survey is bound to
disregard (if, indeed, it can perceive at all) stages either
of development or fluctuation, as even the latest
researches show.[29] Nevertheless, it is possible to distinguish the main economic activities of Republican
Spain, and roughly to assign them their relative importance. When Justin listed the sources of national

wealth, he significantly placed agriculture first : then
follow wine, honey, oil, linen, esparto, horses, and
finally—as we shall see, with equal significance—
mines.[30]   Justin, it is clear, wrote from the viewpoint
of the Spaniard, for whom agriculture was obviously
the staple industry, having flourished long before the
Roman conquest, and not yet impaired. The corn crop
was not, however, evenly distributed : the best yield
was still harvested in southern Ulterior and the eastern
coastal strip, in which areas it may have been regularly
over-produced : it will be remembered that as long
ago as 203 B.C. a surplus had been shipped to Rome.
Abundance of corn in southern Ulterior is reflected
clearly in the coins struck there under the late Republic
(Pl., III, 1, 2, 5). The ear of corn is a constant type at
many towns, either by itself, or in combination with a
plough, a bunch of grapes, dolphins, or tunny-fish.[31]
But the Spanish interior, with poorer soil and a more
rigorous climate, must often have been hard-pressed to
grow sufficient corn for local needs, though the Roman
tendency to shift native communities from the hills to
the valleys probably helped to remedy any shortage.
In general, we may say that the production of corn
sufficed most needs, while certain fertile areas grew
sufficient to form the basis of a thriving export business,
the profits of which (even if conducted through the
hands of Roman middle-men) directly benefited the
growers ; and this is presumably one of Justin's
reasons for placing agriculture at the head of
his list.

With agriculture must be grouped (conformably
enough with English practice) the Spanish fisheries,[32]
which rivalled agriculture both in their antiquity and
their profit. The Phoenician trading-stations which in
early times had studded the south coast had turned

their attention to the fishing industry. This, as was natural in an age of slow communications, was concerned mainly with the preservation of fish in pickle, and with the preparation of a kind of fish-sauce known as *garum*, both of which products won an international reputation ;[33] and in time manufactories on the east coast sprang up as well. The frequent representation of the tunny-fish on the coins of the south (Pl. III, 4), testifies to the importance of the industry, as, for instance, on the coins of Gades, whose fishermen were famous for their Atlantic expeditions. Of the other well-known ' salt-fisheries ', Carteia was among the most important (her coins show us a fisherman at work (Pl. III, 8[34])), while Malaca—an export centre for Rome under the Empire[35]—and Carthago Nova were also depôts of repute. The products of these places were widely distributed through the Mediterranean world, the more so as the luxury of the Roman palate increased. Nor was the fishing industry one which enriched Roman-financed companies at the expense of the Spaniards. Companies there were—certainly during the Empire; but the labour which they employed in the catching or pickling of fish would naturally be local, while the purchase of a fishing concession in Spanish waters would similarly benefit the province as such. Nevertheless it will be noted that the fisheries, like agriculture, could have brought profit only to the west, south, and east coasts : once again the centre was denied advantage.

Very much the same was true of viticulture, which, by the time of Augustus, was sufficiently developed to allow of a flourishing export of wine from Baetica to Italy.[36] Something of this development is reflected in the numerous coins struck in this area bearing the device of a bunch of grapes (Pl. III, 1).[37] In a later

period the production of wine spread up the east coast, the vineyards of Tarraco being much esteemed. By contrast with the vine—a swift and easy crop in the right climate—the olive calls for time, and therefore capital, in its cultivation ; and, although olive-groves are known to have existed in the Republican period, it is unlikely that the production of the famous Spanish oil reached a high level before the time of the Empire : only one town in Baetica—Ulia (Montemayor)—depicts the olive in the late Republican coinage in Spain (Pl. III, 5).[38] Here again the emphasis, such as it is, is on the south. An exception is possibly provided by the case of honey, which is known to have been produced (doubtless for local consumption rather than for commerce) in Celtiberia.[39] Insufficient evidence exists to say if the breeding of stock (horses, pigs, etc.), which became common in the centre and north during the Empire, had yet developed into a profitable concern.

A more certain source of national wealth is to be seen in the textile industry. Fine wool was being produced during the Republic, but was not, perhaps, so widely known as the linen made from the flax of Tarraco and Saetabis (Jativa). The cultivation of flax need have been no capitalist concern, and the profits of it therefore benefited Spain directly : the same was true of the ancient and famous esparto fields lying around Carthago Nova, from which were produced the coarser textiles needed for rope, matting, and the like.[40]

We have now briefly reviewed the principal products and commodities to be associated with Republican Spain—exclusive of mineral products, to which we shall presently return. Our evidence, wherever it is at all satisfactory, points to the east coast and to the

southern parts of Ulterior as the areas of the greatest
productivity : in the centre and north, if rational production was possible at all, there can have been little
surplus available for commercial profit. We have seen
that in many cases—as, for instance, with corn, wine,
and textiles—there were opportunities for the invest-
ment of Spanish capital and for the employment of
Spanish labour, both to Spanish profit. In regard to
the local consumption of Spanish products, the producer's profits would be gross profits, for he could act
as wholesaler and retailer combined. But his profits on
goods exported abroad were probably more often nett.
A characteristic feature of the Imperial period is the
existence of *societates*, guilds or companies, composed
of Roman middle-men, doubtless self-financed, who
managed the export of a particular product, or products, from a particular port in Spain to its market
outside the province—usually Rome.[41] It is probable
that, under the Republic, such Roman *societates* existed
controlling the output of the more important mines ;
and it would not be surprising if the phenomenon had
spread to commerce as well : the only break between
Republic and Empire was political, not commercial.
In addition to the guilds of Roman merchants, wherever
they were to be found, the Spanish producer had to
reckon also with companies serving Phoenician interests, as on the south coast (and particularly at Gades)
or with those including a pronounced Greek element,
such as at Emporium. The activities of a number of
energetic middle-men, Romans, Phoenicians, or Greeks,
along the areas of greatest productivity must have
compelled many Spanish producers to regard a swift
and mounting 'turn-over' as the surest guarantee of
personal profit.

Last upon Justin's list of the national sources of

wealth comes the mining-industry. The richness of the Spanish mines had been the main cause of foreign interference in the peninsula since remote antiquity, and continued to be a primary cause of Roman interest in the province. It is impossible to give here more than a brief résumé of the distribution of Spanish minerals, which is a question that demands—and has received—detailed treatment elsewhere.[42] But it is necessary to sketch this distribution, and to refer to the methods by which the mining-industry was controlled under the Republic.

Of the precious metals, gold was to be found in most of the mountainous parts of Spain, and accordingly in the larger of the rivers. With the advance of Roman dominion under the early Principate it became possible to open up the gold deposits of Cantabria and Asturia : the latter were particularly rich, producing in Pliny's time some 20,000 pounds' weight annually.[43] But central and southern Spain also yielded gold, principally in the Sierra Morena (later to become notorious for Tiberius' appropriation of Sextus Marius' mines), while its presence in Baetica is also recorded. During the Republic, however, if not under the Empire, silver was the most renowned of Spanish minerals. It was silver which had made ' Arganthonius ' a famous king of Tartessos, which had attracted the zeal of adventuring Greeks, which had furnished Hannibal with the sinews of war, and, after him, the Romans, in the form of *argentum Oscense*. Again, when Caesar triumphed after the battle of Munda, it was silver which was chosen as the symbol of Spanish territory. Mention has been made already (see note 35 to Ch. III) of the great mines of Carthago Nova, which in Polybius' time employed 40,000 men and produced 25,000 drachmae daily. Apart from this, however, silver of varying qualities was found throughout Spain, notably at Ilucro, Sisapo (Almadén), Ilipas, and Vipasca (Aljustrel): *argentum Oscense* may be taken as indicating the mineral wealth of the Ebro district; and ancient authority credited the free-lance miners of Baetica with the ability to win nearly twenty pounds' weight of silver in three days.[44]

Among the baser metals, copper was found in great quantities in Spain, chiefly in the districts near the Baetis and Anas (cf. Pl. XII). Mines were worked at Corduba, in the Sierra Morena, and at Vipasca,—all of them rich, but none of them surpassing the mines at the modern Rio Tinto, still in full production and famous throughout the world. It is possible that the Republic laid more store on Spanish silver than on copper: during the Empire, when Spanish gold and silver mines became worked out, and a vast copper and bronze coinage had to be sustained for world-circulation, Spanish copper may have appreciated in value. Lead was another base metal of practical value, indispensable in an age when the laborious working of iron and steel made it difficult to use them for such purposes as the manufacture of piping, boxes, coffins, and sundry personal objects. Its distribution-area coincided roughly with that of copper, but centred mainly in the modern Murcia, particularly at Ilucro, from which was produced lead exported in great quantities from Carthago Nova: a later age saw Spanish lead travelling to India in return for the jewels of the East. Tin (' white lead ') was produced in the Lusitanian area and the extreme north-west: iron was mined in the north and centre (Bilbilis and Toletum forged it as a staple industry); and a whole host of lesser minerals and mineral salts were to be found distributed widely, the cinnabar-mines of Sisapo being the most renowned.

It is safe to assume that, with the exception of the gold, iron, and tin mines of the north and north-west, most of the mineral areas here summarized were worked under the Republic: but to say on what system they were worked is a more difficult question. The mining of gold was usually, perhaps, a State pre-rogative,[45] though not always, as Tiberius' seizure of Sextus Marius' mines shows:[46] the increasing ten-dency under the later Republic to coin in gold must have necessitated some kind of State control of the market price of gold, and with this there may have come increased stringency in the supervision of gold mines. For silver no fixed rule can be found. Mines such as those of Carthago Nova were presumably under the general supervision of the State (though they were not State-owned),[47] but the fact that silver and lead frequently occurred together in other and lesser deposits may have resulted in the selling or leasing of such deposits, either to individual prospectors, or to companies. This system applied also to the mining of lead: at Carthago Nova there have been found lead ingots stamped with the names of those (presumably shaft- or mine-owners) who exported the metal thence;[48] and *societates* are known to have existed at Ilucro and Sisapo very early during the Empire, if not during the Republic.[49]

To sum up, we may therefore say of the Republic that Spanish gold was generally regarded as inalienable from the State, but that silver, lead, and probably copper also, were usually mined by companies or individuals by right of purchase or lease. In the State-owned mines labour would most naturally be supplied by slaves: elsewhere the steadily increasing ownership of mines by Roman companies seems to have resulted in a proportionate influx of Italian labour.[50] Spanish

mines thus supplied Spain with no marketable com-
modity : the profits mainly left the country, and even
of the labour much was furnished from abroad. Hence,
perhaps, the position of the mines last on Justin's list.

Economic development, combined with the traffic of
the mines, presupposes simultaneous development in
the system of communications.[51]   Rivers provided
some parts of Spain with an ancient and easy means of
transport.   The Baetis, for example, which served a
large, busy, and densely-populated area, was navigable
for large boats up to Hispalis, for the smaller to Ilipa,
and for the smallest up to Corduba itself.   The Tagus
and the Durius were also useful waterways for part of
their course, and the same was true of the Ebro : it
has been observed that the coins of Dertosa show two
types of vessel (Pl. III, 6), the lighter of which may
have been employed for river traffic.   This natural
system of waterways was increased and extended by
the construction of canals by the Romans.[52]   Of the
Republican system of roads there is disappointingly
little evidence (see Map III).   The earliest highways
must have been dictated by the necessities of warfare.
Thus the early years of conquest, 218–206 B.C.,
undoubtedly began the systematic improvement of the
ancient coastal route from the Pyrenees to Carthago
Nova, and the construction of branches inland ; and
the operations at the head of the Baetis valley similarly
prepared for the future connection between Carthago
Nova and the Baetis river-road route.   The conquest
of the Ebro valley, and later of Celtiberia, likewise
necessitated some kind of military highways, along
which armies might be fed, reinforced, or even rapidly
withdrawn.[53]   For these early developments we
are obliged to depend on the evidence of logic, and
upon our knowledge of the Roman character, which

always built for the future. Polybius, in a not altogether explicit passage[54] in which he states the various distances along the ancient Gades–Pyrenees route, might easily be taken as proving that by about 120 B.C. this road had been reconstructed and furnished with milestones. But this is to read too much into the passage. By the first century B.C. this road was possibly systematized from the Pyrenees to Carthago Nova, and even a part of the northern branch from Saetabis towards Saltigi and Libisosa (Lezuza)—the future link with Corduba. The work of completing the link, and relaying or repairing the whole route down to Gades itself, and setting up milestones, was more likely the work of Augustus, though it is true that even before his time some sort of a road east of Corduba had existed (the Sierra Morena mines necessitated this), as the presence of a pre-Augustan bridge at Corduba proves.[55]

Two pre-Augustan bridges existed also at Ilerda, north of the Ebro :[56] and from Ilerda comes, too, a pair of Republican milestones which may point to a regular road from Tarraco or Barcino (Barcelona) towards Osca *via* Ilerda.[57] Another milestone of pre-Imperial date comes from the modern Caldas de Mombuy, north of Barcino, and suggests an inland and secondary road branching (like that to Ilerda) from the main coastal artery.[58]

Such evidence as we possess indicates, therefore, that the building of regular roads (which were everywhere of primarily military origin) was chiefly characteristic of Citerior. Nevertheless, military operations had frequently proved to be necessary in Ulterior : these, however, were presumably served by existing tracks which had long connected the ancient network of Turdetanian communities. The Roman achievement during the Republic was to progress slowly in the substituting of works of engineering for the former unmetalled tracks which they found ; and in so doing they gave an obvious stimulus towards social unity and internal trade, besides facilitating the development of the capitalist export trade.

This brief survey of the development in Republican Spain would not be complete without some reference to the coinage,—always conspicuous among a country's economic aspects, and, in the case of Spain at least, an illuminating index for internal progress and activity. The origins of coinage in Spain have already been discussed, and reasons have been given for supposing that silver, with a varying amount of bronze, was coined at a large number of mints in Citerior from a date early in the second century, the silver being absorbed by Rome in the payment of taxes and the bronze forming a medium of internal exchange in Spain. This system appears, from a study of the mints, to have been characteristic of Citerior alone, or mainly so, as second-century silver, with appropriate types and legends, is lacking for Ulterior. But the silver coined in Citerior circulated widely in Spain, being found commonly in Ulterior, and it may well be that Citerior found it convenient to exchange its silver for the commodities which Ulterior was able and ready to furnish in return. In both provinces there were certain other coins in circulation as well,—in Citerior, the silver *drachmae* struck at the ' Greek ' mints of Rhode and Emporium (Pl. I, 1 and 2) ;[59] and, in Ulterior, bronze coins of Phoenician type produced at such towns as Gades :[60] these supplementary coinages would naturally have a less wide circulation. In addition to these different series, there were current increasing numbers of Roman coins proper, chiefly *denarii*, with some bronze (mainly *asses*) besides.

With the fall of Numantia and the collapse of all but sporadic Celtiberian resistance, there was a radical change, for it seems probable that the Iberian silver coinage—the *argentum Oscense*—came to an end : this conclusion is suggested partly by the evidence of finds, and partly by the fact that Iberian silver never reaches the stage of bilingual legends common among the bronze of the later Republic. The cessation was presumably dictated by political motives : its effect upon Spanish economics was probably not serious, for, while Spanish silver must henceforth have been sent to Rome in the form of bullion, the country was in any case now permeated by Roman *denarii* disseminated by Roman legions during three-quarters of a century of intermittent war. There is no reason to suppose that the coinage in bronze was stopped : it is, indeed, from the bronze of the first century that much of our most interesting evidence is derived, for it reflects in a number of ways the gradual adoption of Roman ideas in various parts of the country,—Citerior and Ulterior.

At first the innovation may consist only of the choice of a Roman type, recommended by its familiarity in currency, or of the use of a Roman symbol as a mark of value, or of a symbol signifying a Roman value. Thus the ' Apollo ' heads of Carbula and Obulco are based on those of the *denarii* struck in such numbers by Piso at Rome in the first half of the first century B.C. : orthodox, if crude, ' Roma ' heads appear on the Iberian-inscribed bronze of Saguntum (Pl. II, 1),—a series of increased weight which may, as has been suggested, have been introduced at the time of the re-settlement after 133 B.C.[61] What appear to be Roman symbols are found on bronze of Iliberris, Obulco, and Ulia (all with X, ? $=\frac{1}{10}$ *denarius*

=*as*), and of Caura, Ilipa, Itucci, Orippo, and other
mints besides (all with Λ, ? =*as*): the same marks are
found on the later Latin-inscribed coins of Carbula
and Laelia. In the same way the S on the coins of
Carteia, Searo, etc., stands for S(*emis*): at Abdera the
S is found with the regular Roman type of the
' Jupiter ' head. Coins such as these, attesting romanization by type or symbol,[62] may perhaps be regarded
as characteristic of the half-century after the fall of
Numantia, when a natural emphasis would fall on
Roman coins and coin-denominations in Spain as a
result of the cessation of the Iberian silver.

Then followed the bilinguals, probably towards the
middle of the first century B.C. In Citerior, indeed,
their occurrence is somewhat rare : but a combination
of Iberian and Latin legends is found on coins of Celsa
and Osicerda (Pl. II, 6, with types imitated from the
denarii of Caesar struck in Gaul in 50–49 B.C.),[63]
Saetabis, and Saguntum, the latter mint resorting to
the Roman ' prow ' type (Pl. II, 1). In Ulterior,
however, the transition is more plainly seen.[64] The
obverse types, indeed, like those of Citerior, are
stereotyped, and retain the designs common to the
previous issues. But the reverse types are frequently
bilingual, and are vivid evidence for the forces of
change in this province. They occur regularly at Arsa,
Asido, Baelo, Iptuci, Itucci, Lascuta, Oba, Turriricina,
and Vesci : the coins of all these mints combine Latin
with the native Turdetanian alphabet in their legends.
To these may be added Castulo and Salacia, where the
coins were marked besides with the mint-authorities'
names in native characters. Two other coin-issues
are worthy of notice, though they are not in
fact bilingual : first, that of Clunia, with the legend
CLOVNIOQ <OM>,—a mere transliteration of the

Iberian ethnic name (Pl. II, 3);[65] and second, an emission of Emporium marked MVNIᐸᴿ or ᴹNNᴿ, that is, with a mixture of the Roman and Iberian alphabets.[66]

With rare exceptions, it is impossible to give these bilingual and transitional coinages any very close dating. Certain of them began about the middle of the first century B.C.; and it is probable that they continued in most cases down to the reorganization of provincial coinages carried out by Augustus. Be that as it may, they give, when grouped together, a striking glimpse of the infiltration of Roman influences into Spanish urban life. Their distribution also is significant, for there were of course many other simultaneous pre-imperial issues, a few with wholly Latin legends (as at Emporium, Celsa, and Turiaso, in romanized areas: cf. Pl. II, 3 ff.), but the great majority retaining their Iberian, Turdetanian or Phoenician ethnics; and in this condition the coinage of Spain was to continue until Augustus' reconstruction.

Apart from their bearing on the infiltration of Roman influences, the Spanish coins of the late Republican period argue strongly for increased urbanization and for increased internal intercourse in Spain. In both provinces the total number of active mints is large: but the need for local coinages *in bronze*—a more or less 'small-change' series—does not arise until a population is settled enough to engage in the regular process of urban trade. That these bronze coinages exist in such variety is powerful evidence for the peaceful development of the area in which they were produced—an area corresponding to the whole Roman dominion of the pre-Numantine era. Here we may postulate settled communities, impelled to commerce (by the general economic development of the

8

country) both within themselves and with each other : the coins of the various mints are found widely diffused. It was upon a yet increased and extended urbanization that Julius Caesar was to lay unmistakable emphasis.

CHAPTER VI

JULIUS CAESAR AND THE URBAN EXPERIMENT

THE sketch of Spanish economic development given in the preceding chapter allows an approximate estimate to be made of the extent of romanization among the native communities of the later Republic. Of its quality, however, there is little indication; and this is hardly surprising, for, though economics may and usually do exert a profound influence in a country's collective existence, that influence is more easily measured in terms of material culture than in considerations of political progress. Whatever the modern historian may mean by romanization (and this is not always clear), it may be asserted that the citizen of Rome or Italy would—if he could now be questioned—give to this word the sense of cultural assimilation along the lines of Roman political institutions. With romanization in this sense economics had little to do. It is quite true that thriving commercial connections would encourage increasing familiarity with Roman ideas : the Spanish producer might receive his Roman money from a Roman middleman, knowing his goods to be destined for the market of Rome itself, and—if he paused to count his blessings, such as they were—he might reflect that the healthy condition of his business was due, above all, to the security implicit in the Roman administration of his country. But to see romanization in this relationship alone is to limit its significance severely, as an outside factor, super-imposed rather than absorbed,—an external pheno-menon lacking all root in the inner Spanish consciousness.

Nevertheless, it is this narrow view of romanization that should probably be applied to the Spain of the late Republic. The policy of the government was not yet bold, generous, or far-sighted enough to realize the necessity of using Roman-organized urban units in provincial territory at once as a model of what com-munal life and communal responsibility should be and as a bait to tempt the local politician to assimilate his methods to those of the Roman political system. Although Spain by now contained many centres of Roman influence, these were not situated in such a way as to affect the less commercial and less civilized parts of the country, being chiefly characteristic of the east and south coasts and of the Baetis valley. Nor were they, for the most part, accurate or obvious models of Roman urban administration, for scarcely any displayed a purely Roman character. Tarraco, still an unprivileged town, was an important Roman nucleus, but it has yielded bilingual inscriptions, and long enjoyed an Iberian coinage.[1] The same is true of Saguntum: this town too, romanized as it was, seems to have been denied the recognition of municipal status until the last years of the Republic.[2] Further south Valentia—a true veteran colony of the second century B.C. (see above, p. 79)—possessed a double *ordo*, or local senate, perhaps a sign of two irreconcil-able elements in the colony.[3] The famous old town of Castulo (watch-dog of the Sierra Morena mines, and a fickle watch-dog at that), possessed (like Saetabis)[4] Latin rights under the Republic, and was nevertheless sufficiently well permeated with native influence to call

herself by the transliterated and hybrid name CAST-LOSAIC,[5] analogous to the CLOVNIOQ of Clunia's coins. Gades, a rich and thriving port, second only to Padua in the number of its men possessing the equestrian property-qualification of 400,000 *sestertii*, was almost wholly mercantile, and could scarcely be classed as a residential city in which political organization was of primary importance.[6]   Carteia was hybrid in its origin (above, p. 76); and even Metellinum, a true colony founded in 80 B.C., was little more than a military outpost.[7]   In Citerior the most thoroughly Roman town was probably Carthago Nova :[8] this was matched in Ulterior by Italica and Corduba. But none of these towns enjoyed any privileged status that might be taken as indicating the model community : a *vicus civium Romanorum* was not a positive stimulus towards romanization along political lines. Taken as a whole, neither province was sufficiently familiar with Roman municipal organization to understand its advantages.   Debarred from the ordered and uniform institutions which this urban self-government involved, native communities could scarcely be expected to welcome Roman manners and ideas, still less to seek them voluntarily.

Nevertheless, the extension of Roman peace over an increasingly wide area must have resulted in the chief pre-requisite of urban organization. In many cases local communes were, doubtless, encouraged to coalesce, and to exchange the benefits of insignificant independence for the more tangible advantages brought by amalgamation into one substantial *oppidum stipendiarium*. Evidence for this transitional stage is lacking—it was not the kind of process to attract the attention of the ancient historians, or to leave any other and independent traces,—but it is only by some such general impulse towards amalgamation that the work of Julius Caesar in Spain (as of Augustus after him) can have become at all possible.

Caesar's activities in Spain have, indeed, received a curiously uneven treatment at the hands of historians, most of whom have confined themselves to the military operations which he undertook during the two phases of civil war in Spain, the first against the legates of Pompey, the second against Pompey's sons. For the career of Caesar himself these phases are of obvious importance ; but, though their repercussions on Spain were in many ways serious enough, they were not in themselves integral parts of the romanization of the provinces—rather the reverse. The Sertorian war had, it is true, assumed the semblance of a civil war within the Roman state, but it was at all times much more than this, being actually a trial of strength between Rome and the nationalist energies of Spain harnessed, through romanization, by a Roman commander. Emphasis upon Caesar's civil conflicts in Spain is excusable enough if, at the same time, due account is taken of his provincial policy as such. Even if it is the case that the evidence for his provincial policy in Spain is to some extent indirect—the product of inference rather than of explicit record—we are not thereby justified in neglecting it. Our method therefore will be to omit reference to the campaigns of the civil wars except in so far as they bear directly on Spanish political problems (these campaigns have been described in excellent detail elsewhere),[9] and to concentrate upon Caesar's attitude to the provincial problems which confronted him. Here, as elsewhere, he richly deserves praise, laying the foundations upon which Augustus was later to build so wisely and so well : gifted with a singular imagination, brilliantly

combined with powers of practical organization and direct action, he no sooner diagnosed the symptoms of disease in Spanish national life than he initiated the first of the many steps of reform which were to culminate in the Spanish policy of the Flavian dynasty.

His first knowledge of the country was gained during his period of office as quaestor in Ulterior in 68 B.C.[10]   Seven years later he returned to the same province as propraetor (61–60 B.C.).[11]   Of the events of his governorship we know comparatively little : but that little is significant.   He effected an important change in the law of debt, by which creditors might be entitled to claim two-thirds of the income of their debtors (the radical nature of this measure attests the extent and prevalence of debt—the outcome of a period of economic development and rising exports).[12] His other great achievement was military, its successful result being the clear prelude to his comprehensive reforms of later years.   It consisted of a vigorous offensive campaign undertaken in the area between the Tagus and the Durius.   This area was not indeed quite unfamiliar with the threat of Roman arms, for D. Junius Brutus had, three-quarters of a century earlier, earned his name ' Callaicus ' by a successful expedition to the extreme north-west (above, p. 79 f.). But it had never been formally conquered ; and it is probable that the northern limit of Ulterior had never subsequently been extended beyond the Tagus, the military colony of Metellinum serving as a base for the area between Anas and Tagus.   Not content with the conquest of the territory up to the Durius, Caesar employed a naval arm, operating from Gades, which subjected the coastal communities north of the Durius and even extended its activities as far north as Brigantium (Corunna), thus initiating the penetration of

Callaecia and Asturia which Augustus was to complete. His joint offensive by land and sea once swiftly accomplished, Caesar returned speedily to Rome to claim his triumph and to seek the consulship. But, swift as his campaign had been, it had begun the process by which the Baetis valley was to be detached from the economically and culturally different Lusitanian area lying to the north and north-west of it.[13]

The next few years saw Caesar's steady rise to power in Roman politics, assisted by an astonishing and dazzling record of military success in Gaul. Of the administration of Spain in this period history is silent, being concerned mainly with the political duel in Rome; but one important experiment was tried when Pompey, in 55 B.C., received a long-term command of the two Spanish provinces, with permission to govern them from the capital by means of subordinate *legati*.[14] An arrangement such as this, while it obviously foreshadowed the Principate, was equally clearly to the advantage of Spain, if Pompey exercised care in choosing his *legati*: that he did so is perhaps to be inferred from the fact that, in the later years of civil war in Spain, the Pompeian following was substantial: 'Caesar . . . knew that the favours and following of Pompey in the nearer province were great,'[15] and Pompey's backing was not confined to Citerior. It was, possibly, during Pompey's absentee governorship that Corduba was raised to the status of a colony.[16]

Not until 49 B.C., the peak of the political crisis, did Caesar visit Spain again, and then it was to win his victory at Ilerda and to receive the submission of Pompey's *legati* and their respective armies. He found it politic to grant concessions (of citizenship, property,

or tax-immunity) both to those whose support he required to keep as well as to those whose allegiance he wished to transfer to his own side.[17] For wide or general reforms this was not the moment, nor had he time to make them : nevertheless his conferment of citizenship upon the people of Gades (whose affairs he was asked to regulate) showed, perhaps, the direction in which his provincial policy was tending.[18] Grants such as these, even if they lacked constitutional force, could scarcely be revoked in the face of a power like Caesar's.

Caesar's campaign against the sons and partisans of Pompey, after the latter's death in Egypt, was ended by his victory at Munda in 45 B.C., and left him supreme, in Spain as elsewhere. But Spain was by no means wholly for him ; particularly in the Baetis valley was there a strong pro-Pompeian feeling, shared by such important towns as Corduba, Hispalis, Ucubi (Espejo), and Urso, with Ulia as the only significant exception. Opposition to Caesar's cause, due originally (as we must suppose) to Pompey's beneficence in administration, was strengthened by the rapacity and violence of Caesar's subordinates in the hour of victory : Caesar himself did not neglect considerations of partisanship when he planned his Spanish reforms. Nevertheless, in the face of all opposition, he took but a single year to carry out his whole programme of reconstruction, and, after consideration of its ample scope, no fair critic will deny the justice of his settlement, the correctness of his instinct, or the sureness of his touch. His work remained unimpaired throughout another thirteen years of civil war elsewhere.

It was in the extension of the colonial system that his finest achievement lay. Emphasis upon colonization was now, indeed, natural enough in any Roman politician of democratic outlook, for this was one of the most obvious methods by which unemployment in Rome (due to the steady increase in size and economic idleness of the *plebs urbana*) could be remedied.[19] But to take this view of colonization to the exclusion of any other was to study the interests of the capital alone, irrespective of what provincial conditions required for their betterment. Caesar did not make this mistake: his keen appreciation of the diverse necessities imposed by peace and war was clearly reflected in his twofold view of the purpose of colonies, i.e. as outposts of defence in undeveloped country, where romanization might best be learned by familiarity with the organization of a semi-military base, and as purely civilian centres in well-pacified districts ready to profit by the example of Roman municipal institutions in their most complete form. Nowhere is the dual nature of the Roman colony better shown than in Caesar's policy in Spain.

Of these two classes of Julian colonies in Spain, the former may now be examined. Caesar's experience of the country had been gained mainly in Ulterior: it was in Ulterior that reform was most urgently needed. The previous chapter indicated the agricultural and economic stability of the district comprising the Baetis valley and its near environs. A glance at the map will show how geography contributed towards the economic unity of this district, shut off as it was by a mountain ridge on its north from the parallel valleys of Anas and Tagus. But hitherto this economic independence of the Baetis area had been harshly yoked to an administrative system which treated its affairs as inseparable from those of the districts to the north, where conditions had never been formally settled, and brigandage was still a reality: the relation of the

Baetican to the Lusitanian area was much the same as
that of Achaea and Macedonia towards the slowly
developing province of Moesia under the Julio-
Claudian emperors. Actual risk of war from Lusitania
there was now none : yet the Baetis economic area still
lacked the definite northern limit which its economic
activities demanded. Caesar had doubtless marked
this anomaly during his governorship of Ulterior,
especially during his northern campaign ; and he now
quickly removed it, or at any rate diminished it. The
colony of Metellinum was, as we have noted, probably
the northernmost of the regular Roman positions in
Ulterior. Caesar's earlier campaign had left Metellinum
behind in the wake of his triumphant progress—his
main operations had lain between Tagus and Durius—
and it was to the Tagus that he seems now to have
extended the official frontier of Ulterior, basing it upon
the key-positions of Scallabis (Santarém) and Norba
(Cáceres),

Evidence for this assertion, even if it is indirect, is
strong and cannot easily be rejected. Scallabis appears
in Pliny's description of Spain as *Colonia Praesidium
Iulium*; Norba as *Colonia Caesarina*.[20] Augustan
colonies are as a general rule to be recognized by the
inclusion in their title of some form of the word
' Augustus ', as (for example) Augusta Emerita, Lucus
Angusti, Caesaraugusta (see below, pp. 135 ff.) : the
names ' Iulius ' or ' Caesar ', unsupplemented by
' Augustus ', are not characteristic of the foundations
of the first Princeps ; and his successors usually contrived to advertise their own colonial settlements by
the use of the name applied specifically to distinguish
them (e.g. Tiberius, Claudius, Nero), or by their
gentile name (e.g. Flavius). These known examples of
later usage therefore compel us to regard *Colonia*

Praesidium Iulium Scallabis and *Colonia Caesarina Norba* as original foundations of Caesar himself : [21] ' praesidium ', moreover, describes precisely the function of Scallabis in Caesar's time, whereas for any later period such a name would be far less appropriate. The Scallabis–Norba line, then, may be accepted as Caesar's creation ; and it may well be that the Tagus frontier line was regularized as far up the river's course as Caesarobriga—yet another place-name which seems to point to Caesar's activities, though the -briga termination suggests that this was no more than a purely native community, without political privilege, which in some way earned Caesar's favour.[22]

It will, perhaps, be objected here that Caesar's extension of the northern boundary of Ulterior to the Tagus only aggravated the administrative weakness mentioned above, and that Ulterior, so far from being shaped as a geographical and economic unit centred on the Baetis, was in fact now to be administered under a wide system which was bound to disregard the claims of the Baetis valley to independence. This objection might be sustained if there were not also evidence showing that Caesar created, in the extreme south-west of the peninsula between the lower courses of Anas and Tagus, a coherently municipalized area to which geography closely linked the new Tagus frontier line. Here again the evidence is indirect, being once more derived from nomenclature ; but cumulatively it is strong. The area in question (equivalent to the southern half of modern Portugal), free from extremes of height, possessing much fertile soil, and with all the advantages of a seaboard, was rich in agricultural and mineral possibilities : though it had probably never been subjected to any regular Roman influences, it was nevertheless now peaceful, safe from the brigandage

which the neighbouring heights of Estremadura
encouraged. The modern Beja, which dominates this
area, is the site of the Roman *Colonia Pax Iulia*, otherwise known as *Colonia Pacensis* ;[23] and this foundation
too must be assigned to Caesar : its position would
suggest (like its name) that, whereas Scallabis and
Norba were *praesidia* against unrest beyond the Tagus,
Pax Julia had no more to do than keep an existing
peace around her, in an age when Caesar's victories
had brought peace to all the Roman part of Spain.
This triangle of Caesarian colonies was strengthened
by other foundations of a lower status. Olisipo (the
modern Lisbon), later known as *Municipium Felicitas
Iulia*,[24] was to become the famous port of the Tagus
estuary : the date when it received municipal rank is
uncertain, but its name marks it as a unit in Caesar's
Lusitanian system. Ebora (Evora), often surnamed
'Cerealis', is described by Pliny as *Municipium Liberalitas
Iulia* (cf. Pl. III, 7),[25] and bridged the gap between
Pax Julia and the Tagus colonies : here again, whatever the date of the municipal charter, the original
settlement must be ascribed to Caesar ; and the same
is probably true of Myrtilis (Mertola) to the south.
Thus the south-west corner of Spain was covered by a
framework of colonies, and of towns in which municipal institutions, if not expressly guaranteed by the
immediate grant of a municipal charter, were nevertheless inherent in the names given to them. *Praesidium Iulium, Caesarina, Pax Iulia, Liberalitas Iulia,
Felicitas Iulia* : the names recall Caesar's own description of his acts after Ilerda, when ' he gave privileges to
a number of public and private groups, and filled all
other men with bright hopes for the future '.[26]
Indeed, his Lusitanian experiment turned out to be a
striking success. Secured from northern molestation

by the Tagus frontier (itself destined soon to be superseded), this secondary part of Ulterior developed peacefully and swiftly. Pax Julia, possessor of *ius Italicum* under Augustus, had by then dispensed with the need for troops, soon to be restricted to a handful under the governor of the new 'Lusitania' stationed at Emerita (see below, pp. 137 ff.). Mining at Vipasca, trade at Olisipo, agriculture at Ebora, fisheries at Caetobriga,—these are but representative of the industries which, even if they could never vie with those of the Baetis valley, nevertheless brought peace and prosperity to the Lusitanian area, thus insulating the Baetis valley once and for all from the risk of border unrest. The wisdom of Caesar's planning was acknowledged clearly by Augustus when he detached the newly urbanized and unified area from Ulterior and gave it independent status as part of *provincia Lusitania*.[27]

Such was Caesar's use of the military or semi-military colony, peopled with his veteran citizen-soldiers, and reinforced by towns of municipal or quasi-municipal character, in which the Spanish inhabitants had, by their peaceful adaptability, qualified for the grant of Latin rights as an avenue to the Roman franchise. In the Baetis region itself, as also in Citerior, his colonizing policy was for the most part dictated by very different motives, and scarcely affected any part of the country other than what had already grown fairly familiar with Roman customs and Roman administration. Yet, for all this familiarity, there were (as we have already seen) extremely few centres which possessed the colonial or municipal status that was necessary if the moral of romanization—in the Roman view—was to be driven home. Then again, there was the question of the *plebs urbana*. Suetonius relates that Caesar's overseas colonies absorbed 80,000 of the

unemployed at Rome :[28] few out of this number would
be naturally suitable for inclusion in the most important of the 'frontier colonies', such as Scallabis and
Norba, though nothing debarred them from forming
purely civil colonies in a pacified district. A further
consideration was that of partisanship : many parts of
Spain—especially in the valley of the Baetis—had
joined Pompey's cause against Caesar ; and this pro-
Pompeian complexion must be counterbalanced, if
only by the method of flooding the disaffected
areas with colonists owing to Caesar their new start
in life.

In accordance with these considerations, Caesar
founded four colonies of a purely civil character in the
Baetis area—Hispalis (*Colonia Iulia Romula*), Urso
(*Colonia Iulia Genetiva Urbanorum*), Ucubi (*Colonia
Claritas Iulia*), and Itucci (*Colonia Virtus Iulia*), of which
last the site is only conjectural ;[29] and in addition to
these colonies there were other towns, either with or
without political privilege, which received the recognition implicit in the title ' Iulia ' or ' Caesarina ', such
as Nertobriga (Frejenál), Ugultuniacum, Osset, and
Asido (Medina Sidonia).[30]   Of the four colonies, Urso
possesses the greatest interest for the historian, for its
charter has survived.[31]   This, together with its dis-
tinctive title, ' Colonia . . . *Urbanorum* ', shows clearly
that, of the Baetican colonies, Urso at any rate was
composed of the Roman proletariate : the democratic
nature of the foundation allows *liberti*—freed slaves—
to hold office as decurions in the local senate, and lays
down safeguards by which attempts on the part of the
Roman Senate to interfere in the affairs of the colony
shall be checked. Caesar himself takes a personal part
in making the first appointments to office : and among
the other provisions of the charter (doubtless composed

under Caesar's supervision) were directions which prevented over-production in industry, and injunctions
whereby the colonists were required to contribute to
taxation, or to be enrolled in the local militia at the
discretion of the chief magistrates, the *IIviri iure
dicundo*. The fact that these burdens fell on the new
colonists (the *attributi*) as well as on the old inhabitants
of Urso (the *incolae*) reminds us that the process of
colonization at all four of these settlements was
attended by forfeiture of territory by their original
dwellers : for all four towns had supported the
Pompeian side.

Caesar's foundations in Citerior, too, though their
origin and nature were different on the whole from the
colonies of the Lusitanian or Baetican areas, were of
great importance. That at Celsa (Velilla) was indeed
the earliest—he had founded it in 48 or 47 B.C. in
association with Lepidus (governor of Citerior),
doubtless as an anti-Pompeian makeweight in an
important strategic position : later Lepidus' share in
the foundation was discreetly ignored, and *Colonia
Victrix Iulia Lepida* became *Colonia Victrix Iulia Celsa*
(cf. Pl. IV, 5, 6).[32]   The other Julian colonies in
Citerior were Tarraco (*Colonia Iulia Victrix Trium-
phalis*) (cf. Pl. IV, 7, 8) and Carthago Nova (*Colonia
Victrix Iulia Nova Karthago*). Each of these cities had
long been famous as a centre of administration as well
as of the export-trade : their advancement to colonial
status (probably achieved without any marked influx
of Roman settlers) had long been deserved. So too
was that of Dertosa, the vital town at the crossing of
the Ebro, now given the title of *Municipium Hibera
Iulia Ilercavonia* (cf. Pl. III, 6),—a prelude to its
promotion to colonial dignity under Tiberius.[33]

Only one other of Caesar's settlements remains to

be noted, that of Acci (Guadix), made a colony with the title *Colonia Iulia Gemella*. This foundation was composed, as the coins show us, of veterans of Legions I and II (hence the name ' Gemella ') ; and its composition was suitable in view of its responsibility for guarding the dangerous and difficult neck of the Sierra Nevada, beyond which lay Carthago Nova. Acci was granted *ius Italicum* ;[34] and its significance as being Caesar's one pre-eminently military colony outside the Lusitanian area is shown by Augustus' final reform of Baetica, in which Acci, Castulo, and the Saltus Tugiensis were transferred from Baetica to the new province of Tarraconensis (see below, p. 140).

This list of Caesar's colonies and municipalities is long : the time taken in completing the necessary arrangements was surprisingly short. But Caesar knew his Spain well, and in general his provincial policy was definite and swift. Much has been argued about the existence and scope of a possible *Lex Julia Municipalis*,[35] perhaps to be recognized in the Table of Heraclea. The controversy does not admit of certainty : but it does not lie beyond the bounds of credibility that Caesar did in fact frame a law which defined the most obvious and vital necessities in municipal government, in Italy as elsewhere ; and that, in the event of the revision or creation of a local charter, reference might be made to the model law wherever local circumstances allowed it. If this was indeed the case, then to Caesar may go the credit for attempting to formulate a clear and constant relationship between municipalities and the central government. An increase in the number of municipalities would result in an increased uniformity of administration : but this would not necessarily involve increased bureaucracy or a growth of local apathy, for the

9

administration in question conferred on privileged communities a large measure of self-government, determined and guaranteed by the local charter. Caesar thus extended the scope of local responsibility, besides adding the stimulus of the desire for Roman citizenship to those who sought it. But Roman citizenship was not, perhaps, to Caesar the same precious thing which others made it, if we may judge from the composition of the colony of Urso, or from the huge numbers of unemployed whom he colonized abroad. To gain the citizenship as the reward for success in local self-government was not necessarily to transfer interest from the local municipality to Rome: so many citizens existed outside Rome. Therefore by a great multiplication (and consequent slight cheapening) of the franchise in the provinces, Caesar avoided the evil policy of his successors, whose more sparing grants of the franchise tended to attract to Rome those who gained it, thus constantly robbing the provinces of their ablest political representatives. Had his life been longer, the world might have witnessed the beginnings of a new policy of imperial representation—the result of political emancipation in the provinces.

But Caesar's death came too soon to allow any such development. Nor was there time for any explicit signs of his personal popularity to appear in Spain. The records of stone give us no evidence—inscriptions, dedications, or the like—that his reforms called forth any widespread gratitude or veneration. Only the official titles of the various new foundations recall his actual work: and this work is itself often laid at the door of expediency. But this is a mean and ungenerous view of history, and one which is refuted by Augustus' own adoption of many aspects of his

predecessor's forward policy. It is certain that the lack of any record of contemporary gratitude to Caesar is due only to the world-wide preoccupation with the gathering signs of civil war which followed his early death.

CHAPTER VII

AUGUSTUS' RECONSTRUCTION OF SPAIN

IN the person of Augustus the Roman provinces were destined for the first time to recognize a man remarkable not only for his wisdom and the scope of his imperial aspirations, but also for the power and the opportunities which enabled him to try out his experiments everywhere on the widest possible scale. Spain was to experience the full measure of his beneficence in the course of his reign, which brought with it a great increase in administrative and economic vigour. At first, however, thoughts of administrative reform were overshadowed by a problem at once more immediate and more serious. After his unequivocal victory over Antony in 31 B.C. at Actium, Augustus (to anticipate by four years the granting of this title) was free to make a calm and systematic survey of the Roman provinces and to undertake whatever reorganization appeared to be necessary. It was no mere accident that directed his attention, at an early date, to Spain. Invaded for the first time by Roman armies nearly two centuries before, this great and diverse peninsula had perhaps been a cause of more inconvenience and expense than any other of the provinces. It was true that a large part of it was more or less peaceably settled, and that, in Caesar's time, Roman influence had spread as far north as the wild territory of Callaecia; moreover, Rome had long since begun to profit from the agricultural and mineral

wealth of Spain. Nevertheless, a large part of the country was still untamed: the fierce mountain tribes of Asturia and Cantabria still lay outside the limits of Roman authority, although official triumphs had not infrequently been celebrated by Roman commanders as a result of intermittent hostilities in the years following Caesar's death. Clearly, Spain as a whole could not be considered a settled and solid province until Asturia and Cantabria, remote yet dangerous sources of brigandage, had been drilled into obedience. It is surely unnecessary to suppose that Augustus' military activities in northern Spain were mainly, or even partly, dictated by the desire to exploit the mineral wealth which existed there. Any such theory as this fails to take account of concrete problems of administration. The primary results of the conquest of Asturia and Cantabria were bound to be seen in the increased security of the districts to the south of them and in the eventual reduction of the permanent legionary establishment in Spain.[1]

The events and chronology of Augustus' Spanish war were ill-recorded by ancient historians, and have only recently received careful attention from modern writers.[2] Spanish triumphs were celebrated in 28 and 27 B.C., and we may perhaps assume that these hostilities implied preparation for Augustus' own campaign; this would not be surprising in view of the fact that Augustus himself, in 26 B.C., assumed the leadership of the legions in the Nearer Province.[3] From a base at Segisama (Sasamon) Augustus' forces marched northwards in three columns up the valley separating the Asturian from the main Celtiberian *massif*. On his left flank lay the warlike Astures; these tribes were possibly being held in check at this moment if, as has lately been supposed, it was now that

the legate of Lusitania, P. Carisius, advanced independently from his own province and effected the capture
of Lancia which, lying south-east of the modern Leon,
would thus successfully have screened Augustus from
Asturian attacks. Augustus' own army defeated a
Cantabrian force at Vellica, and thereby pushed its
way through the mountains by the road which runs
past Juliobriga down to the sea at Portus Victoriae
(Santander). By the co-operation of a Roman fleet
from Aquitania, the legions received reinforcements
and fresh supplies. Augustus now turned westward,
and began the systematic subjugation of the Cantabri.
The ancient historians recorded the hardships to which
the Roman troops were subjected in this tedious and
difficult mountain-warfare with savage tribes. By the
end of the season, however, the Cantabri had taken
refuge in their hill-fortresses, and the Romans, more
accustomed to blockading than to guerilla-tactics, had
successfully reduced them to surrender. The campaign had been arduous, and Augustus, whose health
was never good, developed a serious illness which
necessitated his retirement to Tarraco.

The campaign of the succeeding year, 25 B.C., was
therefore undertaken jointly by Carisius and the legate
of the Nearer Province, C. Antistius Vetus.[4] Its object
was the final subjugation of the north-west corner of
Spain. We must assume that the two armies, the one
advancing under Antistius from Cantabria, the other
under Carisius from the middle course of the Douro,
succeeded by their convergence in driving the Astures
into a vast stronghold in the mountains ; this fortress
'overlooked the river Minius'[5] (Minho), and was
called by the Romans Mons Medullius, but its exact
site is a matter only for conjecture. All that is known
is that, after the Romans had invested the fortress

with siege-lines fifteen miles in length, the Astures capitulated and the campaign of this year thus ended.

Two years had apparently sufficed for the conquest of the outstanding tribal areas of Spain : each campaign had ended conspicuously with a siege and a surrender. Augustus himself appears to have considered that the pacification of Asturia and Cantabria was complete, for veteran soldiers in the Spanish legions were paid off (the foundation of Colonia Emerita—the modern Merida—in 25 B.C. was due to this step[6]) and when Augustus returned to Rome from Spain in 24 B.C. the temple of Janus was solemnly closed. But Augustus, no less than the earlier generals of the Republic, underestimated the spirit of the Spanish tribesmen. Almost at once the first of a series of obstinate revolts broke out. Stern fighting is known to have taken place in 24, 22, and 19 B.C. ;[7] in this last year Agrippa was sent to Spain to stamp out the flame of revolt, and it was only after he had taken the most rigorous steps—massacre and enslavement among them—that he brought the hostilities and rebellion to an end. The pacification of Asturia and Cantabria, so often a matter for minor comment by historians both ancient and modern, had taken the best part of ten years to achieve.

A certain amount of local reorganization became necessary in the north as a result of the conquest. Systematically, the hill-tribes were brought down from the high ground and were settled, according to the Roman usage, in the valleys in new towns where they were more accessible to Roman methods and Roman ideas; this process is seen best in Asturia, in the foundation of such towns as Lucus Asturum (Lugo) and Asturica Augusta (Astorga). Simultaneously there became apparent a decline in the brigandage which before had characterized northern Spain, though Velleius is clearly guilty of exaggeration when he records its total disappearance in and after 24 B.C.[8] Much of the newly conquered district was, indeed, warlike and uncivilized, and it was because no great reliance could be placed in its security that Augustus arranged that it should remain under the surveillance of a strong standing army of not less than three legions : the essentially military character of the government in northern Spain is shown clearly by the special treatment which Augustus reserved for the north when organizing the conventual system else-where (below, p. 142 f.). That he was right in doing so is suggested by a cursory mention of Asturian unrest over half a century later, under Nero. Augustus certainly performed his task well, and the fruits of his reward must soon have been apparent, not least in regard to the mineral exploitation of Asturia : as Florus says, ' Sic Astures, nitentes in profundum opes suas atque divitias, dum aliis quaerunt, nosse coeperunt.'[9]

Although Roman domination now extended over the whole of the Spanish peninsula, the character of the Spaniards and the standards of their civilization varied very greatly from one area to another ; to speak of Roman Spain in the time of Augustus would be to conceive of an altogether false unity. The rich farms and prosperous towns in the valley of the Baetis ; the busy mercantile communities of the coastal regions ; the partially romanized elements of the interior who were sprung from vigorous Lusitanian or Celtiberian stock ; and now the fierce and unruly tribesmen of Asturia, Callaecia and Cantabria—what system of administration could ever make a unity of these ? It is this question which makes Augustus' reconstruction of the Spanish provinces a matter of enduring interest,

for the reconstruction was, in fact, the Emperor's own commentary upon the varying levels of Spanish civilization.[10]

The chief feature of the reform lay in the abandonment of the old two-province system in favour of a tripartite division (see Map II). The former province of Hispania Ulterior was henceforth to be bounded, on the north and west, by the southern watershed of the Anas; the resultant province of Baetica (as it came to be called) was still separated on the north-east from Hispania Citerior by the previously existing inter-provincial boundary. All the territory beyond the Anas of which the newly-defined Baetica was now deprived was to form the third, and new, province of Lusitania adumbrated by Caesar; and Lusitania continued to observe the same inter-provincial boundary in relation to Hispania Citerior (or, to give it its new name, Tarraconensis) as had existed before between the old provinces Citerior and Ulterior. In the extreme north, the recently conquered territories were carefully apportioned, Asturia and Callaecia being incorporated by Lusitania, and Cantabria by Tarraconensis; the extension of the inter-provincial boundary ran approximately by way of the river Astura and thence up to the northern coast. Lastly, the newly-defined province of Baetica was declared a 'public' province, being henceforward under senatorial instead of imperial control.

It is necessary to define as clearly as possible the date and the circumstances of this far-reaching reorganization. According to Dio Cassius,[11] the changes took place in 27 B.C. In this case, therefore, they would have formed part of the empire-wide classification of the Roman provinces, as armed or unarmed, which was the prelude to Augustus' first great constitutional settlement in that year. Even apart from the testimony of Dio, however, it is tempting on various grounds to assign the reconstruction to 27 B.C. In that year the plans for the projected campaigns in Cantabria and Asturia were being formed. The area comprised in 'Baetica' was by now free from the need of possessing a regular military force, and the imminence of war in northern Spain clearly demanded the transference to the north of all such troops as were not required in the south. Ever since the days of the Punic domination in Spain the valley of the Baetis had formed a natural territorial unit. In making over this unit to senatorial administration in 27 B.C., therefore, Augustus would have been doing no more than recognize an age-old argument. A series of later dates has, nevertheless, been suggested for the reform by various historians,[12] but in no case does there appear to be sufficient justification for disregarding the evidence of Dio ; and Dio's dating is here accepted.

General considerations, of both geography and administration, show that the reconstruction was a wise one. The old two-province system, the necessity of which had been so correctly divined in the early years when Roman Spain was no more than an interminable coastal strip, had now outgrown its usefulness. For many years past the northward extension of the Further Province had become increasingly difficult, for, whereas the governors of Citerior had at all times been able to penetrate inland up the valleys of the Ebro and the Sucro and thence down the courses of the Tagus and the Douro, the less fortunate commanders of Ulterior had been forced to scramble across a succession of mountain ranges—the Sierra Morena and the western spurs of the Guadarramas—which left the valley of the Baetis sequestered and ever further in the rear.

Nor had the northern frontier of Ulterior been at any time satisfactorily defined, even after the reorganization which Julius Caesar had achieved; the artificial combination of a series of parallel river-valleys could never result in a unified province. Augustus' reform restored the valley of the Baetis to its rightful state: geographically, it was self-contained, and its cultural and political level was higher than that of the rest of the peninsula. Lusitania suffered nothing by the change: its political and economic conditions were never those of Baetica, and it was now free to develop along the lines so brilliantly suggested by Caesar. The independence of modern Portugal is a tribute to Augustus' shrewd wisdom.

The boundaries of Portugal, however, differ sharply in the north from those which at first marked the new province of Lusitania; Portugal excludes Galicia and Asturias. This discrepancy is significant. All that part of Lusitania which lay to the south of the Douro was, by the time of Augustus, peacefully settled: the fact that the governor of Lusitania was, as a rule, only of praetorian rank was the corollary of the fact that his province needed only the most modest of garrisons—consisting, after Augustus' reign, of nothing but auxiliary troops. To this peaceful area were added, by Augustus' reconstruction of the Spanish provinces, the wild and uncivilized districts of Callaecia and Asturia. Clearly, the old two-province system, with its theory of 'parallelistic' command, was reborn when the new conquests were thus apportioned. It is not known by what method of liaison the governors of Lusitania and Tarraconensis contrived the armed surveillance of Callaecia, Asturia, and Cantabria. Possibly it became the usual practice that the governor of Tarraconensis should exercise a general supervision over all

these districts together. If this is so, the policy directly
foreshadowed the modification of his first plan that
Augustus was at length obliged to make. About the
end of the first century B.C., Callaecia and Asturia were
separated from Lusitania and incorporated in Tarraconensis,[13] the governor of which was henceforth able
to apply a joint administration of a special nature (considered below, p. 143 f.) to all the newly-acquired
districts. This change of boundary in the north was
accompanied by one in the south, Tarraconensis being
enlarged by the addition of a tract (comprising Castulo,
the Saltus Tugiensis, and the mountainous region
round Acci)[14] for which adequate armed protection—
always desirable—was now assured.[15]

The pleasing Roman acquiescence in unimportant
inconsistencies is well shown in Spain by the survival
of various anomalies which recalled the earlier systems
of provincial division. It was, for instance, still
possible for Baetica and Lusitania to form one unit for
the collection of the 5 per cent Inheritance Tax.[16] In
the south, several curious ties continued to exist
between Baetica and the region which Tarraconensis
incorporated. A procurator responsible for the collection of imperial dues in Baetica is found paying for
repair-work done both in Castulo and on the Castulo-
Sisapo road.[17] Titus' '*curator* and *praefectus fisci* in
Baetica' is commemorated in Castulo.[18] The coastal
town of Baria still ranked as part of Baetica when Pliny
wrote,[19] though it lay well over the eastern border;
and there were a number of other territorial 'islands'
elsewhere,[20] the continuance of which was tolerated,
doubtless in response to local wishes and considerations of local finance and economics, when a more
rigid and mechanical system than that of Rome would
have swept all such exceptions away.

Within each of the three Spanish provinces some system of subdivision was necessary for administrative purposes. The earliest subdivision of which we know was the *conventus*. This, as its name implies, was a regional centre at which the people of a district might gather, for the dispensation of justice and the transaction of other civil business. The practice was, clearly, one which was only feasible where the conditions of life were settled, and it is therefore not surprising to find that, when Julius Caesar, then a praetor, made an assize-tour in Spain in 61 B.C., the district concerned lay in Baetica.[21] But it is most unlikely that the conventual regions were at all systematically plotted out in Caesar's day; all that he probably did was to stop at certain of the larger towns as and when the pressure of legal business demanded his presence. Nevertheless, the nucleus of the conventual system now existed, ready for the development which took place during the reign of Augustus, under whose administration the several conventual areas, linking country towns and villages with one or other of the various Assize towns, were clearly defined. The four *conventus* of Baetica (those grouped round Corduba, Hispalis, Astigi—the modern Ecija—and Gades) must have been among the first to be so defined; and in Lusitania the formation of *conventus* round centres at Emerita, Scallabis and Pax Julia must have been greatly accelerated (even if the process was not already complete) when Augustus' boundary-modifications set the Douro as the northern limit of the province. In Tarraconensis the two great cities of Tarraco and Carthago Nova had for a long time been administrative centres of the first importance, and developed naturally into conventual headquarters under Augustus. The foundation of the Augustan colony of Caesaraugusta (Saragossa) on the

Ebro created the focus of a third *conventus* for Tarraconensis, embracing the Ebro valley in its middle and
upper reaches together with the watershed on both
sides and certain parts of central Celtiberia. So much
may safely be inferred, for the Augustan epoch, from
Pliny's description of the Spanish *conventus*.[22]

The *conventus*, then, are first heard of in relation to
the romanized valley of the Baetis ; they are Assize-
groups, intended to facilitate the dispensation of civil
justice and the transaction of civil business ; they are,
in fact, the corollary of a civilian population living in
peace. It is precisely this fact which lends so much
significance to a discrepancy between Pliny and Strabo
in their accounts of the internal organization of the
Spanish provinces. For Pliny, Tarraconensis comprised seven *conventus*—those enumerated above together with those grouped round Clunia, Asturica,
Lucus Augusti, and Bracara (Braga). Strabo, on the
contrary, gives in an important passage[23] a description
of organization in northern Spain which differs dia-
metrically from that of Pliny. According to Strabo,
the governor of Tarraconensis—a *consularis*, as befitted
his command over three legions—had three subordinate legates : two of these legates were *legati legionis*,
one exercising control over Callaecia with two legions,
while the other, with the third legion, watched
over Asturia and Cantabria ; and the third legate
(evidently a civil officer, as Strabo assigns him no
troops) administered the *togati*, i.e. peaceable inhabitants, of central Celtiberia. The governor himself,
meanwhile, concerned himself with administrative
duties further south, especially at Tarraco and Carthago
Nova.

It is impossible to reconcile the accounts of Pliny
and Strabo, for they differ too radically. Albertini,

however, has ably argued that the sources on which Pliny based his account of Tarraconensis were post-Claudian in date, and, if this is so, there is justification for regarding the organization of northern Spain described by Strabo as an intermediate stage of government preceding the establishment of regular *conventus* in that area at a later date. Strabo, indeed, has his obscurities, not the least of them being his allocation of two legions to Callaecia and only one to the vast Asturia–Cantabria tract; and it is permissible to suppose that by Callaecia he understands that area which belonged to Lusitania before Augustus' boundary-modifications of *c.* 2 B.C. (cf. note 27 to this chapter). This would allow us to assign the two legions to the most mountainous and obstinate part of northern Spain; the third legion would suffice for the surveillance of the remaining area eastward to the Pyrenees. Of Strabo's general accuracy, however, there can be little doubt. Callaecia, Asturia, and Cantabria were deemed to require a strong standing army for many years to come. In these circumstances the administration of these regions was bound to be military, and though the ultimate change to the conventual system was doubtless envisaged and even encouraged, *conventus* proper were at first an utter impossibility.[24]

The delineation of Baetica and Lusitania on a basis, in each case, of cultural and geographical unity thus left Tarraconensis in a peculiar position—a vast province, some of it highly romanized, some of it but newly conquered, and some of it, though peaceful, not more Roman than Celtiberian. Consequently, in both judicial and financial matters Tarraconensis admitted of variations from the strict system. The governor himself must have required subordinate assistants; these officers, so frequently mentioned on later inscriptions

as *legati iuridici*, were assigned by the emperor to a provincial governor and varied, both in their number and
their competence, according to circumstances. In the
north, their presence (as legal assistants and commissioners) must have been especially necessary until the
increasing pacification of the country allowed the
legionary legates to take over their functions
themselves.[25] The chief financial officer—*procurator
Augusti*[26]—in Tarraconensis also had his subordinate
officials, prominent among them being the *procurator
provinciae Hispaniae Citerioris per Asturiam et Callaeciam*
—a designation which, though not attested before the
end of the first century A.D., probably reflects the
increasing importance of a long-established post in that
district.[27]

General improvement in financial methods was,
probably, one of the reforms that rendered the
Principate so welcome in the provinces. From
Augustus' time onwards, the governors of the Spanish
provinces, senatorial or imperial, were salaried officials,
in conformity with general usage elsewhere. The
proconsuls of Baetica, even if they did not owe their
selection entirely to Augustus' estimate of their
abilities, were responsible to a senate guided by
Augustus' wishes: the propraetors of Tarraconensis
and Lusitania were responsible to Augustus alone.
The financial powers of the procurators were derived
directly from the emperor, and thus the procurators,
though outwardly subordinate to the imperial legates,
could in effect keep a check upon them. It is true
that the proconsuls of Baetica experienced no such
check from their own financial officers, the quaestors,
whom they themselves appointed; but imperial
procurators were found in Baetica too, for the collection of special and isolated imperial dues (see above,

p. 140), and if they failed to notice a proconsul's dishonesty, the local *concilium* (of which more will be said later) might complain of this to the central government. The provincials were therefore guarded against the excesses of the last two centuries, and, although cases of extortion are recorded, they are distinctly uncommon.[28]

So far as the details of taxation are concerned, little more is known about the period of the Principate than about that of the Republic. There is no evidence for estimating the total taxation-yield of Spain. The personal and property taxes in force during the Republic were continued, and the risk of unjust imposition or equally unjust immunity was greatly reduced as a result of Augustus' development of a regular census-system.[29] Certain indirect taxes were also either continued or now introduced. Of these the *portoria*, or customs-dues, were among the most important. They were not, indeed, an imperial innovation. But the system of the Spanish *portoria* under the Principate suggests that the Republican usages were greatly modified; not only was the actual rate—2 per cent—unusually low, but it is also probable that the whole of Spain formed a single customs-area, from which it would, of course, follow that inter-provincial intercourse in Spain was fostered and that the Roman Government was content with the income derived from the sea-borne and Gallic traffic alone.[30] In addition to the *portoria* there were the 5 per cent Inheritance Tax, mentioned above, and levied on Roman citizens only; the 5 per cent Manumission Tax, which naturally affected persons of substance for the most part; the 1 per cent Sales Tax, of general application, and therefore of a low rate; the 4 per cent tax on the sale of slaves; and others of lesser importance and less frequent application.[31] There is no reason to think these taxes excessive; nor was the collection of them likely to result in extortion.

The chief administrative changes which Augustus effected in Spain have now been reviewed: these changes formed the framework for his provincial policy in Spain. Under the Principate provincial policy was a question which turned mainly upon the attitude which successive emperors adopted towards the extension of the franchise. It is to Julius Caesar's lasting credit that he had been the first to see clearly in the wider extension of *civitas* the means both of romanizing the provincial communities and also of stimulating these communities to absorb new influences. Moreover, those whom he made *cives* were occasionally, as his experimental colonies in Spain show, of non-Roman characteristics. Augustus, however, though he inherited many of Caesar's political ideals, was less lavish than Caesar with the franchise, which he did not regard as the principal method of romanization. For him, Roman citizenship was to be the reward only of those in whom the true Roman pattern was already visible, and he seems to have looked upon the intermediate stage of *Latinitas* as a good means of avoiding the abuse of full *civitas* by those whom he did not consider to be ready for it. Caesar would have been content with (and might even have preferred) a heterogeneous body of *cives*: Augustus desired them to conform to type and to formula. The comparatively slow rate of increase in Roman citizens throughout the Empire during his reign which his *Res Gestae* records reflects his policy faithfully.[32]

When all is said, however, it must be admitted that

Augustan Spain showed no inconsiderable proportion of towns possessing full franchise. Naturally, this proportion was highest in the most highly romanized area—Baetica: here, out of 175 communities, some 46 had privileged status, nine of them being colonies, ten of them *municipia*, and the remainder being towns with Latin rights. In Tarraconensis, indeed, the number of colonies (12) and *municipia* (13) was greater; but on the other hand less than 20 towns had Latin rights, and the balance of unprivileged communities was relatively far greater. Lusitania—in a sense the newest province of the three—contained only some 45 communities in all; these included five colonies, one *municipium*, and three towns with Latin rights. The total number of privileged towns in Spain was thus about a hundred.[33] Nor must Augustus' success be estimated by these facts alone. Municipalization was accompanied by urbanization,—the process which made Vespasian's later reforms possible. The increasing tendency of smaller communes, often mere *vici* or *pagi*, to amalgamate into one large stipendiary town was doubtless encouraged by Augustus as part of his centralizing policy, and during the first century of the principate a considerable proportion of such rural communes seems to have undergone amalgamation of this kind.[34]

If Augustus declined to make the franchise the keynote of his Spanish policy, it remains to be found where the imperial emphasis lay. The answer lies in his substitution, for the Julian system of civil colonies, of that of military foundations. It is of course true that the Augustan colonies varied in the degree of their militarism. Astigi and Tucci (Martos), for instance, in Baetica, were semi-military in origin owing to their settlement by ex-legionaries, but they became purely civilian centres, as their inscriptions show: parallel examples in Tarraconensis are provided by Barcino, Ilici, Libisosa, and Salaria. The colony of Caesaraugusta (which occupied a position of great administrative importance on the Ebro, and was for a time privileged, like Corduba, to strike silver *denarii* in the imperial series proper) contained military detachments (below, p. 150); but its inscriptions are those of an administrative centre pure and simple. The clearest and finest example of the Augustan system was undoubtedly to be recognized in the colony of Emerita, queen of the province of Lusitania, if not of all Spain. Though it had been founded originally on a military basis as a home for veterans discharged after the first phase of the Asturio-Cantabrian war (above, p. 135; cf. Pl. IV, 1–4), this city soon lost its essentially military characteristics, and quickly assumed an administrative importance in Lusitania parallel to that of Tarraco and Corduba in the other provinces. Tarraco and Corduba, however, even though their promotion to colonial status was comparatively recent, were by now old cities, having grown up with the extension of Roman power in Spain; and over a long period of years they had, like such other early settlements as Carthago Nova and Italica, unconsciously absorbed all that was truly Roman in spirit, organization, art, and architecture. Emerita, on the other hand, was a colony which could boast no previous history at all: thus it serves as the best possible pattern of what Augustus wished his new foundations to be. From the first, its administrative competence was strongly in evidence: its establishment was commemorated by locally struck coins of silver and bronze; and the inscriptions show vividly how great was the volume of official business

transacted at the provincial capital. Indeed, the growth of a purely municipal spirit (fostered at Tarraco and Corduba by long years of slow development) seems to have been hampered at Emerita by its sudden creation as a provincial centre of the first magnitude : it was later found necessary, on more than one occasion, to supplement the numbers of its citizens (below, pp. 180, 187). But what Emerita lacked in municipal tradition was compensated by its commercial prosperity (attested by the many nationalities recorded on the inscriptions) and by its outward magnificence. Throughout our period it seems to have enjoyed a high degree of imperial favour : the theatre built originally by Agrippa was restored under Hadrian ; of the two bridges, the later one (spanning the Anas)—a long and magnificent structure in use to-day—belongs to the time of Trajan ; and with all this there were two aqueducts, an amphitheatre, a circus, and reservoirs,—a truly worthy setting for the capital of a province. Emerita is a fine symbol of Augustus' provincial policy as applied to Spain, that is to say, a colonial policy based at first on military lines, subsequently assuming civil and administrative importance, and advertising (by its material splendour and comfort) the benefits of Roman rule and Roman customs among the peoples of the province, who might thus become increasingly familiar with the nature of Roman municipal institutions.[35]

Augustus' military preoccupations are further reflected in the character of his road-building (see Map III). While he was content to keep up the existing roads in Baetica, and to leave the construction of new roads in Lusitania to his successors, he applied himself actively to augment the communications in Tarraconensis. Two milestones suggest the early construction of a road between the vital points of Bracara and Asturica, by way of Aquae Flaviae (Chaves); a third indicates the building of a parallel route to the south; another, found north of Bracara, shows a third radiation from this centre. At the eastern end of the province Augustan milestones have been found on the Celsa–Ilerda road, while in the north-east a milestone of the end of the reign is evidence for the building of a road across the Pyrenees into Aquitania. All these roads were military: of the others, those in the neighbourhood of Carthago Nova and Castulo were doubtless designed to facilitate mining operations, while the great Via Augusta was of course a commercial route, much of which (to judge from the frequency of Augustan milestones in and around Corduba) Augustus found it necessary to rebuild.[36]

At the end of Augustus' reign three legions—IV *Macedonica*, VI *Victrix*, and X *Gemina*—were permanently quartered in Spain. The coins of Caesaraugusta under Augustus and Tiberius show the numbers of these legions in conjunction with *signa* or *vexilla* (Pl. IV, 9), and it is likely that detachments from them may have been stationed there at this time, and even possible that the whole of IV *Macedonica* was at one time quartered there. The headquarters of VI *Victrix* and X *Gemina* were in the Asturia-Callaecia district, where circumstances demanded that the bulk of the legionary forces should be: IV *Macedonica* was presumably stationed permanently somewhere in Cantabria until its hypothetical removal to Caesaraugusta. Military police of a kind were doubtless required elsewhere. The town of Acci, for instance, had been originally settled by ex-legionaries; Carthago Nova had contained a *vexillatio* in the pre-Augustan

period; and Italica contained one under the early Principate, possibly (as Mommsen suggested) as a guard against Moorish attacks from northern Africa. The first *vexillatio* of which we hear at Tarraco is of the Flavian period; but it must be remembered that the command of the *praefectus orae maritimae* centred in Tarraco, and the marines commanded by this officer may have sufficed for the police duties arising there.[37]

CHAPTER VIII

SPAIN AND THE PRINCIPATE

THE thorough reorganization of Spain described in the preceding pages was the result of a rigorous central government directed by the enlightened policy and the unquestioned power of one supreme statesman —the Princeps. The contrast between the administration under Augustus and his successors, and that which had characterized the Republican régime, was such that only the newly conquered and least civilized elements in Spain can have failed to appreciate it. Material comforts and an improvement in the standard of living seldom pass unnoticed among those on whom they are conferred. It is sufficient for our purposes to point out but two of the improvements which the Principate effected or encouraged,—the multiplication of places of amusement (few towns of any consequence lacked their theatre or amphitheatre by the end of the first century), and the provision of good water-supply in districts where the nature of the ground made this difficult (the superb aqueduct at Segovia, and its only slightly less imposing fellows at Emerita, Tarraco, and Toletum, are products of the early Empire (Pl. IX)). No one could deny such benefits as these; and there were many more besides. Tacitus, indeed, in describing the very institution of the Principate,[1] recorded its willing acceptance by the Roman provinces, now tired of political jobbery and

the greed and venality of Roman officials. The establishment of the Principate, with all its constitutional implications, might well be a matter of wide concern in Rome and Italy—the hallowed area of the Senate's domestic control. Elsewhere the constitutional issue between Princeps and Senate was of little account: the provinces were more interested in the policy which dictated their government, and this policy, in the long run, connoted the person of the Princeps by whom it was defined. As long as his personal influence continued to assure Spain of a succession of able and honest governors and of a unified, steadfast and beneficent provincial policy, provincial gratitude was bound to find its focus in the person of the Princeps.

In dealing, therefore, with those institutions— whether religious or civil—which grew up in the early years of the Principate and had as their essential feature the veneration of Augustus, the reasonable historian will be careful to reflect on all that Spain (in common with other provinces) had to thank him for.[2] The court poet may have had his axe to grind when he exclaimed, ' deus, deus ille, Menalcas ! ' But in the provinces the impulse to such feelings was spontaneous. For Rome, Augustus was *divi filius* through his family connection with the illustrious Julius, now deified. For the Spaniard, the title possessed a deeper significance : Augustus was a man of superhuman achievement, and honours of more than human measure must therefore be paid to him. It was surely no accident, no mere exhibition of provincial non-conformity, that the bronze coins struck at Tarraco after his death bore, instead of the orthodox *divo Augusto*, the legend *deo Augusto*.[3] That this should happen at Tarraco was, of course, not surprising; Augustus had stayed there in 25 B.C., recovering from the illness contracted during the Cantabrian campaign. (It may even have been at this time that the altar dedicated to Augustus at Tarraco (Pl. IV, 8) was erected, though the similar altar at Emerita was certainly erected later in his reign.) It was at Tarraco again that the first temple in honour of Augustus was erected, after his death, by permission of Tiberius.[4]

Nevertheless, the sentiments to which Tarraco gave expression so clearly were no more than the index to what was happening elsewhere in Spain. Augustus would have been an improvident statesman if he had not attempted some means whereby this devotional enthusiasm might be bound up officially with the business of provincial administration as a whole. In the provinces of the Greek east, now long accustomed to the cult of living rulers, the means lay ready to hand: the provincial assemblies, or κοινά, already met at regular periods, under the presidency of their high-priests, for the celebration of religious festivals in honour of their particular local deities, and the substitution of the cult of 'Roma et Augustus' in place of the previous cults took place easily and naturally. For the western provinces the problem was more difficult. Although it is true that isolated priesthoods in honour of Augustus existed, in Italy and elsewhere, nevertheless the west possessed no ready-made machinery, such as there was in the east, by which the imperial cult could be universally and quickly introduced. In order, therefore, to foster the growth of *concilia*—assemblies analogous to the eastern κοινά— it was first necessary to create religious centres of an artificial kind. This was brought about by the erection of the various provincial altars, dedicated to the worship of Rome and Augustus, of which that at

Lugdunum is the most famous example. For the due observance of the worship, a hierarchy and a ritual must be found ; and from this there finally emerged the western *concilia*, one to each province, meeting yearly under the presidency of the *flamen provinciae* for the transaction of the religious functions, together with such civil and financial administration as the existence of the *concilium* involved.[5]

The growth of *concilia* in the three Spanish provinces cannot be traced through all its steps, for, although a *concilium* ultimately existed in all three, their development does not appear to have been simultaneous. As has been remarked, the date of the altar erected in Augustus' honour at Tarraco, though it certainly fell within his lifetime, cannot be determined exactly ; all that can be said of the establishment of the *concilium* in Tarraconensis is that its nucleus had been formed before Augustus' death, and that its organization was probably perfected when Tiberius, in A.D. 15, consented to the building of a temple to Divus Augustus at Tarraco. For Baetica, the evidence is even more uncertain, but it may probably be assumed that the request made by this province to Tiberius in A.D. 25 that he might sanction the building of a temple in honour of himself and Livia presupposes the existence of an embryonic form of *concilium* in Baetica :[6] Corduba became the regular meeting-place. In Lusitania, the *concilium* is attested by the frequent mention of the flaminate on inscriptions, and the appearance of the altar on the post-Augustan coins of Emerita suggests that it was at that city that the assembly met, though the date of its establishment (possibly late in Augustus' reign) is uncertain.

At first, the practical functions of the *concilia* were doubtless confined to the observance of the cult of

'Roma et Augustus'—Rome and the reigning Princeps—together with the business necessitated by the existence of the *concilium*, i.e. election of the high-priests, voting of complimentary decrees and statues, holding of games, examination of accounts, and the like. But, although such duties may appear to be somewhat restricted, the office of *flamen*, which conferred the title *flaminica* upon the holder's wife, was one of great honour, zealously pursued. Indeed, it was probably regarded as one of the highest attainments to which a provincial could aspire; and those who had held the position were careful to have the fact duly commemorated on inscriptions. Such inscriptions frequently record a *flamen's* town of origin, and it is of interest to observe that, apart from an inevitable proportion of flamens derived from large cities like Tarraco and Carthago Nova, the office was apparently most highly prized in Lusitania and the northern half of Tarraconensis—the less romanized area where active encouragement of the imperial cult might most beneficially be undertaken. Additional importance began to attach to the flaminate during the course of the first century of the Principate. Owing to the frequent practice by which the *concilia* despatched delegations to Rome bearing birthday or other messages to the Princeps, there arose some sort of liaison between province and emperor. This was not destined ever to develop into a regular system of provincial representation, as might perhaps have been possible, for there was no obligation upon an emperor to transact provincial business through the *concilia* while the easier and probably more efficient method of acting through the provincial governor still remained. Nevertheless, there were certain questions, affecting an entire province, which did not admit of the

governor's acting as an intermediary, and the chief of such questions was that of the misdemeanour of a governor himself or his officials. Representations of provincial complaints by *concilia* in cases of this kind were, during most of the first century A.D., commonest in the eastern provinces; but the practice is attested in the case of Spain in the period of the Flavians and Trajan, while under succeeding emperors it may have been extended so as to cover other and less serious business.[7]

The religious duties incumbent on the *concilia* were, then, essentially provincial in their scope and application; but the expression of municipal loyalty was not ruled out, and there were instances of individual towns which possessed a priest for the observance of their own municipal cult of the Princeps:[8] it might, of course, happen that the same man achieved both positions, high-priest of both his town and his province.[9] Augustus' death naturally produced further diversity in the matter of priesthoods; as a *Divus*, he might become the object of an individual cult, administered by a special priest, and the worship of a *Divus* could be combined with that of the reigning Princeps, or with that of Roma.[10]

Although it would be unsafe to declare that freedmen were never admitted to the provincial flaminate in Spain, it is at any rate unlikely that opportunities for their admission were anything but rare. This conclusion is suggested partly by the great frequency with which bodies of *VIviri Augustales* are recorded on the inscriptions of all three provinces. Whatever may have been the origin and the early duties attaching to the office of *sevir*, its later significance is clear. It was a priesthood which was open to freedmen, and which existed for the cult of Augustus, at first in connection with the Lares. The *seviratus* involved its holder in much ceremony and expense, and accordingly the office was particularly suitable for the wealthy freedman class, which was otherwise debarred from any but the lowest administrative posts. Apart from Asturia and Cantabria, where the ownership and manumission of slaves would naturally have been less frequent than elsewhere, colleges of *seviri* (serving six together) are found in a great number of Spanish towns. As their records indicate, *seviri* were often men of great eminence (either in their own town or in their *conventus*) on whom additional local honours might also be conferred.[11] The association of wealthy freedmen with the *sevirate* was thus the means of stimulating the loyalty of a large and influential class of men towards the Princeps; many of the freedmen of Spain were of eastern stock, and, without this stimulus, might have been slow in adopting the vigorous consciousness of a western province in relation to the emperor.[12]

Such were the official methods by which Augustus successfully contrived to convert the devotional enthusiasm of Spain into a political asset : both the *concilia* and the *seviratus Augustalis* stood the test of experiment, and were destined to continue with comparatively little change until the third century of the Empire. A brief mention has already been made (above, p. 157) of the institution by certain towns of private priesthoods, of a purely municipal kind, for the observance of the imperial cult. An interesting and significant development took place when this practice was extended so as to include the cult of members of the imperial house other than the Princeps himself. This innovation was perhaps made during the reign of Tiberius : Anticaria (Antequera), which

had a *Pontifex Caesarum*, included the name of Livia, as ' Genetrix Orbis,' in a dedication made in honour of her and Tiberius, and Olisipo provides an instance (probably falling within the reign of Tiberius) of a *flamen* for the cult of Germanicus Caesar and Livia. The change was a natural one ; the divine lustre of the Princeps himself shone brightly on the members of his family also.   To honour the imperial house was to honour the Princeps, and it is not surprising to find at Urgavo (Arjona)—a town remarkable for the frequency of its compliments to the imperial family— the existence of a *Pontifex Domus Augustae* at some date within the first century A.D.[13]

The foregoing instances have all been concerned with religious observances, official and unofficial. No account of the Spanish estimate of the Principate would be complete without a reference to the honorific dedications, to the Princeps and his family, of which the inscriptions of Spain furnish so many examples. These dedications (whatever the occasions which produced them) were unofficial, and they are therefore all the more valuable as showing the spontaneous loyalty of the Spanish provinces.   Although they are found in all parts of Spain, they are mainly charac-teristic of the more civilized and highly romanized areas of Baetica and southern Tarraconensis. As might be expected, Augustus was frequently the object of such dedications, the unofficial nature of which is clearly shown by the widely varying forms of imperial title which were used : Urgavo, for instance, in an outburst of enthusiasm, named Augustus *pater patriae* in 6 B.C., four years before that title was conferred.[14] But the members of an emperor's household were, in this connection also, not disregarded. A number of loyal dedications were made in honour of Tiberius

and of Gaius and Lucius Caesar, doubtless owing to
the place which these princes held at various times in
Augustus' dynastic scheme; and various members
of Augustus' house were honoured in a remarkable
series of dedications at Ulia.[15] The custom continued
during the reign of Tiberius,—Livia, Drusus, and
Germanicus being frequently the objects of such
dedications,—but declined progressively during the
remainder of the Julio-Claudian dynasty; somewhat
significantly, the latter part of Nero's Principate is
almost entirely devoid of Spanish dedications. From
this it might be inferred that Spanish interest in the
Principate declined as time went on: Augustus, its
founder, had been the common benefactor of the
civilized world, and his schemes for the succession
had naturally been of universal interest. That succession once assured and achieved, the person of the
Princeps might well become merged in the institution of which he was the centre: moreover, in the
later period of the dynasty of Augustus, scant attention
was paid by the reigning Princeps to the question of
advertising his heir in the provinces, either by means
of the provincial coinage or by other methods.[16] And
yet the average provincial could never have forgotten
that it was the personal character of the Princeps that,
in the long run, determined the tenor of provincial
policy; and it is difficult to avoid the conclusion that
the decrease in the number of dedications signifies,
at first, a less enthusiastic attitude to Augustus' successors than had been adopted towards Augustus
himself, culminating, by Nero's reign, in something
like a definite personal antipathy to the emperor. An
attempt will be made in the following chapter to
estimate the achievement of the Julio-Claudian policy
in Spain; it may thereby be possible to compare the

benefits conferred by Augustus' successors on Spain with those of which Augustus himself was the author.

Something has been said of the divinization of the Princeps and of the Imperial house which took place in Spain; and it may be asked at this stage, first, what policy the Roman administration pursued with regard to the many indigenous cults of the peninsula, and, secondly, to what extent the Roman Pantheon was encouraged or spread among the Spaniards. In brief, the answer to these closely related questions is that the official Roman attitude was one of wide toleration. The evidence for this conclusion is drawn mainly from inscriptions: these show that in Lusitania and in the northern districts of Tarraconensis the native worships flourished without hindrance, and these areas were (as has been seen above, p. 156) just those which were chiefly characterized by their enthusiastic adoption of the imperial cult. It would therefore appear that, provided the less civilized parts of Spain were punctilious in the observance of the imperial cult, they were freely permitted to continue in the worship of their local deities. In Lusitania the most prominent of such deities was Endovellicus, the centre of whose cult was at Villaviçosa, south-west of Badajoz; but elsewhere the worship of a goddess, romanized into the form Dea Turubrigensis and often identified with Proserpina, was frequently to be found; and various lesser deities had their cults also. In Tarraconensis the cults were more varied and more numerous, and most of them were free from any romanizing contamination, though some of these deities, such as the 'nymphae' and 'lares' which are met with, were given outwardly Roman names. Equally indigenous were certain of the celestial cults which existed in Spain, of which those of Sol, Luna, and Lux Divina are examples.

In contrast to the native cults of Spain, the deities of the Roman Pantheon were worshipped chiefly in the areas most subject to the influence of romanizing centres; Jupiter, Juno, and Minerva were most frequently honoured, as might be expected. There is little ground for thinking that the cult of the gods of the Roman State was widely diffused on its own merits: many cases which at first suggest such diffusion are to be regarded as the result of the identification of a native deity with the appropriate Roman equivalent: the identification of Proserpina and Dea Turubrigensis has been mentioned, and Jupiter, Mars, and other of the Roman gods experienced the same process. It may be assumed safely that the State gods of Rome were naturally revered where Roman influences were paramount, but that little, if anything, was done to compel their acceptance elsewhere. The same toleration is seen in the comparatively large number of Oriental and other foreign cults which are attested: that of Isis was the commonest, but Serapis, Sabazius, Cybele, and Attis are also recorded, together with other cults, such as those of Mithras and the Matres Aufaniae, the importation of which may have been due to the demobilization of legionaries.[17]

Religious toleration was thus among the concessions made by Rome to Spain, and national cults remained unaffected by the Principate. It remains to inquire what was the official attitude of the imperial government towards the question of Spanish nationalism in general. Too often we speak of the romanization of a province, or of the spread of Roman influences in a province, without sufficiently distinguishing what is implied in this process. Subjection to the imperialism

of an external power implies certain obvious obligations, in particular, that of conforming to the recognized and habitual political institutions of that
dominant power ; and this is true no less of an imperial
organization like the British Empire of to-day than of
the Roman Empire of old, for this conformity is an
administrative necessity.   In these days, however,
conformity of political institutions is only a cloak
under which there may be found a wide diversity of
other and non-political institutions, the nature of
which may be summarized in the brief phrase ' national
cultures.'   What, then, was the policy of Roman
imperialism with regard to the national culture of
Spain ?   It was said of Claudius, one of the most
broad-minded of provincial administrators, that he
wished to see ' all Greeks, Gauls, Spaniards, and
Britons dressed in the toga '.[18]   Does this imply that
political conformity with Rome was to be so far-
reaching as to blot out the national character of the
non-political institutions in the provinces ?

If it is thought that the decay of national characteristics in Spain would be hastened by the political
uniformity of the imperial régime, it should be remembered, first, what anomalies and inconsistencies existed
within the actual fabric of the administrative system.
Some of these have already been touched upon in the
preceding chapter (above, p. 140), but there are many
others as well—for instance the sharp distinction
between the status of *liberti* in Caesar's municipal
foundations, where they might become decurions,
and their position in the foundations of Augustus,
which excluded them from this office.   But there is an
even more remarkable instance.   Of the purely
western provinces of the Empire, Spain, together with
Africa, Gaul, and certain areas in the Alpine and

Danubian districts, had been accustomed during the time of the Republic to a native coinage of a purely local kind. It is true that the Republican administration had curtailed the work of the Spanish mints to the issue of bronze alone (above, p. 111), but the point of real interest is that, after the establishment of the Principate and until Gaius' suppression of all local western coinages in favour of a single mint at Rome, the privilege of issuing true local coinages was confined alone to Spain and Africa.[19] The coins of the various town-mints of Spain naturally bore the head of the Princeps on the observe, and often referred by their legends to other members of the imperial house, as circumstances suggested, particularly in those cases where colonies struck their own coins.[20] But there was no insistence by the central government on the form of imperial title to be used, nor upon the status of the officials responsible for issuing the coins; both the titles and the officials vary widely from place to place,[21] while finally the choice of reverse types was entirely a matter for local decision. When it is remembered how important a part in Augustus' imperial reforms was played by the reorganization of the coinage throughout the Empire, this discrimination in favour of local Spanish coinages is highly significant. Whatever political uniformity might be imposed on the Spanish provinces, it did not extend to the local currencies—a sphere in which the imperial prerogative might have been expected to assert its habitual claim. Nor did it apply to religion (as has been seen above), or to language either: the *patrius sermo* survived at any rate into the second century of the Empire.[22]

Attempts have been made, however, to show that one of the main objects of the Roman administration

of Spain, in both the Republican and the Imperial epochs, was the weakening or dissolving of the various natural racial groups of which the country consisted, —in other words, that the Roman policy in Spain was, at all times, ‘divide et impera’. The basis of this charge is the system of *conventus*, which, on this theory, are regarded as disruptive subdivisions of an artificial character designed to cut across Spain's previously existing tribal divisions. It is true that during the first century of their occupation of Spain the Romans had been considerably troubled by the number and the vigorous independence of these tribal divisions, as a moment's reflection upon the wars against the Lusitanians and Celtiberians will show. And yet, in the time of the Republic, Rome had certainly recognized, if not the need for tribal groups, at least the fact that they existed : this may be clearly inferred from the appearance upon the native Celtiberian silver coins of such tribal names as those of the Vascones, Ilergetes, and Laeetani. Moreover, if the application of the *conventus* system, as developed under the Principate, is to be the criterion of the continuation of a policy of disruption, then obviously serious inconsistencies arise. When Augustus undertook the conquest of the Callaeci, Astures, and Cantabri, the areas inhabited by these obdurate tribes were, as was noted in the last chapter, precisely those to which the system of *conventus* was not applied : the first conventual areas to be delineated were, on the contrary, those in Baetica, and it was only in Lusitania and the civilized parts of Tarraconensis that the example set in Baetica was followed. To suppose that the *conventus* were a clever disruptive organization is to mistake their purpose completely : they were no more than an administrative convenience, and their scheme was dictated only by the distribution of the main administrative centres. In the time of Augustus the survival of tribal sentiment in the greater part of Spain was no more sinister a phenomenon than the existence to-day of such bodies as the Yorkshire Society or the Men of Kent.[23]

There is, indeed, considerable evidence for the uninterrupted existence of tribal divisions in various parts of Spain : the dedication set up by ' Callaecia ' to C. Caesar[24] will serve as one example, while reference may also be made to the practice by which bodies of auxiliaries raised in a certain area were designated by the name of that area.[25] A federal instinct is further illustrated by the records of the *hospitia* which existed at Asturica, Pallantia, Clunia, and Pompaelo ;[26] these instances, unlike the solitary case of Lacilbula in Baetica,[27] were all in that northern part of Spain where a disruptive Roman policy would, if it had existed, have been most anxious to prevent them. Yet another case of federation is to be found in the united action of those communities which, in Trajan's reign, combined to raise sufficient money to build the famous Alcantara bridge.[28]

It may therefore be concluded that imperial administration in Spain was not inconsistent with the expression of national feeling : political conformity, inherent in the system of *conventus*, and encouraged by the increasing numbers of colonies and *municipia*, was an administrative necessity, but it did not necessarily conflict with those traces of nationalism which still survived after two centuries of Roman government. Not unnaturally, it was in the north that survival was most frequent and longest enduring : elsewhere, political conformity with Rome had, through long years of peace, tended to produce a

parallel uniformity of culture and spirit. But, to some extent, there was still a sense of nationalism all over Spain, independent of the distribution of the conventual centres, the primary object of which was only to facilitate the transaction of provincial business.

The ‘Roman Peace’ which Augustus conferred on Spain was not disturbed by the army revolts to which the Empire’s northern frontiers were subject in A.D. 14: the fine structure planned and built by him was not, therefore, imperilled, and the peace of the Spanish provinces remained unbroken. A survey of the relationship which existed between these provinces and the Principate which guaranteed, or at least dictated, the quality of provincial policy in general has enabled us to form certain conclusions regarding the significance of the Principate in Spain, the popularity of the Princeps and his house, and the question of toleration, religious and otherwise, in Spain. In the healthy atmosphere engendered by Augustus’ enlightened reforms the provincial system was free to develop apace. If there was any deeply rooted or widespread resistance to the imperial régime, no trace of it has come down to us : it would be gratuitous to suppose that the oath dictated to the Lusitanians in A.D. 37 by Ummidius Quadratus was anything but the customary oath of allegiance,[29] or that the unrest in Asturia in Nero’s reign represented more than a local disturbance in a notoriously wild district.[30] Everywhere the arts of peace, and not those of war, were fostered ; and one of the most striking results of the imperial administration was to be seen in the increase of intercourse between the members of the various communities—an increase for which inscriptions afford clear proof,[31] and which was doubtless encouraged by the imperial emphasis on a good road system.

One final aspect of the relationship between Spain and the central administration still remains to be considered. Something has already been said, in the preceding chapter, about Augustus' attitude to the extension of the franchise in the Roman provinces. It is possible that, to the mind of an orthodox Roman statesman, the romanization of a province may have been judged largely by the number of provincials attaining to full *civitas*, which implied the closest conformity with Roman political institutions, and which under Augustus was withheld from all except those in whom the Roman pattern was visibly reproduced. Nor was Augustus' policy in this respect retrogressive: Roman political theory had for long years taken it for granted that *civitas* was the goal of provincial aspirations, and Caesar alone had seen in the franchise an opportunity for provincial development of another kind. While the orthodox view of the franchise continued supreme, it followed that men whose political ambitions included the desire to assist in the administration of their province as a whole were discouraged from so doing; local political eminence would bring with it a grant of *civitas*, but the focus of *civitas* was Rome, and not the province. In brief, the Roman provincial system, under both Republic and Empire, lacked the means whereby provincial politicians in their various towns could combine into a political body capable of representing the political views of their province to the central government: the *concilia*, as we have seen, were primarily religious bodies, and any slight political competence that they may have attained came only at a later date, when orthodox Roman policy was too

familiar to be dislodged. Roman theory was certainly not mistaken in its estimate of *civitas* as a potent means of romanization ; what it failed to realize was that Rome's constant absorption of provincial talent resulted in a crying need for some machinery whereby this talent could be used in provincial administration. Under the Flavian emperors, indeed, this need was partially understood : Vespasian's policy of 'adlecting' eminent provincials into the Senate frequently brought it about that a province—especially in the Greek east—was governed by one of its members. But even this system, as its success depended entirely upon the imperial estimate of individual provincial worthies, denied the provinces, as a whole, the benefit of general representation. In the time of the early Empire, therefore, provincial status and provincial self-administration were mutually exclusive ; and although Spaniards are very occasionally found occupying administrative posts in Spain, such posts are always of a very minor character.

It is easy to criticize Augustus too severely in this matter. He was but the founder of an empire : the immediate details of administration he left complete, but he did not thereby rule out the possibility of development by his successors, and if they were to fail, the fault would not be altogether his own. The acceptance of Augustus' imperial legacy was an almost crushing responsibility, as Tiberius, with little need for dissimulation, publicly declared.[32] In the following chapter we shall attempt to trace the development of the Augustan policy during the half-century which followed his reign.

CHAPTER IX

SPAIN UNDER THE JULIO-CLAUDIANS

THE untried experiment of the dynastic principle was severely tested in the half-century following Augustus' death, but the allegiance of the army to the imperial house, and the growing efficiency of the imperial civil service, enabled the successive emperors to deal with the complex problem of provincial administration sufficiently well to preserve the continuity of Augustus' masterly system. Tiberius and Claudius have rightly been credited with a sane and enlightened provincial policy; Gaius has more recently found his apologists; and the Principate of Nero was remarkable, if for nothing else, for the rehabilitation of the Roman name in the east. For Spain, indeed, the evidence during this period is not abundant: the establishment of the Augustan system, rather than its secure consummation, was what chiefly arrested the attention of ancient historians, to whom sudden change offered more attractive material for analysis than steady progress. The information to be gathered from coins becomes more limited; and even the inscriptions, although they are still plentiful, speak with a less spontaneous voice than those of the reign of Augustus. Nevertheless, the main outlines of Julio-Claudian policy may be discerned, and it will be seen that the march of events in Spain during these fifty years followed closely—perhaps too closely—the directions implied in Augustus' own policy.

The main contribution of the Julio-Claudian emperors to Spanish progress seems to have consisted in the extension and improvement of the road-system (see Map III).[1] During the Principate of Tiberius a road was driven north from Emerita towards Salmantica, and this certainly reached the Tagus-crossing north of Norba at Garrovillas, where a milestone dated A.D. 25–6 was found.[2] Ten years later the Via Augusta called for repair in the neighbourhood of Corduba,[3]—an indication of the volume of traffic which had passed along it since Augustus started to build this section not quite forty years before (above, p. 150), and a reminder that even those parts of this great trunk road which lay in the senatorial province of Baetica came under imperial supervision. It was in Tarraconensis, however, that Tiberius' road-building activity was most conspicuous. In the north, in A.D. 32–3, a road was being constructed from Bracara to Aquae Flaviae (Chaves) and beyond, on the way to Asturica ;[4] the same year saw work being done in the extension of the trans-Pyrenean road on which a beginning had been made at the close of Augustus' reign ;[5] and in the following year the route from Asturica to Caesaraugusta was being opened up.[6] In the south, a new branch was constructed leading north-west from the Via Augusta up into the Sierra Morena : a milestone gives the date of this work as A.D. 32–3, and, as it was in A.D. 33 that Tiberius confiscated the gold-mines of Sextus Marius,— ' Hispaniarum ditissimus ',—from whose fame the Montes Mariani (the Sierra Morena heights) were so named, it may be concluded that the emperor was quick to begin the exploitation of a newly acquired source of mineral wealth.[7] New roads were also made in the vicinity of Carthago Nova.[8]

The brief reign of Gaius, and especially the later half of it, saw further useful work being done. Communications between Iria Flavia (Padron) and Lucus Augusti were now, apparently, undertaken,[9] and the coastal route between Scallabis and Bracara, which was in hand in A.D. 40, must have been instrumental in opening up the north-western area of Lusitania.[10] The Via Augusta also received attention, as was henceforth the rule.[11]   Under Claudius a new road was driven south-east from Bracara, in the direction of Emerita,[12] and a continuation was made of Tiberius' road on the Emerita–Salamantica line.[13]   In A.D. 43–4 there was great activity in the north-west of Spain, at Bracara, Aquae Flaviae, and perhaps Compleutica also.[14]   The presence of a Claudian milestone of A.D. 44–5 at Tudae (Tuy), at the crossing of the Minius, implies the completion of Gaius' coastal road northward from Scallabis ;[15]   elsewhere, progress was made also with the road which Tiberius had begun between Asturica and Caesaraugusta.[16]   Among other work of Claudius' reign should be noticed the road pushed along the foot-hills of the Pyrenees from Ilerda to Osca,[17] and—perhaps most interesting—the relaying of large sections of the Via Augusta between Carthago Nova and the Pyrenees between A.D. 47 and 50.[18]   Nero's reign, though in other respects of little benefit to Spain, saw no interruption in the extension of the road-system.   The Emerita–Salmantica road, already developed under Tiberius and Claudius, now needed repair,[19] and in one place at least a new section of it was laid.[20]   In Baetica the usual repairs to the Via Augusta were undertaken.[21] In Tarraconensis the route between Lucus Augusti and Asturica now first received serious attention.[22] Of the other milestones of this province the most

interesting is that which, found at Otañes, suggests a
new road leading northwards from Segisama towards
the coast in the neighbourhood of Flaviobriga (Bilbao),
that flourishing port of the future.[23]   The Otañes
milestone is remarkable for being dated after A.D. 59;
it would appear that Nero's last years were lean years
for Spain so far as road-works—and perhaps material
benefits in general—were concerned.

The inscriptions which fall later, in the period of the
Flavians and Trajan, indicate that the construction of
new roads, though naturally continuous, was limited
in comparison with the Julio-Claudian period; henceforward, the repair of the earlier roads was the chief
necessity. It may therefore be claimed for the Julio-
Claudian dynasty that it left Spain provided with the
essential roads which military or economic considerations demanded, and that subsequent emperors had
only to elaborate and supplement the earlier network,
which may perhaps be regarded as the greatest continuous piece of work achieved in Spain by the House
of Augustus. It is of some interest to observe the
distribution of the Roman roads in Spain. The
majority of them lie within the northern half of
Tarraconensis, linking together the chief towns in the
mountainous districts of Callæcia, Asturia, and Cantabria, and running along the valley of the Ebro—for
two and a half centuries the corridor to the extreme
north; in the southern half of Spain a number of
roads radiated from Emerita, and the great Via
Augusta furnished a trunk route from south-west
Spain up to Gaul, throwing out subsidiary roads as it
passed through Baetica, and linked up also with the
Montes Mariani and with Carthago Nova. The region
most thinly provided with roads was, thus, that which
an earlier age had known as central Celtiberia, i.e.

that mountainous plateau from which sprang the head-waters of the Durius, the Tagus, and the Anas. But this was an area the inhabitants of which were partially romanized,[24] and, although the arts of peace—agriculture, trade, and mining—certainly necessitated (and indeed presupposed) the existence of roads of a sort in the central plateau, the warlike character of the newly conquered tribes in the equally mountainous district farther north demanded the speedy construction of first-class military roads there as an essential factor in the preservation of the Roman peace. It has, indeed, sometimes been supposed that the chief object which the northern roads were intended to serve was the development of the mining industries.[25] Ultimately, it is true, this became their chief function; but at first it was more important to keep the peace than to work the mines. In Lusitania, the early development of a road-system radiating from Emerita was made necessary by the manner in which the Durius, the Tagus, and the Anas all impeded north-and-south communications: it may be assumed that, wherever possible, a beginning was made in the bridging of some of the more important river-crossings. The roads of Baetica must have been made, in many cases, long before the time of the empire; so populous and so civilized an area could not, even during the Republic, have dispensed with adequate communications. Here, indeed, mining operations had, for many years already, called for good roads, quite apart from the claims of trade and commerce: and we may conjecture that the constant attention paid by the emperors to the Via Augusta did but set the seal upon an otherwise excellent road-system.

In contrast to their activity in the building of new roads, the Julio-Claudian emperors followed a policy

which was in other respects conservative, tending
usually to consolidation rather than to innovation.
The reign of Gaius, indeed, brought to an end a
privilege for which Spain had previously been conspicuous. Something has already been said of the
significance of the permission, granted by Augustus
to the various chief towns, to coin local bronze coins
(above, p. 164). This concession had continued
(though not without restriction) even under Tiberius,
who, regarding the Gallic revolt of Florus and Sacrovir
as a symptom of a nationalist movement, had cautiously
terminated the issues of bronze struck under the
auspices of the ' Concilium Galliarum ' at Lugdunum.[26]
Under the administration of Gaius, however, no local
Spanish bronze was struck at all, and it may therefore
be inferred that his suppression of the Spanish town-
mints occurred at the very beginning of his reign,
being perhaps a prelude to his even bolder step of
transferring the imperial mint from Lugdunum to
Rome. Deprived as they were of fresh supplies of
locally produced small change, the Spanish provinces
were obliged to rely henceforward on the output of
the senatorial mint at Rome ; but it was not until the
time of Nero, at the earliest, that senatorial bronze
coins circulated in sufficient numbers to meet the
economic demands of the western provinces, and for
some years to come, therefore, Spain (in common with
Gaul and Britain) had recourse to the local striking
of imitations of the official senatorial bronze. Large
numbers of these local copies have been found in
Spain, based chiefly upon the ' Agrippa '-type *asses*
which belong probably to the reign of Gaius and
upon the ' Minerva '-type *asses* which were issued
profusely under Claudius.[27] The official attitude of
the government towards this practice seems to have

been one of toleration, or at any rate connivance : the imitations differed in an important respect from the earlier autonomous issues in that they bore imperial, and not local, types.   Once suppressed, the autonomous mints were not destined ever to re-open ; from the time of Claudius onward the gold and silver coins of the imperial mints, and the bronze of the senatorial mint, were the only legal currency.[28]

As regards the extension of the franchise by means of the promotion of towns to privileged status, even the most liberal estimate would still fail to show Julio-Claudian policy in Spain as anything but conservative and, indeed, retrograde.   Under Tiberius no such extension (apart perhaps from the promotion of Dertosa) would seem to have taken place,[29] and, even if the autonomous town-mints had continued to operate in Gaius' reign, it is doubtful, in the absence of supporting evidence, whether the coins thus struck would have told us of any increase in the number of privileged communities.   The list of provincial colonies founded by Claudius is no mean one, but it does not include the name of any Spanish foundation.[30] Nor is there any evidence that Claudius created new *municipia* : there is nothing to suggest that the two Spanish towns the names of which incorporate that of Claudius—Baelo Claudia and Claudionerium—received municipal privileges.[31]   In the case of Baelo, indeed, it may be that the title 'Claudia' implies some form of compensation made in respect of revenue-losses incurred when Claudius detached certain towns on the coast of Mauretania from their dependence on Baetica (see below, p. 178).   The reign of Nero is not known to have added to the already existing number of privileged towns.   If, therefore, we are to define the Julio-Claudian policy with regard to the franchise

and its extension, it may be said that, even if isolated grants of *civitas* were from time to time made, such grants were not either frequent or liberal enough to be considered worthy of historical record, or to find commemoration on contemporary documents. The Augustan system remained unaltered; and consequently the more highly romanized provinces, such as those of Spain, were denied the increase of privileged towns which fell to the lot of the more backward parts of the Empire. This was an anomaly the gravity of which was emphasized by the magnitude of subsequent reforms.[32]

In the sphere of administration, however, at least one salutary and progressive change took place, most probably during the reign of Claudius. For his invasion of Britain in A.D. 43 Claudius employed four legions, of which three had previously been stationed on the Rhine; and, in the subsequent rearrangement of the Rhine forces, three legions were brought up to compensate those which had been withdrawn. Among them was IV *Macedonica*, from Spain: the reduction of the Spanish standing army by one-third suggests the increased peacefulness of the northern area over which that army watched. This inference is supported by other considerations. In the discussion of Augustus' administrative reforms given above in Chapter VIII, it was seen (p. 142 f.) that the accounts given by Strabo and Pliny of the organization of Tarraconensis were mutually exclusive, and reasons were adduced for supposing that Strabo (with his omission of Callaecia, Asturia, and Cantabria from the *conventus* system prevailing elsewhere) was describing the organization of Tarraconensis in its first, or Augustan, state, while Pliny's allocation of *conventus* to the areas centring upon Bracara, Lucusaugusti, Asturica, and Clunia

(Map II) holds good for a date later than that of Strabo's scheme. The precise dating of Pliny's material relevant to Tarraconensis is hard to determine. It was certainly pre-Flavian, as is shown by a reference (IV, 110) to *Amanum portus, ubi nunc Flaviobriga colonia*; and that it may have been of early Claudian date is suggested by Pliny's record (III, 19) that the inhabitants of Icosium, in northern Africa, were attached to the Spanish town of Ilici for administrative purposes—a state of affairs which could hardly have continued after Claudius' formation of the province Mauretania Caesariensis about A.D. 44. To accept a Claudian date for Pliny's sources is therefore to hold that Claudius superseded Augustus' almost wholly military administration in northern Spain, substituting for it the civil order—implied by *conventus*—previously established over the rest of Spain. General considerations make this view a likely one. Three-quarters of a century had elapsed since the Augustan arrangement had been established: romanization had progressed in the north sufficiently to allow a large reduction in the standing army; and, three decades later, northern Spain was not thought unfit to receive its own share of the Flavian benefaction.[33]

The administrative changes just described were the last, of any consequence, to take place until Vespasian introduced his great municipal programme, and they probably belong, as we have seen, to the early years of Claudius' reign, when his provincial administration was still of a high level. Claudius' personality, indeed, was not of a kind likely to make him unpopular in Spain. We find him committing no such act as that of Tiberius, who associated Seianus with himself in the *duumvirate* at Bilbilis.[34] Such instances of Claudius'

personal participation in Spanish affairs as survive are of a different kind : his name and those of a number of *privati* appear together on a dedication put up on the completion of some work at Castulo ;[35] the erection of the first public statue of Claudius at Ipsca (Cortijo de Iscar) in A.D. 46 is made the occasion of special commemoration ;[36] an inscription found at Cabeza del Griego attests the institution of a body of *Sodales Claudiani*—whether in his lifetime or afterwards is uncertain.[37] Finally, it is worth noting, as evidence of the increasingly close relation between the provinces and Rome, that two inscriptions (both dedicatory) give him his censorial title, although the censorship had been in abeyance for sixty-eight years : one of these comes from Nabrissa Veneria,[38] the other from Ipagrum (Aguilar de la Frontera).[39]

With Nero there came a swift deterioration in Rome's provincial relationships. At first, indeed, his extreme youthfulness was compensated by the competent administration of his advisers. To the provincials, however, as to the armies, he remained a mere figure for some time ; and the early dedications in Spain appear by their wording to emphasize nothing so much as the fact that Nero was a lineal descendant of Augustus.[40] Later experience was to be more instructive, and was to strain seriously the link between Rome and the provinces which had previously been forged. As we have already noted, there was little work on the Spanish roads after A.D. 59, and thereafter a most valuable form of imperial propaganda lapsed for a decade. Public and private inscriptions bearing Nero's name ceased in Spain about A.D. 62, and the world-wide process of rapacity and impiety by which attempts were made to refill the imperial exchequer after the fire of Rome in A.D. 64 was not calculated to inspire a resumption of them. It is not surprising to find that, at a time when the imperial ties were momentarily weakening, there were spasmodic outbreaks of trouble among the Astures and in the Balearic Isles as well.[41]

Galba's rise to power was not, however, caused by Spanish dislike of Nero : the record of his eight years' governorship of Tarraconensis was not such as to win him provincial backing on a wide scale, if we are to believe Suetonius, and it is probable that his support was confined almost entirely to the one legion then in Spain, namely VI *Victrix*.[42] With Otho it might have been otherwise, if circumstances had allowed the Spanish provinces to express their opinion of him. He had governed Lusitania for the long term of ten years, apparently without impropriety ;[43] and this early promise seemed likely to be fulfilled during his brief reign, in which, to judge from the account of Tacitus,[44] he foreshadowed the Flavian policy in Spain. The passage is worth quoting : ' Eadem largitione (i.e. with the same generous instincts as marked his domestic policy in Rome) civitatum quoque ac provinciarum animos adgressus, Hispalensibus[45] et Emeritensibus familiarum adiectiones, Lusonibus[46] universis civitatem Romanam, provinciae Baeticae Maurorum civitates dono dedit.' The reversion to the pre-Claudian arrangement with regard to the dependence of African towns upon Baetica is indeed surprising, although (so close was the ethnological tie between Spain and north Africa) certain coastal towns in Africa may have been quite willing to enjoy the undoubted commercial advantages which this connection with Baetica would involve. But the wholesale extension of the franchise is the most interesting of Otho's reforms. He had been a capable administrator, and

had spent a decade in Spain ; and, being himself free from the hereditary dogmas of the Julio-Claudian line, he may well have considered that Augustus' provincial policy, in its relation to the franchise at least, had become too much of an heirloom. Had he lived to reign without rivalry or conflict, Otho—and not Vespasian—might have been the author of the second great reconstruction of Spain. His successor had little interest in the provinces, and left no mark on the administration of Spain.

The history of Spain during the half-century of the Julio-Claudians is uneventful, so far as the main details of administration are concerned, and may be summed up in the phrase 'continuity of policy.' Such continuity was, indeed, of the greatest value in a country which had been the scene of opportunist methods for more years than its seniority among the Roman provinces deserved. Spain was now entirely at peace, and this peace was not disturbed either by the army revolts of A.D. 14 or by the military rivalries of A.D. 69. Administrative policy was clearly defined ; the principle of the responsibility of governors was firmly established ; and governors might on occasion remain in their provinces long enough to acquire a really personal interest in their welfare. All this was of the highest value, not least because it encouraged and hastened the material development of a naturally rich and prosperous country. But development of another kind was lacking : although there was no lack of opportunities for Spanish self-advancement in agriculture, trade, and commerce, the continuation of the Augustan franchise system, coupled with a failure to increase the number of privileged communities, ensured that only a very small proportion of Spaniards should have any stake in the government of their communiti es. Administration was still for the most part an external affair, in the hands of Romans : the imperial policy was not concerned with the high conceptions of imperial citizenship or dominion-representation ; and thus it came about eventually that Spain, though one of the richest of all the Roman provinces, and also one of the most highly romanized, was no exception to the disease of apathy which attacked Rome's foreign possessions. Imperial government had omitted, in the important years of adolescence, to teach her the art of self-government.[47]

CHAPTER X

THE MUNICIPAL REFORM OF THE FLAVIANS

VESPASIAN achieved supreme power only to find the State bankrupt, the legions depleted or demoralized, and provincial conditions in more than one place seriously disturbed. Of his ability to deal with these problems there could be little doubt. A long and successful military career, intimate knowledge of many of the provinces, a practical attitude towards finance,—all these qualities strengthened the new Princeps, 'the father of grown-up sons', in approaching the task of imperial reform; and in his sons was centred his hope of its consummation: 'either my sons shall succeed me,' he said, 'or no one'. The Flavian dynasty is frequently regarded as having produced an autocracy: in fact, the Flavians did no more than tear down the veil which had so long served to shroud the essential basis of the Principate, and alter (by the infusion of fresh blood from the provinces) the composition of a Senate which was unreliable if not effete. In the administration of the provinces as a whole there was no essential change, unless it was to be seen in the sharp improvement of the regulations by which it was conducted.

In Spain, indeed, the anxious transition from the Julio-Claudian dynasty to the Flavian dynasty produced little, if any, disturbance: the change from

Princeps to Princeps was of military rather than general importance. But the final triumph of the Flavian cause was destined to open up, almost immediately, a new provincial era for all Spain.[1] Vespasian's interest in the peninsula is perhaps to be seen in the persons of those whose appointment to Spanish provincial command he approved. Tarraconensis, from A.D. 70–73, was governed by the great administrator of Moesia under Nero,—T. Plautius Silvanus Aelianus, a former military colleague of Vespasian's, tried and trustworthy. In A.D. 71 M. Ulpius Trajanus, a man of Spanish origin and father of the future Emperor, took up office as proconsul of Baetica : the contrast between his previous command of Legio X Fretensis under Vespasian, during the Jewish Revolt, and the entirely peaceful government of Baetica should not suggest any diminishing importance in the order of the posts which he held.[2] The name of Otho's successor in Lusitania is not known, though L. Baebius Avitus, appointed procurator in A.D. 69, was continued in office for ten years.[3]

Vespasian's careful choice of *personnel* was suddenly explained when, in A.D. 73 or 74, it was announced by imperial edict[4] that Latin rights were forthwith to be extended to a very large number of hitherto unprivileged towns. The ancient writers, sometimes slow to appreciate provincial reform, duly recognized this signal measure : 'universae Hispaniae Vespasianus Imperator Augustus iactatum procellis reipublicae Latium tribuit ', wrote Pliny the Elder ;[5] and echoes occur in the pages of Josephus[6] and Aurelius Victor.[7] But our clearest evidence for it consists of the nearly contemporary records inscribed on bronze—the Leges Salpensana and Malacitana,[8] together with the many scattered references, yielded by inscriptions and

historians, to *municipia Flavia* or to men enrolled, by their enfranchisement, in the Flavian tribe, Quirina.

The nature and scope of Vespasian's Spanish reform must be examined in some detail. That the edict, which first announced it, fell in A.D. 73 or 74 (thus coinciding with Vespasian's assumption of the censorship) may be deduced from the fact that the earliest instances of enfranchisement under the new regulations occurred in A.D. 75. Such enfranchisement was according to the conditions governing grants of *Latium minus* : that is to say, in every one of the new *municipia* created by Vespasian the six chief magistrates elected every year received full Roman citizenship,[9] both for themselves, their parents and their wives, as well as for their children and grandchildren in the male line of descent.[10] Thus, in comparison with the increase in the citizen-roll effected by the later application of the system of *Latium maius*—which conferred citizenship upon all members of a local senate, together with their relatives in the same degrees—the extension of citizenship by *Latium minus* may at first appear limited and cautious. Reflection, however, will correct this view. In a *municipium* composed of already highly romanized elements *Latium maius* was obviously appropriate, being the quickest method of bridging the nationality-difference which distinguished a *municipium* from a *colonia* (whose inhabitants were Roman citizens).[11] But the communities for which Vespasian's grant was designed were, on the whole, far from being highly romanized, as an estimate of their numbers and distribution clearly indicates : his object in conferring these rights was not to acknowledge an existing state of highly developed political organization throughout Spain—this was yet to come—but to prepare the way for this in communities which he deemed ready for the experiment.

Pliny, as we have noted, records that Vespasian's grant of Latin rights embraced all Spain. Pliny's own lists of the Spanish communities (based on material mainly of the Augustan age) comprise over 520 towns, of which just under one-fifth are represented as possessing political privilege, i.e. positive rights—*civitas* or *Latinitas*, as opposed to mere *libertas*. It is difficult to estimate the number of communities which received political rights in the period between Augustus and Vespasian; but this number certainly did not exceed 70—a maximum figure, reckoned for safety—if indeed it came anywhere near it.[12] Unprivileged communities at the beginning of Vespasian's reign may therefore have numbered at least 350. These are the towns to which *Latium minus* was now granted; and research has traced over a quarter of them, 23 being clearly designated as *Municipia Flavia*, while 11 show their origin by the inclusion in their name of some form of the title 'Flavius', and a further 56 by the incidence of the Flavian tribe-name 'Quirina'.[13] Of these 90 new *municipia*, 41 lay in Tarraconensis (with 1 in Majorca), 38 in Baetica, and 11 in Lusitania; and these figures may be taken as an approximate guide to the distribution of the remaining and unrecorded three-quarters.

Faced with his self-imposed task of raising 350 or more communities simultaneously to the rank of *municipia*, Vespasian therefore first issued his edict (which was presumably binding no less in senatorial Baetica than in the two imperial provinces), and followed this up by the detailed work of issuing charters, one to each community affected, and by all the various acts of readjustment and reorganization

which his great reform necessitated. There is no reason to doubt that most of the charters were drawn up to a common pattern: such uniformity would obviously save labour as well as expense. Even so, the labour involved was gigantic, and continued well into the reign of Domitian, to whose reign the charters of Salpensa (Facialcazar) and Malaca belong. The case of Malaca, indeed, is a good example of the innumerable readjustments which had to be undertaken. Previously Malaca had been a *civitas libera et foederata*—a vigorous community, composed originally of Phoenician traders, whose autonomy, guaranteed by bilateral treaty with Rome, covered everything save the direction of foreign policy. Stimulated by the Flavian reform, Malaca now abandoned autonomy in favour of incorporation; and no more striking tribute than this could be paid to the value set on the franchise and upon its appropriate municipal system.[14] Other examples of incidental reorganization are abundant. Urso took the opportunity to have its charter republished; Cartima (Cartama) may have followed the lead of Malaca in voluntarily sacrificing free status;[15] Curiga (Monasterio) and Ipsca each underwent a process of amalgamation;[16] Sabora (Cañete la Real) petitioned the Emperor to be allowed to move its site from the hills to the plain;[17] the affairs of Carbula (Almodovar del Rio), now sunk to the poor status of a *pagus*, demanded attention;[18] at Emerita there was an increase both of *territorium* and of inhabitants;[19] boundaries, whether communal or regional, received adjustment;[20] and, as a corollary of these alterations and adjustments, there was of course frequent necessity for reorganizing the collection or allocation of revenues where local changes upset existing arrangements. It is not unlikely that, in certain of the newly created

municipia, prominent townsmen took some share in
the vast work of reorganization, perhaps at the
original suggestion of such governors as Plautius
Silvanus and Trajan.[21] But that special commissioners
were sometimes required is shown by the existence
under Titus of a *curator* in Baetica (see below, p. 193).
To this officer there must have fallen such business as
the financial readjustments caused by the transference
of Sisapo and Mirobriga from Baetica to Tarraconensis ; and similar commissioners elsewhere may have
supervised the financial changes occasioned by the
transference of the Vettonian region from Tarraconensis to Lusitania.[22] But Titus' *curator*, and any
others who may have existed, had more to do than
this, for the increase in the citizen-roll affected radically
the taxation business of each province. *Latinitas*
did not, of course, bring with it *ius Italicum*, i.e.
exemption from land-tax (indeed, with increasing
development, the *municipia* possibly began to be
assessed at an increasing rate) ; but those who gained
the franchise, while ceasing to pay *tributum capitis*,[23]
became liable instead to the 5 per cent tax on inheri-
tances ; and the consequent changes in the machinery
of tax-collection must have been considerable. With
such innumerable details of administration the provincial governor could scarcely be expected to deal
unassisted, especially as his term of office might not
be of any fixed duration ; and hence the need for
specially appointed officials.

After a decade or so, however, the work of reorganization was probably fairly complete. With the
shifting of a considerable part of local government
from the provincial governors to the communities
themselves, the process of decentralization had now
begun, and the work of administration became simpler

and less costly. Fragmentary though the extant
charters are, they leave no doubt of the standard of
municipal consciousness and industry required. Complete independence in local affairs there was not and
could not be ; and the number of municipalities—
such as Singilia (El Castillon) and Sabora—where the
title *liberum* denotes exceptional freedom in local
administration is significantly small. Nevertheless the
control of local revenues by municipal magistrates, and
the power of jurisdiction in all except certain criminal
cases reserved for the decision of the local governor
or his deputies, were concessions ample enough to
stimulate keenness and patriotism in the conduct of
local business. It would be interesting to know how
far the *personnel* and business of the provincial *concilia*
were affected by this increase in local autonomy ; but
unfortunately there is no evidence which allows even
a conjecture on this question, which is potentially one
of the most interesting of the period under review.

Vespasian's astonishing reform in Spain was not
paralleled by any similar reconstruction elsewhere. It
is therefore difficult to resist the conclusion that, of
the non-municipalized provinces, Spain—and Spain
only—had reached the stage of internal development
suitable for limited self-government. Indeed, we may
go further, and say that Vespasian's act of mass-
enfranchisement suggests that he considered the
reform to be overdue, for otherwise (since he had no
need to gain the support of the Spanish provinces by
measures of enticement) he would surely have introduced it more gradually. But there was now none of
the party bitterness which had complicated Caesar's
Spanish reconstruction : of the provincials, as distinct
from the legions which garrisoned them, it may be
said (in the words which Tacitus puts into the mouth

of a senator of the times) that while one hoped and prayed for a good Princeps, one put up with any one got.[24]   Indeed, public opinion in Spain wore a peaceful enough complexion ; and to this was due the fact that, from A.D. 71, the garrison could now be reduced to a single legion, VII *Gemina*, representing the barest of concessions to the frontier-army principle in a non-frontier country.[25]   This general pacification was one condition of municipal reform : the second condition was familiarity with Roman political practice.   Such familiarity was the result of the steady and peaceful development of the country under the Julio-Claudians : economic progress was now to be matched by political emancipation.   It would be wrong, however, to suppose that the newly created municipalities were predominantly Roman in character, for there is nothing to suggest that, in the remoter parts of Spain at least, the nationalist characteristics of the type tolerated by Augustus had weakened or vanished : that these characteristics still existed is plain from the continued existence of Spanish auxiliary regiments.[26] But, viewed as a whole, the temper of the country was peaceable and orderly, and allowed Vespasian to grant privileges to towns which had absorbed the essentials of the Roman political system without serious loss in their sense of local personality.   In this sense it may be said that ' Vespasian first returned to the policy of Caesar ',[27] if it is at the same time allowed that Vespasian's estimate of the Roman citizenship was narrower and more conservative (as was natural in a *novus homo*) than that of Caesar, the noble born.

Liberalism was not, however, the same to Vespasian as altruism ; nor was the reputation which he earned in his lifetime other than that of prudence and hard-headedness—qualities which seem to have made the

reign of Titus so pleasant an interlude for Roman society between the administrations of his father and his brother. Spain benefited must repay her benefits; and it may now be asked how this was possible. The changes in taxation have already been noticed (above, p. 188): a progressive reduction in the receipts from direct taxation was accompanied by an increase in those from indirect taxes, and possibly by an increase in the rateable value of Spanish communities for purposes of the *tributum soli*; and the difference between the respective amounts may not have been large. Suetonius alludes in a well-known passage[28] to Vespasian's raising, and occasional doubling, of provincial taxation; but there is no evidence to show that in Spain the increase was any other than what might result from the measures and changes described above. Indeed, so far as Spain is concerned, the chief increase in revenues was probably derived from the mines, which (as will be seen later) were placed in a special administrative category about this time, and were henceforth very strictly controlled.

More important, perhaps, than any positive gains in taxation-revenues were the direct economies to which the Flavian reform led. We have already noted the lightened burden of the Spanish provincial governors under the new régime: this must have involved a reduction of administrative staff, unless it can be shown that a widespread and general need for subordinate *legati iuridici*—regional deputies to deal with legal decisions—had already shown itself.[29] A more radical and permanent economy was to be seen in the reduction of the legionary establishment of Spain to one legion,—a step which was not made at the cost of undue reliance on auxiliary troops: some half-dozen auxiliary cohorts and *alae* were stationed in the north-

west : half as many auxiliaries seem to have sufficed
for Lusitania : *vexillationes* of the legion were posted at
Tarraco and Italica—each an important administrative
centre ; while Tarraco contained also two cohorts
perhaps under the command of the *praefectus orae
maritimae*,—a coastguard official whose naval base may
have been transferred about this time to Barcino.[30] In
Baetica responsibility for maintaining the peace of the
province must have rested with the several communities, as it certainly did at Urso. But while Spain itself
now justified this definite and lasting reduction of its
own garrison-forces, it also began to supplement the
numbers of the legions stationed elsewhere in the
Empire. Enrolment in the legions was conditional
upon possession of Roman citizenship. In Italy there
was becoming evident an increasing reluctance to
serve in the legions, as the various rivals for power in
A.D. 69 had found. If recruits could not be found in
Italy, they must be produced from the provinces ; and
Vespasian, by increasing the number of *cives* throughout Spain, increased thereby the number of those
eligible for legionary service. To the provincial, as
opposed to the conservative or even degenerate
Italian, the legionary career was not without its attractions. Foreign service, steady pay, an opening—
through the highest steps of the centurionate—to the
Roman Civil Service itself,—these were no inconsiderable inducements to swell the army to which Rome and
Italy were becoming more and more indifferent. The
Roman army benefited also from the large number of
auxiliary troops whom Vespasian and his successors
were able to recruit in Spain, and particularly in the
north-western district : in this connexion may be
noticed the curious anomaly that no *diplomata*, that is,
certificates of citizenship after discharge from auxiliary

service, have yet been found for units enrolled in
Spain; and this fact has produced the tentative conjecture that Spanish auxiliary recruits may have been
henceforth granted the franchise upon enlistment, as a
means of keeping up the numbers of the auxiliary
contingents in an increasingly pacific age.[31]

Vespasian's reconstruction of Spain provided him
with an opportunity for introducing another reform,
the effects of which, if not so tangible as those of steady
finance and increased recruiting, were of considerable
political importance. Allusion has already been made
to Titus' *curator* in Baetica. This same official (whose
inscription,[32] damaged, and now lost, lacks the name)
was, early in his career, *flamen Augustalis in Baetica
primus*, that is to say, the first official priest of the
imperial cult in Baetica. The growth of the imperial
cult, its encouragement in the less highly civilized
areas, and its association with the machinery of the
provincial *concilia* in Tarraconensis and Lusitania, has
been described above (pp. 154 ff.). Doubts have been
expressed about the genuineness of the present inscription; but in reality its remarkable contents are all in
its favour. Moreover, even if it could be proved to be
false, its vitiated testimony would not be an irreparable
loss. It is well known that the imperial cult, as
organized by the *concilia*, while being a product of the
eastern provinces of the Empire, was first applied to
those western districts where no antipathy, in the form
of conservative Roman tradition, would bar its
growth. Lugdunum, Emerita, Tarraco (the congress-
centre for central and northern Spain), quickly took
their place in the scheme: in Baetica, however, to
which Tiberius denied a temple in his honour in
A.D. 25,[33] the imperial cult may have been deliberately
retarded. The reason for this is not difficult to see.

The imperial cult in the time of Tiberius was a solemn undertaking,—an intercession of thanks for the destiny of Rome and the greatness of the founders of the Empire. Half a century had done much to modify the status of the Princeps ; and, if only because the deification of a dead Emperor and the divinization of his house were the general rule, it was not now difficult to realize the political expediency which underlay the rule. Thus, in the early Empire, thanks were not demanded from those whose political complexion might make their thanks no more than formal. Now, formal or not, the imperial cult was an integral part of the imperial sanctions to rule ; and all alike must support and observe those sanctions. Baetica, in short, was now brought into line with Tarraconensis and Lusitania : a special *flamen* was appointed for the formal inception of the cult, and presumably for the institution of the provincial *concilium*. Whatever the success of the cult in Baetica, the *concilium* was to serve its limited function of representation in a proper fashion, as subsequent events showed.[34]

A source of additional, and this time more tangible, profit was ensured by Vespasian's development of the north-western districts, Asturia and Callaecia. Already, as we have seen, the reign of Claudius had probably placed these districts on the same general administrative footing as the rest of Tarraconensis. Even now, however, their cultural level must have been considerably below that of the remainder of the peninsula : populous they may have been—a fact which explains the large number of auxiliary units there recruited— but this only served to complicate the problems of an area already difficult enough owing to the wildness of the country, the hardiness of its inhabitants, and the richness of the mineral deposits which invited a yet

more systematic exploitation. It seems that Vespasian countered these difficulties by a variation of the administrative system which affected Tarraconensis as a whole, appointing regional procurators—they would have been called District Commissioners to-day—who were subordinate to the governor of Tarraconensis, though within their own districts they exercised a fully deputed authority in civil and administrative business.[35] Under such a system the peculiar needs of Asturia and Callaecia would be certain of receiving the full attention which might have been denied to them in the absence of these special deputies. There was, indeed, much to engage the attention of these Flavian procurators. Asturica and Bracara were among the number of tribal centres which received municipal charters; and the occurrence of place-names incorporating some form or other of the name 'Flavius' is noticeably frequent in these districts, implying that, even where a formal charter was not granted, urbanization was encouraged (as a necessary prelude to municipalization) and was recorded by the allusion to the Flavian name. Only by some such hypothesis can we explain the well-known inscription from Aquae Flaviae (Pl. X), which records the names of ten small *civitates*, together with that of Vespasian, in the commemoration of some unspecified enterprise—perhaps the building of the Tamega bridge—or act of gratitude.[36] This process of unification must necessarily have been helped on by the activity of the Flavian emperors in extending the road-system of the north-west: the Via Nova, a direct route from Bracara to Asturica by way of Nemetobriga and Bergidum, was begun under Vespasian and continued under Titus, and was clearly intended to bisect the area enclosed by the circular road-system constructed under the Julio-Claudians.[37]

With urbanization and road-works proceeding apace, the imperial government could the more easily press on the development of mining in the north-west : it is not always remembered that Pliny's report[38] of the annual gold-yield of the north-west and west dates from the Flavian period. Gold, indeed, was a prime necessity in the Empire at this period : the growing luxury of the times resulted in its increasing immobilization in articles of luxury, and yet the volume of gold currency in free circulation had to be maintained—in fact, it was necessary to raise it ever higher—partly in order to fulfil the economic needs of a growing Empire, partly to counterbalance the constant absorption of gold coin by peoples outside the frontiers of the Empire.[39]

The supposition that the imperial government found it increasingly necessary to keep a strict control of the world-sources of the more valuable metals may be illustrated from the *Lex Metalli Vipascensis*, the charter of the mine of Vipasca (the modern Aljustrel, in Portugal).[40] This *lex* is a document, incomplete in its present form, engraved on bronze in letters which have generally been assigned to the later part of the first century of our era. Though it refers explicitly to a *lex metallis dicta*, i.e. a general statute for the control of mines, and to a *lex ferrariorum*, which may have revised or supplemented the *lex metallis dicta* in its application to iron mines, this document contains no internal evidence of date sufficient either to uphold or to destroy the purely epigraphic dating proposed above. It is, however, safe to assume a Flavian or Trajanic date, for another bronze document,[41] found subsequently at Aljustrel, seems clearly to be an appendix of Hadrianic date, containing amendments or elucidations of the original *lex* such as were applicable

to the Vipasca mine. And, since Spain occupied so much of the attention of Vespasian and his sons, it is to their period rather than to that of Trajan, always more interested in the east than in the west, that the document may be assigned: it may even be that the Spanish mines, by calling themselves for fresh organization and control, prompted the Flavians to frame a general mining charter in such a way that it was applicable over the whole Empire.

Incomplete though the Vipascan bronze is to-day, it nevertheless reveals one fact of paramount interest. In an age which had witnessed the extension of Latin rights to virtually the whole of Spain, Vipasca appears as a non-urban and unprivileged community, rigorously controlled by a Procurator of Mines whose authority (apparently supreme except in cases of life and death) may have embraced all mines, of whatever kind, in the area in which Vipasca lay. Scarcely less important is the allusion made in the Vipascan law to the *lex metallis dicta*—a general Mining Statute. For Vipasca itself mined only silver and copper; and it is therefore clear that the imperial government of the day, not content with absolute control of gold mines alone, had extended the principle of state ownership to mines of the less precious metals as well:[42] by this means, of course, it was able to control the output, and consequently the market-price, of all the metals mined under its direction. Nor was it necessary (save in the now rare cases of privately-owned mines) to express a formal claim to state ownership: this was done tacitly, if the Government made the leasing of a shaft or shafts conditional upon the acceptance by the leaseholders of strict procuratorial administration both of the shafts and of the pit-head settlement, the costs of this administration being met by the rents which the leaseholders paid.

Administration of the mines therefore implied state-ownership; and the document leaves us in no doubt of the revenues which accrued to the *fiscus*.[43]

The Flavian epoch, then, probably saw all the principal mines, of Spain at any rate, and possibly elsewhere too, come under the direct control of the state: by the Hadrianic period, to judge from the supplementary and later document, the state automatically claimed one half of the metal produced—a heavy royalty that had to be paid in addition to the initial fees exacted for the registration of mining-rights; and, were the earlier document complete, it is possible that this system would be found to apply to the pre-Hadrianic period as well. The revenue derived from this strictly directed system must have been immense: and, if its organization may be attributed to the Flavian dynasty, Suetonius' report of Vespasian's raising and occasional doubling of provincial tributes will come several stages nearer explanation, the word 'tributes' standing loosely for revenues in general. Nevertheless, although the mines were now made to yield more under this rigid procuratorial administration, the accompanying regulations for the social welfare of the pit-head communities were not inconsiderable. 'The lessee of the baths, or his partner, shall entirely at his own expense warm and keep open the baths . . . from sunrise until noon for the women, and from 1 p.m. to 8 p.m. for men, subject to the approval of the procurator who will be in charge of the mines. He shall properly furnish water running into the tank over the heating chambers, up to the highest mark, and in the plunge, for the women as well as for the men. The lessee shall charge each man half an *as*, and each woman an *as*. . . . The bronze articles which he shall use he shall properly wash, dry, and coat with fresh grease at least once

every thirty days. . . . The lessee shall have wood in
reserve at all times. . . .' Strict monopolies are
imposed, by means of paid licences, for cobbling, barbering, and laundering : the barber ' shall have this
privilege, that no one in the village of the mining-
district of Vipasca, or within the district, shall practice
barbering for profit.' Similarly, ' no one shall have the
right to clean and press, for pay, unworn or soiled
garments save him to whom the lessee, his partner, or
his agent shall have leased or granted this privilege.'
Monopolies to-day are often associated with profiteering : but under the eye of the Procurator of the Mines
profiteering was probably not easy : that these social
regulations were framed for humanitarian purposes
may be deduced from yet another rule : ' School-
masters shall be untaxed by the Procurator of
Mines.'[44]

The chief Spanish reforms and readjustments which
may be connected with the Flavian dynasty have now
been reviewed. To Vespasian may be given the praise
for his bold and unerring instinct which brought about
the greatest social and political revolution in the history
of Roman Spain,—a revolution which was not complete until the reign of Domitian. With the historical
results of this municipal reform we are not immediately
concerned: the following and final chapter will
attempt to assess them. Our present emphasis is upon
the reform as such,—its tacit recognition of Spanish
adaptability and romanization, its encouragement of
local pride and enterprise, and its promise of economy
and simplification in the administration of the Spanish
provinces. These features demonstrate admirably the
nice balance, discernible in the Flavians (and not lacking in Augustus himself), between a desire for genuine
progress and an insistence that progress must to some

extent pay for itself. Flavian Spain certainly progressed : equally certainly it helped to pay, and without
undue inconvenience, for the costs of progress. Few
men alive at that time were qualified to say whether
this progress was too late, or the cost too great.

CHAPTER XI

THE AGE OF TRAJAN: PROSPECT AND RETROSPECT

WITH her dignity increased, her initiative stimulated, and her administration simplified, Spain emerged from the Flavian epoch into that mid-day sun of peace and prosperity which, sedulously advertised by the socially conscious emperors of the second century, illuminated the provinces with a radiance not lost upon the rhetoricians of the age.[1] The new century was, indeed, a manifest turning point in the history of Rome. For six centuries she had suffered the pains of expansion: in the train of conflict, while she had laboriously shaped the Mediterranean basin into one vast political unit, had followed the inevitable problems of social and economic reorganization; and over all her difficulties she had risen supreme. Under Trajan it seemed that territorial expansion was not to stop short with the Mediterranean area: his eastern campaigns pointed the way to the destruction of the one organized menace still remaining to confront Roman dominion,—the power of Parthia, destined to become really serious once more in the third century. Hadrian, however, decided that the limit had been reached: his predecessor's new conquests in the Near East fell rapidly away; and from now onwards the imperial government was chiefly occupied, not with the expansion of the Empire, but with its protection against the dangers of disintegration, external and internal,—dangers which were aggravated during the military anarchy which beset the Empire in the course of the third century.

Beyond the reign of Trajan, therefore, the present survey will not be extended. With him expansion reaches its climax; and at the same time a new imperial philosophy is achieved, whereby the Emperor is Emperor not by the accident of birth, but by his natural fitness to rule. Trajan was, moreover, a Spaniard by origin, born at Italica in that province of which his father had been governor : it is thus the more appropriate to end our narrative at the point when Spain gives Rome the first of the ' provincial ' Emperors. Nor will it be a violation of historical method to fix this limit, for (as will be seen) the age of Trajan supplies evidence enough for discussion of the problem of imperial and municipal decay (if decay it was) which bulks so large in the history of the later Empire.

In conformity with an era of peace and plenty heralded over most of the Empire at large, the Spanish scene in the time of Trajan must have appeared varied and brilliant.[2] The Emperor's own care and activity on behalf of his parent country were strongly marked. The Flavians, after a period of intermittent neglect of Spanish affairs, had inaugurated the age of political emancipation : Trajan's reign seems, by contrast, to have recaptured something of the material splendour which had everywhere made Augustus' principate so memorable. His government was assiduous in repairing or extending the already complex system of roads, not only in the more recently developed north-western areas,[3] but in the centre and south as well :[4] with this road-work may be coupled the construction

of two bridges,—one the magnificent co-operative
enterprise at Alcantara,[5] still spanning the Tagus
(Pl. XI), the other crossing the Tamega at Aquae
Flaviae [6],—both dedicated to Trajan, and standing
as examples of an enlightened progress of which there
were doubtless many other instances elsewhere. An
age of building is generally also an age of high industrial and commercial activity, which itself demands
(and creates) a rise in the standard of urban life. In
this Spain was not behindhand. It is not here possible
to sketch, even briefly, the complex social life of
Trajanic and post-Trajanic Spain.[7] But the reader,
if he glances at any classified list of epigraphical or
literary evidence,[8] or studies the excavation-reports of
a representative town or of a country-district, especially
in Baetica,[9] cannot fail to realize the abundant activity,
the diversity of life, the wealth of callings, and the
high level of material comfort which characterized
Spain from the time of Trajan onwards. Professions
and trades, commerce, religious cults, the beguile-
ments of leisure, education, the social and medical
services,—all these aspects of provincial life blend into
a vivid picture of an advanced and critical civilization.
Hence the dedications of thanks set up in gratitude to
Trajan,[10] as to his successors, and the memorials
commemorating the benefits of his times.[11]

This picture, seemingly so attractive and persuasive,
has been very variously appraised by recent historians
of the Roman Empire.[12] To some it has appeared
in most essentials to give a true view of the imperial
commonwealth in the second century, if not later. In
the opinion of others it is misleading, perhaps false,
being no more than the gloss put upon contemporary
conditions by those most able to profit from them or
to express gratitude at their profit.[13] Between these two

standpoints still lies an uncomfortably wide gap, which may possibly never be bridged satisfactorily: the Empire of the second century and later, though it saw the technique of imperial propaganda developed to an extraordinarily skilful pitch, failed to produce a historian in whom the faculties of free criticism and analysis were sufficiently strong to enable him to study the social conditions prevailing in the provinces. To a large extent this difference of opinion is caused by a difference of approach to the problem. Those who ask 'What *did* Rome give to the provinces?' will obviously not return an answer welcome to those whose question is, 'What did Rome *not* give to the provinces?' Therefore, in attempting to assess the sum of romanization in Spain and to define the qualities of Roman administration, we must attempt also to define the defects of those qualities if we are to avoid extremes of judgment.

Chief among the benefits which Rome conferred on her Spanish provinces was that of peace. As a peninsula, Spain was, indeed, free from the danger of external invasion once the Roman hold on the Pyrenees and the line of the Ebro was established and assured. But the peace which Rome gave was primarily internal. Spain, with her innumerable hill-top communities, each with an independent leader and a free existence, was physically incapable of peaceful co-operation without the presence of Roman troops to ensure it.[14] The task of establishing the supremacy of Roman soldiers in Spain belonged mainly to the Republic. It was long-drawn-out, often because of the inefficiency or stupidity of Roman commanders; and thus arose a list of conquered armies and a literature full of the horrors of Spanish warfare, themselves the cause of a reasonable prejudice against Spain as a grim and

recalcitrant land. But Roman patience, not unmixed with Roman desires to exploit the natural riches of Spain in a costly age of expansion, finally prevailed; and with the reign of Augustus there came the end of large-scale fighting. There still remained the suppression of local banditry, and the true pacification of the northern areas. Nevertheless, local division and internecine strife were now finally ended. On the peoples of Spain the inauguration of peace, guaranteed by Roman troops, had the obvious effect of turning them from an existence of watchful isolation to a mode of life in which agriculture and local industries were the prime concerns. Population, which shrinks in intermittent warfare, is restored to a higher level in peace: increased population and a settled existence necessitate more food, produced more scientifically, or more and better industries, in order that food may be bought from elsewhere. The resolution and enthusiasm natural to war yielded to the calmer activities necessary to peace; and with it all there is apparent, in Spain as elsewhere, a genuine thankfulness—one of Augustus' chief mainstays—felt by all to whom productive life is dearer than the horrors of a worthless death. Not until the troubles of the third century arose was Spanish public opinion harshly reminded that the continuance of peace could not always remain the responsibility of the central government alone. City-walls were then hurriedly built up, with scant attention to the quality of materials or workmanship; and nothing speaks more eloquently of the preceding years of security than the Spanish reaction to this panic scare.[15]

In this sense, perhaps, the change from multiple and insignificant independence to modified self-government under the secure protection of Rome and the Roman peace, though it was in itself an excellent change, may have contributed to that growing lack of responsibility and enterprise which begins to be apparent in Spain from the second century onwards. This does not mean that Spanish productivity declined: on the contrary, it probably increased. But the peaceful condition of the country, and its consequently growing productivity, inevitably attracted the keener spirits among the Roman business and capitalist circles; and, in the absence of unlimited Spanish capital or strong Spanish competition, the economic exploitation of Spain by Roman interests was a foregone conclusion. Already, as we have seen, Republican Spain had probably tempted Roman speculators to invest capital in export and industrial concerns. With the country formally pacified, the stream of immigrants was bound to increase, in numbers and diversity, especially as the economic life of Italy began to show signs of stagnation. Romans, Gauls, Africans, Greeks, and Orientals settled in the various administrative or commercial centres:[16] Roman capital was probably prominent in the formation of business companies;[17] to such companies probably fell a large and lucrative share in the export trade of the oil, wine, and fish-sauce conveyed in the jars whose fragments compose to-day the Monte Testaccio at Rome—a vast heap of sherds (predominantly Spanish), 150 feet high and half a mile in circumference.[18] The promise of the Republic is fulfilled under the Empire: with mines monopolized (as they were by the Trajanic period) by the state; with foreign capital controlling a substantial part of the export business; with wheat certainly,[19] and oil and wine probably, over-produced regularly in the south for export abroad regardless of the comparative agricultural poverty of the centre and north; and finally with the growth of large estates,

latifundia, originally representing the vested interests of absentee landlords in Rome or Italy and subsequently taken over for imperial control as the practice of confiscation grew up,—we have, in brief, an economic system (which might be called deliberately unscrupulous if it had not been simply unplanned and opportunist) by which Spanish supply goes primarily to meet the demands, not of Spain, but of Rome and other large consumer-towns, which pay for Spanish exports in money usually destined (less a natural deduction for the Spanish wholesalers) for the pockets of Roman capitalists whose concern those exports are. Of anything like a balance of trade there is no indication : the list of Spanish imports is meagre in the extreme.[20] We may therefore say of the Roman peace in Spain (adapting the words used by Schulten in a different context)[21] that, while it came itself as a characteristic benefit, it also brought with it the characteristic evil of secure and uninterrupted economic exploitation by Roman capital,—a process not checked by any administrative safeguard.

The economic affiliation of Spain with the artificially controlled markets of Rome was accompanied, and to some extent encouraged, by the increasingly artificial nature of the administrative system under which Spain was governed. In the early days of the Roman occupation when Rome, burdened with war after war, was attempting desperately to govern her provinces by opportunist methods frequently inadequate to the demands made upon them, the administration of the Spanish provinces was of a mainly military character, natural to a country in which Roman governors seldom completed their term of office without having first led their troops on some aggressive or punitive expedition. Political instruction, peaceful collaboration, nascent urbanization,—all these were ideals which, though not excluded (as the records of the Scipios, Cato, Sempronius Gracchus and Sertorius himself indicate), were normally not prominent owing to the unrest and danger caused by a fluid and undefined northern frontier. Nevertheless, in those areas beyond which the tide of warfare had receded for good, political instincts had steadily developed; and, divided though Caesar's provincial policy was between the needs of Rome and the needs of the provinces, his Spanish reforms are profoundly significant of the political potentialities of the now settled parts of the country. But Caesar's policy was abruptly and prematurely terminated; and thus it fell to Augustus—that catholic administrator with a conservative outlook—to shape the political system by which Spain and the other predominantly peaceful provinces should be controlled.

It may at once be said that the Augustan system of provincial administration was remarkably well organized and remarkably elastic: Augustus' Spanish reforms, even though they were by no means regardless of economic considerations, show clearly his efforts to vary the nature of the government in accordance with the varying levels of culture which the country included. For this axiom of elasticity he and his successors deserve full praise; and the provinces themselves welcomed an era in which the fair and regular assessment of taxes, the payment of salaries to government officials, and an organized judicial system automatically reduced oppression and extortion to a minimum.[22] It was, however, significant of Roman imperial policy that oppression and extortion, though rare and severely punished when they occurred, continued to be possible. For, now no less than

before, Rome herself was still the political mistress of the world : this was an axiom, only momentarily endangered in A.D. 69 and not thereafter seriously disputed until the reign of Gallienus, which underlay the attitude of the earlier emperors towards the Roman citizenship, prompted their use of the process of *adlectio* into the Roman Senate, and sanctified such a cult as that of *Roma Aeterna* in the darkening years of the third century.[23] Briefly, the question is this : Was Roman citizenship an appropriate stimulus or reward for local enterprise or progress in the provinces ?

As a reward it was certainly very highly prized, not least because of the infrequency with which it was conferred under the Julio-Claudian Emperors, whose cautious policy in this respect towards Spain has already been examined. It was, moreover, on a presumed and general eagerness to win Roman *civitas* that Vespasian based his whole Spanish reform : municipalization through widespread grants of *Latium minus* was plainly a poor and halting innovation unless there was a general desire to stand for local magistracies. And yet, even if we admit that the traditional and axiomatic value of Roman citizenship could scarcely be questioned—much less disregarded—in the Rome of the Flavians and Trajan, we may still feel that the system which rewarded a career in local politics with political rights in another and distant city was a curious one, and that Rome had perhaps never freed herself from the provincial philosophy most natural to that distant age in which her ' provinces ' consisted in fact of adjacent territory, such as Latium, where the exercise of civic rights was a concrete possibility, and not merely a flattering but unpractical potentiality.

If Roman *civitas* was regarded as a prize—and there is no doubt of this—then it must clearly have acted as

14

a powerful stimulus to those intending to take up a political career in a provincial *municipium*. From the time of Vespasian onwards (until Caracalla's desperate and freakish enfranchisement of the whole Roman world), we might, therefore, think of the Spanish municipalities as so many urban units all fostering internal keenness and enterprise. In very many this was, no doubt, the case—especially in the more recently civilized districts of the north and north-west, where a new and high-sounding prize was more acceptable and less deeply analysed. Elsewhere, various factors may have combined to weaken the stimulus. Whatever the degree of municipal self-government conceded in the several urban units, the provinces of Spain came no nearer to any system of provincial self-government,[24] —an ideal, indeed, which receded ever further owing to the constant short-circuiting of local talent by conferment of *civitas*, which turned men's eyes to Rome rather than to Spain. If a province as such had no self-government, its people were unable to co-operate in any systematic economic or social policy ; and even if it is urged that the provincial *concilia* were concerned with business far wider than religious organization and the detection of oppression or injustice,[25] the silence of history does not entitle us to suppose that their functions encouraged or achieved anything in the nature of the formation of a genuine political or economic committee, with provincial (as opposed to Roman) interests to the fore. This concentration of provincial interests upon the political organism of Rome was bound to result in a *laissez-faire* attitude towards purely municipal and provincial problems : it is likely that this was the principal cause of that disinclination to assume municipal magistracies which had probably become evident even in Flavian

times.[26]   The evil was only aggravated by the fact that local magistracy and membership of a local senate often involved considerable private expenditure.[27] Local politics thus tended to become the monopoly of the local magnates : general interest in, and critical control of, local finances thus slackened ;[28] and this is the prelude to the introduction of *curatores*, special financial commissioners for the direction of municipal affairs, who were only too frequently confronted (if we may judge from the younger Pliny's experiences in Bithynia) with debt and corruption in public places. *Curatores* are the product of the age of Trajan : there is, indeed, no reason to suppose that they were anything but a rare necessity in Trajanic Spain,[29] for it was still a far cry to the days of general scarcity alleviated by the demoralizing benefactions of the rich ;[30] but a combined process of economic and political decline which began to affect most of the Empire at large cannot have left Spain untouched.

Politically, therefore, as well as economically, Spain stood in an organized and cumulative dependence to Rome. This process was not without its effect on the development of Spanish literature and art.[31] The list of Spanish writers who lived during the first century and a half of the Principate is, indeed, no mean one : the two Senecas, father and son, and Lucan, all born at Corduba ; the geographer Pomponius Mela ; Columella of Gades, the expert on the increasingly difficult problems of agriculture ; Quintilian, the literary purist of Calagurris who rose to a salaried position under Vespasian ; Martial, native of Bilbilis, the brilliant and pungent epigrammatist of a decadent Roman society,— these names are landmarks in Latin literature of the Silver Age ; and with them may be mentioned the lesser poets and orators of the Corduban school, such as M. Porcius Latro, Junius Gallio, and Sextilius Hena. Their achievement was considerable, but, although their common origin may perhaps be traced in common characteristics of style, they did not constitute a coherent school of literature, based on a common cultural tradition. All, save Pomponius Mela, spent the greater and creative part of their lives in Rome or Italy, where their views were shaped and their output dictated by essentially non-provincial factors. Moreover, by the second century the list of Spanish writers, speakers, and thinkers is virtually exhausted : Spain, which gives two emperors to Rome, yields the literary supremacy to Africa, itself destined to produce an imperial dynasty in the *Severi*. Nor was the failure of the literary fount counterbalanced by the development of any indigenous artistic style. Spanish adaptability, which had been seen so plainly in the hybrid Greco-Iberian art of the fourth century B.C. and onwards, had not (it seems) lessened with the years. The art of Spain under the Empire is the art of Rome, in architecture, pottery, sculpture, and painting : native characteristics, whether they were originally strong or not, were (like the much more vigorous Celtic influences in Britain) irreparably lost in the invading flood of practical architecture and unimaginative, representational art which the Romans brought with them.

Thus in culture, as in politics and economics, Spain took her cue from Rome. Although, with the growth of social consciousness in the Roman administrative classes, this dependence was automatically saved from becoming politically despotic or oppressive by the parallel development of the conception of *libertas* (freedom from arbitrary rule), it was nevertheless accelerated by the introduction and extension of bureaucratic methods by the central government. It was finally assured by

the tacitly recognized and universally active principle that ' Rome could dispense with attempts to justify her imperial work by the superiority of the culture which she could offer to her peoples, and be content with the knowledge that the *Pax Romana* enabled them the better to live lives of the kind which were their own.' [32] This axiomatic superiority of the Roman culture—complex though that culture now was owing to its absorption of many originally un-Roman elements—was successfully enough established and maintained to become, as it were, the sentimental bricks and mortar which bound the provinces into a heterogeneous unity so close as to survive the various disintegrating factors of five centuries. A central and centralizing ideal such as this was, indeed, of immense value and significance. Nevertheless, it may be said that a philosophical ideal divorced from active enterprise is somewhat of a negative benefit to those to whom it is presented. Athens in the fifth century B.C., though her imperial technique was frequently selfish or ill-advised, had been able to unite the best of the civilized world in a common enterprise against Persia. This involved making subjects out of allies, as she quickly found, and hence in the end came her failure. Rome, on the other hand, developed an Empire whose very vastness excluded any common ideal of active enterprise : faced with the alternative either of reversing the Athenian method and making allies out of subjects, or of denying provincial independence in favour of political dependence sweetened by a centralizing bond of sentiment, she not unnaturally chose the latter alternative, thus keeping under her own direct control the economic forces of the Empire as a whole. It was, perhaps, in Christianity that the Empire was to realize its first common enterprise of an active nature : but with that aspect of Roman Spain we are not concerned.

Such, then, are the qualities and defects of the Roman administration of Spain. The qualities are brilliant,—secure peace and swift material development; an elastic system of government, free from uniformity, and tending towards local autonomy; and a common sentiment: to these virtues may be added others, such as a fair system of taxation, good legal facilities, and wide religious tolerance. The defects are those which became ingrained in the Roman character during its centuries-long struggle for world-supremacy, —insistence on economic control; the projection of Rome (and the Roman politico-administrative system) over all provincial acquisitions, leading to provincial apathy, and so to provincial decline and bureaucracy; and the consequent refusal to convert a pacified and passive unit of Empire into an active and responsible member. To the already threadbare controversy about romanization no solution is here offered in the case of Spain: it is doubtful if the word should mean more (from the provincial point of view) than familiarity with the ideas of a race adept at administration, famous for its lawyers, its speakers, and its builders, and memorable for the massive economic basis of its huge territorial expanse. From the Roman point of view it meant something very different, namely, the pursuit of a dexterous and efficient system of opportunism, assured of success by Spanish peace, Spanish loyalty to both Rome and the Emperor, and Spanish acceptance of those political privileges which were the most conspicuous reward for that loyalty.

NOTES

CHAPTER I

[1] For detailed treatment of the geography, vegetation, soil, etc., of Spain, reference should be made to A. Schulten *s.v.* 'Hispania' in Pauly-Wissowa-Kroll's *Real-Encyclopädie der classischen Altertumswissenschaft* (henceforth cited as *P.-W.*) cols. 1979 ff., and to the same writer's *Hispania (Geografía, Etnología, Historia)* (Barcelona, 1920). Much material of a general nature is to be found throughout the pages of L. C. West, *Imperial Roman Spain : The Objects of Trade* (Oxford, 1929).

[2] See, for example, Justin XLIV, 1, 4.

[3] According to Regel, *Landeskunde der iberischen Halbinsel*, p. 121, cited by Schulten, *Hispania (Geografía, etc.)*, p. 55.

[4] The question of the Ligurian elements in ancient Spain has been discussed by Schulten, *Hispania (Geografía, etc.)*, p. 108 f., and by the same writer in *Fontes Hispaniae Antiquae* (cited henceforth as *F.H.A.*) I (Latin edition, 1932), p. 25 f. Fuller discussion is contained in the Appendix (ch. XXIX, pp. 631 ff.) of P. Bosch Gimpera, *Etnología de la Península Ibérica* (Barcelona, 1932), cited henceforth as Bosch, *Etnología* ; this monumental work is indispensable as a store of information about pre-Roman Spain.

[5] For Spanish rock-paintings, see Bosch, *Etnología*, pp. 18 ff. with his fig. 10 illustrating the Castillo paintings ; also J. R. Mélida, *Arqueología Española* (Barcelona, 1929)—a convenient summary of Spanish antiquities from the earliest times down to the Romano-Christian period—for reproductions of the Altamira paintings, plate opposite p. 24 and fig. 6.

[6] Cogul and Alpera, Mélida, op. cit., figs. 7, 9 ; Saltadora, Bosch, op. cit., fig. 13.

[7] For Neolithic Spain, see Bosch, op. cit., pp. 63 ff., and Mélida, op. cit., pp. 29 ff. The dolmens and megalithic tombs of Spain and Portugal are studied by E. T. Leeds, *Archaeologia*, LXX, pp. 201 ff.

[8] Cf. Bosch, op. cit., pp. 146 ff.

[9] The African affinities of the early Iberian culture-wave are discussed by Schulten in his *Numantia*, I (*Die Keltiberer und ihre Kriege mit Rom*) (Munich, 1914), pp. 35 ff.

[10] So Schulten, *Hispania* (*Geografía*, etc.), p. 109 f. ; see the same writer on Avienus, *Ora Maritima*, vv. 252 ff., in *F.H.A.* I (Latin edn.), p. 27 f. This view is not accepted by Bosch, op. cit., pp. 325 ff.

[11] See Bosch, op. cit., pp. 146 ff.

[12] The ' cyclopean ' wall of Tarraco is shown by Mélida, op. cit., fig. 34 ; for Los Millares pottery, cf. Bosch, op. cit., figs. 103–4.

[13] See Bosch, op. cit., pp. 175 ff.

[14] See Mélida, op. cit., pp. 73 ff.

[15] The fullest discussion of Tartessos is that of Schulten, *Tartessos: ein Beitrag zur ältesten Geschichte des Westens* (Hamburgische Universität : Abhandlungen aus dem Gebiet der Auslandskunde, Band 8 ; Reihe B, Band 5) (Hamburg, 1922): cf. also the same author in *Hispania* (*Geografía*, etc.), pp. 112 ff., and in *F.H.A.* I (Latin edn.), pp. 126 ff., for a summary of the views of his *Tartessos*. More lately, in his article ' Die Etrusker in Spanien ' (*Klio* XXIII (1930), pp. 365 ff.), Schulten has put forward a theory suggesting Etruscan elements in the earliest colonization of south and south-east Spain ; but Bosch is perhaps to be followed in his view (op. cit., p. 658 f.) that lack of true evidence, whether historical or archaeological, must prevent the Etruscan theory being at present more than a theory. For Bosch's reconstruction of Tartessian culture, see his pp. 258 ff.

[16] See Bosch, op. cit., p. 242.

[17] The Biblical references are quoted in full in *F.H.A.* I (Latin edn.), pp. 127 ff. ; the earliest is contained in 1 Kings xxii, 48.

[18] v. 421.

[19] Bosch, op. cit, pp. 269 ff.

[20] Cf. Psalms 72, 10.

[21] The arguments for lowering the date and minimizing the intensity of Phoenician contacts in Spain are summarized by Bosch, op. cit., pp. 258 ff. ; for the Psammetichus scarab, see his fig. 216, and, for the Aliseda treasure, figs. 217–23.

[22] Schulten's estimate of the extent of the Tartessian dominion at its height is conveniently shown on Plate II of his *Tartessos*.

[23] The facts for this era are collected and discussed by Rhys Carpenter, *The Greeks in Spain* (Bryn Mawr, 1925): it was by Carpenter that the western sea-route of the Phocaeans, traceable in the -οῦσσα suffix, was first pointed out. See also Bosch, op. cit., pp. 288 ff., and Schulten in *F.H.A.* I, *passim*, with the same author's 'Die Griechen in Spanien' in *Rheinisches Museum*, 1936.

[24] Herodotus IV, 152.

[25] Cf. the passages from Hesiod and Stesichorus cited in *F.H.A.* I (Latin edn.), pp. 130 ff.

[26] These distances are defined by the Massiliote *Periplus* (*F.H.A.* I) in Avienus' *Ora Maritima*, vv. 565, 699.

[27] The development of Emporion is discussed by Bosch, op. cit., pp. 310 ff.

[28] See Herodotus I, 163–7, with which cf. Anacreon, fragment 8 (Bergk's edn.) *ap.* Strabo III, 2, 14. The view that the Arganthonius episode was the climax of Greek penetration in Spain, rather than the prelude, is forcibly argued by Bosch, op. cit., pp. 288 ff., where it is suggested that Herodotus' sources were derived from purely Phocaean tradition, as distinct from the essentially Massiliote tradition of the *Periplus*.

[29] For the site of Mainake see Schulten in *Forschungen und Fortschritte*, Jan., 1939. For the Mainake–Tartessos land-route, cf. Schulten in *C.A.H.* VII, p. 774 f., on Avienus' *Ora Maritima*, vv. 178–80.

[30] Published as *F.H.A.* I, edited by Schulten.

[31] On the hybrid Greco-Iberian art, see Rhys Carpenter, op. cit., pp. 57 ff. (perhaps a little too much inclined to exaggerate the possibility of the influence of pure Greek models) and Mélida, op. cit., pp. 158 ff., with figs. 84–9.

[32] See J. G. Milne, in *Numismatic Chronicle*, 1938, pp. 36 ff.; S. Gsell, *Histoire ancienne de l'Afrique du Nord* I, II (Paris, 1920); Bosch, op. cit., pp. 315 ff.

[33] Polybius III, 22,—supported by H. M. Last in *C.A.H.* VII, pp. 859 ff., and by the late R. L. Beaumont's 'The Date of the First Treaty between Rome and Carthage,' *J.R.S.* XXIX (1939), pp. 74 ff. Through the kindness of Mr. A. R. Burn, I have been able to see Mr. Beaumont's paper in MS. form before publication.

[33a] Beaumont, op. cit., arguing that Polybius' ἐπέκεινα means 'south of,' discusses the rival interpretation.

[34] Neither of these colonies is mentioned in the Massiliote *Periplus*; therefore it is likely that both were founded later than *circa* 530 B.C.

[35] Polybius III, 24.

[36] See Bosch, op. cit., pp. 304 ff.; Mélida, op. cit., pp. 117 ff., where care should be taken to distinguish the material of two periods, the one early and the other late. Typical sculpture of the purely Carthaginian epoch is illustrated by Bosch's figs. 252-7 and Mélida's figs. 59-61.

[37] Punic influence in the Baetis valley is reviewed by G. Bonsor, 'Les colonies agricoles pré-romaines de la vallée du Bétis,' in *Revue archéologique* XXXV (1899). See also Bosch, op. cit., fig. 286, for the Osuna reliefs, and pp. 342 ff., with figs. 290 ff., for the evidence from the district of the Oretani.

[38] See G. F. Hill, *Ancient Coinage of Hispania Citerior* (American Numismatic Society's *Notes and Monographs*, no. 50), pp. 18 ff.

[39] I, 10; see here the statements of Gsell, op. cit., I, pp. 440 ff.; II, p. 313 f.

[40] III, 13, 7.

[41] See Bosch, op. cit., pp. 362 ff.

[42] *Id.*, pp. 381 ff.

[43] *Id.*, pp. 453 ff., 621 ff.

[44] Schulten's view is presented in his *Numantia*, I, pp. 16 ff.: the counter-arguments are developed in Bosch, op. cit., chapters XVIII, XXIV, XXV, XXVIII, reinforcing the previous short study of G. Kraft, 'The Origin of the Kelts,' in *Antiquity* III (1929), pp. 33 ff.

[45] So Bosch, op. cit., p. 474 f., on the '*Oretani qui et Germani cognominantur*' of Pliny III, 25.

[46] An excellent summary of Celtiberian culture is that of Schulten in *C.A.H.* VII, pp. 782 ff.

[47] Cf. Strabo, III, 1, 6.

[48] For the culture of the Balearic Islands, see Bosch, op. cit., pp. 187 ff., corrective in parts of Mélida, op. cit., pp. 102 ff. The intensity of Punic influence at Ebusus may be judged from the finds made in the Puig des Molins necropolis there: cf. Bosch, op. cit., figs. 252-7.

CHAPTER II

[1] See *C.A.H.* VII, pp. 665–98.

[2] Fabius quoted by Polybius III, 8, 1; the same tradition appears, e.g. in (Dio Cassius XII) Zonaras 8, 17, and is not absent from Appian, *Iber.* 4–5.

[3] Polybius III, 8, 1–10, 5. Cornelius Nepos, *Hamilcar*, 4 remarks pertinently that Hamilcar *equis armis viris pecunia totam locupletavit Africam.* But ancient historians were on the whole slow to comprehend the relation of economics to history.

[4] Th. Mommsen, *The Provinces of the Roman Empire from Caesar to Diocletian*, tr. W. P. Dickson (London, 1909), I, p. 63.

[5] According to Appian (*Iber.* 46) the Celtiberians of the Numantine district had never seen elephants before 153 B.C., so that even Hannibal probably penetrated no farther than half-way up the Ebro valley.

[6] XXV, 10.

[7] Dio Cassius XII, fr. 48.

[8] See above, p. 16, for Massiliote influence and its extension along the east coast of Spain. Schulten, in *F.H.A.* III, p. 11, comments that, if Hamilcar did in fact conquer a Massiliote town, this is the best explanation of the Roman embassy of 231. It might also be added that such an act of conquest would account for the stiffening attitude of Rome in subsequent years.

[9] Diodorus XXV, 11–12; Livy XXI, 2, 3–7.

[10] Livy XXI, 2, 7; 18, 9 (Livy regards this treaty as a renewal of a previous one to the same effect; but the previous boundary had been at Cape Palos, and the Ebro treaty is an obvious concession on Rome's part); Appian, *Iber.* 7 (where falsity of tradition is obvious in Appian's placing of Saguntum *north of the Ebro*); Zonaras 8, 21; Polybius II, 13, 7; III, 27, 9; III, 30, 1.

[11] The inhabitants of these towns, presumably to be equated with the 'other Greeks' of Appian, *Iber.* 7, and doubtless victimized like those of Saguntum, are so described owing to the false derivation of Saguntum from Ζάκυνθος. In fact, Saguntum was in origin an Iberian fortress, named Arse (?): see discussion and bibliography in Hill, op. cit., pp. 111 ff.

[12] Schulten, in *C.A.H.* VII, p. 788 f., and *F.H.A.* III, p. 17, emphasizes the responsibility of Rome (through her treaty with Saguntum) for the Second Punic War. But this can be exaggerated beyond merely technical limits : the war was a war of set policy. Cf. also *C.A.H.* VII, p. 809, VIII, p. 27 f. ; and Ed. Meyer in *Kleine Schriften* II, pp. 331 ff.

[13] See E. Groag, *Hannibal als Politiker* (Vienna, 1929) ; and, for a bibliography dealing with the Spanish phase of the Second Punic War, *F.H.A.* III, p. 56.

[14] Polybius III, 13–14 ; Livy XXI, 5.

[15] Ancient estimates of Hannibal's penetration in Spain became greatly exaggerated : cf. Livy XXI, 5, 17 ; Justin XL, 5, 6. More sober estimates by modern scholars appear in *C.A.H.* VII, p. 789 f., and *Historia de España* (ed. R. M. Pidal), vol. II (Madrid, 1935), p. 15 f.

[16] See *Historia de España*, cit., figs. 14 and 15.

[17] The Turduli (Livy XXVIII, 39, 3) or Turbuletes (Appian, *Iber.* 10), elsewhere called by Livy (XXI, 6, 1) the Turdetani, seem in fact to have been equivalent to the Mastieni of Murcia and Valencia,—a people with affinities to the former Tartessian culture (see ch. I, pp. 10 ff.) represented in the late third century by the Turdetani proper, and their centre may perhaps be placed at the Turba or Turbula of which Livy (XXXIII, 44) and Ptolemy (II, 6, 60) speak. Bosch Gimpera and P. A. Bleye, in *Historia de España*, cit., p. 14, review the problem, assigning the Turbuletes to Teruel.

[18] Polybius III, 29, 9–10.

[19] Livy XXI, 6, 2–3.

[20] The Roman feelings of shock, not unmixed with shame, are given a dramatic and almost certainly false setting in Livy's story (XXI, 19, 6 ff.) of the reproach of the Bargusii.

[21] Polybius III, 20, 6, speaks of this embassy as going to Carthage after the fall of Saguntum was known in Rome : and it is easily confused with the tradition of the earlier embassy sent to Hannibal during the siege.

[22] These details are derived from Polybius (III, 33, 5 ff.), who found a Carthaginian record of them inscribed on a bronze tablet at the Lacinian promontory in Bruttium—an interesting example of scientific method in ancient historiography.

²³ The numbers of Hannibal's own army appear to be exaggerated in Polybius III, 35, 1 ; and likewise his preliminary losses (by desertion, etc.) in III, 35, 7–8, since Livy XXI, 23, 4–6 allows for a reduction of no more than 10,000 from these causes : cf. *C.A.H.* VIII, p. 35. Polybius III, 39, 2, and Livy XXI, 23, 1–2, attest Hannibal's subjection of the Ebro-Pyrenees coast.

²⁴ H. H. Scullard, *Scipio Africanus in the Second Punic War* (Cambridge, 1930), p. 43.

²⁵ Tarraco is the 'Kissa' of Polybius III, 76, 5, and the 'Cissis' of Livy XXI, 60, 7 ; and is naturally to be identified with the 'Cesse' or 'Cese' of the coins found there in such numbers and variety (see Hill, op. cit., pp. 39 ff.). The town was originally an Iberian fortress built in the traditional style (the 'cyclopean' wall-structures are illustrated in *Historia de España*, cit., figs. 22–4 : cf. plan in fig. 20). On it was super-imposed the edifice of a Roman town—the 'Scipionum opus' of Pliny *N.H.* III, 21. The first historical mention of the site was that of Eratosthenes (*c.* 280–195 B.C.) : cf. Strabo, III, 4, 6.

²⁶ A fragment of the Greek historian Sosylus, friend of Hanni-bal, preserves a reference to this sea-fight, and emphasizes the active assistance rendered by Massiliote sailors to the Roman (and, equally, Massiliote) cause : cf. U. Wilcken in *Hermes* XLI, pp. 103 ff. ; XLII, pp. 516 ff.

²⁷ The record of Cnaeus' advance to the Saltus Castulonensis and Hasdrubal's counter-offensive from Lusitania (!) in Livy XXII, 20–21, is a hopeless confusion, caused either by duplica-tion of other campaigns or by sheer misunderstanding of records. Cnaeus had not the troops for such a venture.

²⁸ Polybius III, 97–99 ; Livy XXII, 22. Doubted by some scholars (cf. Scullard, op. cit., pp. 46–7), the story is perfectly acceptable. The Scipionic camp at Saguntum has been identified by Schulten : cf. *Philologische Wochenschrift*, 1928, no. 7, p. 222 ; *Archäologischer Anzeiger*, 1927, p. 233.

²⁹ The date of the battle of Hibera is disputed, being assigned to 216 or 215. The present writer prefers the earlier, and traditional, date.

³⁰ Livy XXIII, 48–49.

³¹ The annalistic tradition appears in Livy XXIII, 49 ; XXIV, 41–42. Though it contains occasionally probable elements, it

is impossible as it stands, with the Carthaginians falling back to Munda (!), and Roman garrisons installed in the Baetis valley. Attempts have been made (see Scullard, op. cit., p. 49 and Schulten in *F.H.A.* III, p. 81) to see in the Iliturgi and Intibili of Livy a misunderstood reference to towns of the same or similar names north of the Ebro: but Punic operations in Catalonia are as difficult to accept, at this time, as Roman victories in Andalusia.

[32] An inscription of the Imperial epoch (*C.I.L.* II, 3836) commemorates the 'recovery' of Saguntum. Castulo—'urbs valida ac nobilis et adeo coniuncta societate Poenis ut uxor inde Hannibali esset' (Livy XXIV, 41, 7)—was the key both to the Baetis valley and to the mineral wealth of the Sierra Morena.

[33] Cf. Appian, *Iber.* 16.

[34] Topographical problems are difficult, perhaps insoluble. Amtorgis, where Livy (XXV, 32) leaves Cnaeus, cannot be identified (see N. Feliciani, *Studi e Documenti di Storia e Diritto*, 1904, p. 210). Cnaeus retired to Ilorci—'Scipionis rogum' (Pliny *N.H.* III, 9), variously identified as Lorca (Schulten, *F.H.A.* III, p. 91; Ed. Meyer, *Kleine Schriften* II, p. 445) and Lorqui (Scullard, op. cit., p. 50 f.). The latter, lying north of Carthago Nova, is perhaps thus more acceptable. The defeat of Publius can be placed only conjecturally in the neighbourhood of Castulo (see Appian, loc. cit.).

[35] Livy XXV, 36, 14, puts the two defeats 'octavo anno postquam in Hispaniam venerat' (Cnaeus), i.e. in 211 B.C., agreeing with the scheme of Polybius, though elsewhere he contradicts himself.

[36] Marcius' achievement became exaggerated: see Livy XXV, 37-9, and subsidiary accounts in *F.H.A.* III, pp. 93 ff. Nevertheless his actions, for one reason or another, won him Africanus' praise: see Scullard, op. cit., p. 57, note 1, and Feliciani, op. cit., p. 217 f.

[37] See Scullard, op. cit., pp. 32 ff., for the background of Roman domestic and foreign policy in which Scipio grew up.

[38] For Livy's confusion in dating, due to a misinterpretation of Polybius' Olympiad reckoning, see *C.A.H.* VIII, p. 84, n. 3. The election of Scipio and the status of Silanus are discussed by Feliciani, op. cit., pp. 226 ff.

[39] The best English discussion of the Scipionic legend is that of Scullard, op. cit., chapters II, III and IX.

40 There is much divergence in Livy, Appian, and Polybius concerning the disposition of the Punic forces (Livy XXVI, 20, 6 ; Appian, *Iber.* 24 ; Polybius X, 7, 5), and modern criticism has been much exercised : cf. Feliciani, op. cit., pp. 243 ff., and Scullard, op. cit., p. 59, n. 1. Broadly speaking, the Polybian version may be accepted as correct.

41 The topography of Carthago Nova is described in detail by Polybius X, 10,—though with false orientation : for the whole question see Scullard, op. cit., ch. III and appendix I, and *Historia de España*, cit., fig. 17.

42 The carefully marshalled arguments of Scullard, op. cit., pp. 71 ff. (with which cf. *C.A.H.* VIII, p. 85), concerning the 'miraculous' ebb, are here accepted.

43 See the sources collected in *F.H.A.* III, pp. 112 ff.

44 Cf. Valerius Maximus III, 6, 1.

45 The topography and tactics of Baecula are fully dealt with by Scullard, op. cit., pp. 100 ff., 300 ff.

46 According to Livy (XXVIII, 3, 3), Orongis—the centre of a wealthy and fertile district—had been used by Hasdrubal as a base for expeditions ' circa mediterraneos populos.' The town presumably commanded the Baetis valley from higher ground overlooking its middle course.

47 Livy (XXVIII, 16, 14) places the battle of Ilipa in 206 B.C., and some scholars (see *C.A.H.* VIII, pp. 88–9 ; Scullard, op. cit., pp. 304 ff.) are reluctant to accept a dating which results in a year of such crowded and necessarily swift activities. But the activities *were* swift, and were to some extent delegated by Scipio to his subordinates ; and the Livian tradition may stand, thus leaving the capture of Orongis in 207 as an action necessitated through the artificial dispersion of Punic forces in that year.

48 See Scullard, op. cit., pp. 126 ff. The name Ilipa appears, probably through MS. corruption, as 'Ηλίγγα in Polybius XI, 20, 1 : the change from ΙΛΙΠΑ to ΗΛΙΓΓΑ is, as has been shown, easy. Livy's version calls the place Silpia (XXVIII, 12, 14),— clearly not to be equated with the Ilipa he mentions in XXXV, 1 : probably Silpia stands as a euphonized form of Ilipa. See Ed. Meyer, *Kleine Schriften* II, pp. 406 ff. ; Scullard, loc. cit. ; the site is connected psychologically with the Scipionic foundation of an adjacent site at Italica (see p. 51 f.).

[49] Appian, *Iber.* 32, gives the forms Ilurgia and Castax, transformed by Livy XXVIII, 19, 1, into Iliturgi and Castulo : Polybius here fails. Ilurgia is presumably the Ilorci (' Scipionis rogum ') of Pliny, *N.H.* III, 9 : and is to be recognized rather in the modern Lorqui than in Lorca : see Scullard, op. cit., p. 142, n. 2, and our n. 34 above. Castax cannot be identified.

[50] XXVIII, 39.

CHAPTER III

[1] Livy XXVIII, 38 ; XXIX, 13.

[2] Livy XXXII, 27, 6.

[3] Livy XXVII, 38.

[4] Livy XXXII, 28, 11.

[5] For the boundaries, inter-provincial and otherwise, of the two new provinces, see E. Albertini, *Les divisions administratives de l'Espagne romaine* (Paris, 1923), pp. 13 ff. ; Schulten, *C.A.H.* VIII, p. 306 ; Hübner, *C.I.L.* II, Suppl., p. lxxxv. For the position of the southern extremity of the inter-provincial boundary east of Baria, see Artemidorus *ap.* Steph. Byz., s.v. Ἰβηρία : cf. Pliny *N.H.* III, 5, 8 ; Livy XL, 41. Albertini, loc. cit., would place it at the river Mazarron ; Schulten, loc. cit., at the river Almanzora. For its northward course east of the Saltus Tugiensis and Castulo, see Caesar, *B.C.* I, 38, 1–2.

[6] See here N. Feliciani, ' L'Espagne à la fin du IIIe siècle avant J.C.' in *Boletín de la Real Academia de la Historia* XLVI (1905), pp. 363–98.

[7] Possibly commercial : this might help to explain the false derivation of Saguntum from Ζάκυνθος (see above, p. 219), i.e. commercial, and so Greek. Hill (op. cit., p. 120) makes the interesting suggestion that silver from Saguntum formed the basis of the ' victoriate ' coinage in Italy, between the 1st and 2nd Punic wars (cf. H. Mattingly, *Roman Coins* (London, 1927), pp. 13, 23). It seems certain in any case that Saguntum was coining in silver before the Roman invasion of Spain (see Hill, op. cit., p. 117 f.) : and supplies of Spanish silver from *c.* 220 B.C. would facilitate the raising of the date of the first Roman *denarii* from 187 B.C. (H. Mattingly and E. S. G. Robinson ' The Date of the Roman Denarius, etc.,' *Proc. Brit. Acad.*

XVIII (1932), pp. 211 ff.) to about 217 B.C., as suggested by J. G. Milne, *J.R.S.* XXVIII (1938), pp. 70 ff., and *Class. Rev.* L (1936), p. 215.

[8] The *territorium* of Saguntum is a case in point. Disputes connected with it had given Hannibal his *casus belli* in Spain : and after the end of the war the Saguntines had their *vectigal* restored to them by Rome : see above, pp. 27 ff., 44.

[9] See Hill, op. cit., pp. 6 ff., 10 ff.

[10] See Ch. IV, n. 8.

[11] Feliciani, in *Boletín*, cit., pp. 387 ff., makes some useful observations on the economics of third century Spain.

[12] Cf. the operations of Fulvius Flaccus : Livy XL, 16 ; 23.

[13] See p. 64 f.

[14] *C.I.L.* II, 1168-9, 1180, 1182-3 (referring to Hispalis (Seville), opposite Italica).

[15] See Feliciani in *Boletín*, cit. ; also J. J. van Nostrand, ' Roman Spain ', in *Economic Survey of Ancient Rome* III (Baltimore, 1937), pp. 121 ff. (cited as *E.S.A.R.*).

[16] See W. T. Arnold, *Roman Provincial Administration*[3] (Oxford, 1914), pp. 21 ff., 197 ff.

[17] It must be remembered that *civitates stipendiariae* were not the only communities on whom taxes were imposed. Thus a *municipium civium Romanorum*, unless it possessed *ius Italicum*, paid for the territory which it occupied : so, too, an *oppidum iuris Latini ;* and both alike were subject to the indirect taxes imposed on *cives* and non-*cives* respectively, as also was a *colonia*, though this (as it possessed *ius Italicum*) paid no *tributum soli*. See *Historia de España*, cit., p. 394.

[18] See *E.S.A.R.* III, pp. 127 ff. ; Arnold, op. cit., pp. 198 ff. ; Schulten, *C.A.H.* VIII, pp. 308 ff.

[19] Cf. Cicero, *Verr.* III, 6, 12,—' ceteris impositum vectigal est certum, quod stipendium dicitur, ut Hispanis et plerisque Poenorum quasi victoriae praemium ac poena belli.'

[20] Livy XXIX, 3, 5.

[21] This suggestion is usually justified by a reference to Livy XXXIV, 21, 7; but this passage records only Cato's reorganization of the iron and silver mines of Citerior. Nevertheless it is possible that both reforms were achieved at the same period.

[22] See Arnold, op. cit., p. 202 f. ; and below, p. 248, for the negative argument for poll-tax in Spain.

[23] See above, note 7.

[24] Discussed fully by Hill, op. cit., especially pp. 135 ff. ; A. Vives y Escudero, *La Moneda Hispanica*, II–III (Madrid, 1924–6) ; E. Hübner, *Monumenta Linguae Ibericae* (cited as *M.L.I.*) ; E. J. Haeberlin in Schulten, *Numantia*, IV, p. 273 f. See also below, ch. IV, note 21.

[25] Summary in *E.S.A.R.* III, p. 128 f. : this should be read with care if the respective contributions of the two provinces are to be distinguished.

[26] XXXIII, 27, 2.

[27] XXXIV, 10, 4.

[28] Cf. Hill, op. cit., pp. 135 ff. ' According to Hübner ninety out of a hundred (Iberian coins) are of this type.'

[29] Hill, op. cit., pp. 105 ff. It should be noted that the bronze issues of Secaisa were more common than the silver.

[30] See Hübner, *Arqueología de España* (1888), p. 203. Iberian coins found in Gaul are recorded by A. Blanchet, *Traité des monnaies gauloises* (Paris, 1905), p. 184 ; while Hill has written ' On the coins of Narbonensis with Iberian Inscriptions ' in the American Numismatic Society's *Notes and Monographs*, no. 44 (1930).

[31] This observation was made first by Hübner (*M.L.I.*, p. 5) and not, as Hill appears to suggest (*Notes and Monographs*, no. 50, cit., p. 44), by Schulten.

[32] Cf. Livy XLIII, 2, 12. It is wrong to suppose that *vicesimae*, where exacted, formed the *stipendium* of those areas : if this had been the case, there would have been no question of payment at all, and it was the payment, not the *vicesimae*, that caused the trouble in 171 B.C. (cf. Livy, loc. cit.).

[33] *C.A.H.* VIII, p. 311 f.

[34] See O. Davies, *Roman Mines in Europe* (Oxford, 1935), pp. 94 ff. ; T. A. Rickard in *J.R.S.* XVIII (1918), pp. 94 ff. ; L. C. West, op. cit., pp. 40 ff.

[35] Baebelo : ' qui CCC pondo (argenti) Hannibali sub-ministravit in dies ' (Pliny *N.H.* XXXIII, 97). Carthago Nova : Πολύβιος δὲ, τῶν περὶ Καρχηδόνα Νέαν μνησθείς, μέγιστα μὲν εἶναί φησι, διέχειν δὲ τῆς πόλεως ὅσον εἴκοσι σταδίους, περιειληφότα

κύκλον τετρακοσίων σταδίων, ὅπου τέτταρας μυρίαδας ἀνθρώπων
μένειν τῶν ἐργαζομένων, ἀναφέροντας τότε τῷ δήμῳ τῶν Ῥωμαίων
καθ᾽ ἑκάστην ἡμέραν δισμυρίας καὶ πεντακισχιλίας δραχμάς (Strabo
III, 2, 10). The picture of the fabulous wealth of Turdetania in
Strabo III, 2, 9, derives only from Poseidonius.

[36] Livy XXXIV, 21, 7; cf. Aulus Gellius, *Noctes Atticae* II,
22, 29.

[37] V, 15.

[38] Livy XXI, 60, 4; XXVII, 38, 11.

[39] (Dio Cassius) Zon. IX, 17.

[40] Livy XXXII, 2, 5; XXXIII, 21, 6; XLIII, 2.

[41] Iberian characteristics are well sketched by Schulten,
C.A.H. VII, pp. 782 ff.

[42] The head-quarters of the governors in the early years are
uncertain, and presumably varied with the position of the
army, though Tarraco and Carthago Nova in Citerior, and Italica
and (after 151 B.C.) Corduba (Cordova) in Ulterior, were doubtless the chief administrative centres: cf. Albertini, op. cit.,
p. 21 f.

[43] For convenience in reckoning, Cato (195 B.C.) is here
treated as a pair with Appius Claudius Nero, though in fact
Cato's command was supreme.

[44] See above for other (and not necessarily exclusive) explana-
tions of these divergences, p. 58.

[45] See Feliciani in *Boletín*, cit., p. 375.

[46] By Van Nostrand, *E.S.A.R.* III, p. 123. The same writer
(p. 128) estimates the total revenue *per annum* over the years
218–168 B.C. as only 'a trifle more than five per cent of the
estimated entire state income.'

CHAPTER IV

[1] Livy XXIX, 1–3; Appian, *Iber.* 38; Diodorus XXVI,
22; Livy XXXI, 49, 7.

[2] Livy XXXIII, 19; 21; 25–7; Appian, *Iber.* 39.

[3] Bardo is mentioned solely in Livy XXXIII, 21, 6 (see

Schulten in *F.H.A.* III, p. 175), and may have been situated in the lower part of the Baetis valley.

[4] XXXIV, 18, 1–2.

[5] On this place-name see Schulten, *F.H.A.* III, p. 177.

[6] Zon. IX, 17.

[7] Livy XXXIII, 43.

[8] It might perhaps be conjectured that the Greeks of Emporion, displeased at Roman attempts to break their commercial monopoly on the north-east coast, were not averse to inciting against Rome the Indiketes who formed the native element of their joint community.

[9] The MSS. of Livy XXXIV, 19, 10 give the name 'Saguntia' as a Celtiberian base—plainly a confusion of Saguntum with Seguntia (=Segontia). The archaeological evidence for Cato's progress to Numantia is given in Schulten, *Numantia* IV, pp. 33, 181: see also Aulus Gellius, *Noctes Atticae* XVI, 1, 3.

[10] For Cato's operations in Spain, see Livy XXXIV, 8–21; Appian, *Iber.* 39–41. Minor authorities are quoted in *F.H.A.* III, pp. 177–94.

[11] XXXV, 1, 1–2.

[12] Livy XXXV, 1; 7; 22 (Toletum ... parva urbs ... sed loco munito).

[13] Livy XXXVII, 46, 7; 57, 5–6.

[14] Livy XXXIX, 21, 8–10.

[15] Appian, *Iber.* 42.

[16] The concerted actions of Sempronius and Postumius are recorded in Livy XL, 35; 36; 39–40; 44; 47–50. See also Appian, *Iber.* 43–4; Diodorus XXXIII, 24–5; Plutarch, *Ti. Gracchus* V, 2; Florus I, 33, 9.

[17] A total of 55,000 men sent jointly to both provinces is not included in this calculation.

[18] Valerius Maximus IX, 1, 5.

[19] Livy XL, 35.

[20] Further extensive reinforcement is recorded also for the years after 179 B.C., viz. for 177 (doubtless to relieve the army of Sempronius Gracchus), and again for 176, 173, and (at first refused but afterwards granted) for 172. Fresh troops sent out in 169 brought up the regular forces in each province to one legion, apart from *socii*. (See Livy XLI–XLIII.)

²¹ The historical value of these mints as evidence for early Roman penetration in the valley of the Ebro depends, of course, on the interpretation given to Livy's phrase ' argentum Oscense ' (of which the traditional view was adopted in Chapter III) ; and, even so, is corroborative only, as no single one of these mints can be dated exactly. Those who hold that Livy's evidence is confused and anachronistic will say that the ' Oscan ' and other native Iberian coinages must be brought down to a period not much before the Numantine War, and for support they will point to the evidence of the coin-finds at Numantia itself (see Hill, op. cit., p. 139 f.). But they forget that Iberian silver was struck primarily for the payment of tribute, and not for internal circulation ; therefore the absence of finds which can be dated to the years *before* the Numantine War is as natural as the presence of Iberian silver at Numantia and elsewhere *during* that war, i.e. when tribute-money was withheld over a wide area by communities which thus temporarily usurped it as a genuinely local currency.

²² Hill, op. cit., p. 108.

²³ Livy, *Epit*. XLI.

²⁴ See Mommsen on *C.I.L.* II, 2857. (The suggestive 2897 s suspect.)

²⁵ *C.I.L.* II, 5041=*I.L.S.* 15. This bronze tablet is figured in *Historia de España*, cit., p. 70, and discussed in *F.H.A.* III, p. 201 f. ; *E.S.A.R.* III, p. 134 ; and *C.A.H.* VIII, p. 313.

²⁶ Livy XXXIX, 21.

²⁷ *Iber.* 43.

²⁸ Appian, *Iber.* 44.

²⁹ *Ibid*.

³⁰ Livy XLIII, 2. There is also recorded, in Livy, *Epit.* XLIII, an abortive rising at this time under one Olonicus (to be identified with the Olyndicus of Florus I, 33, 13), perhaps caused by the prevalent oppression.

³¹ The earlier case of Gades—an allied town—in 199 B.C. will be recalled in this connection.

³² Livy XLIII, 3 ; cf. *C.I.L.* II, p. 242.

³³ The evidence for the Lusitanian war is contained chiefly in Appian, *Iber.* 56–75, supplemented by minor details in Livy, *Epit.* XLVII ff. ; Velleius, bk. II ; Valerius Maximus, bks. VI, VIII ; Florus, bk. I. The material is fully handled by

P. Bosch Gimpera and P. Aguado Bleye in *Historia de España*, cit., pp. 89 ff., and by A. Schulten, 'Viriatus,' in *Neue Jahrbücher für das klassische Altertum* XXXIX (1917), pp. 209 ff. (Spanish edition, 'Viriato,' in *Boletín de la Biblioteca de Menéndez y Pelayo*, 1920, pp. 126 ff., 272 ff.).

[34] Appian, *Iber.* 57. It is sometimes supposed (cf. *Historia de España*, cit., p. 90 f.) that the Ὀκίλη of Appian should refer to the town of Ocila (mod. Ocella) situated in the territory of the Vettones. This involves a mistranslation of Appian, who says clearly 'some overran Libya at large (τὴν ἄλλην Λιβύην), while others besieged Ocili ': and there can be little doubt that Appian refers to the town in Africa called Zelis by ancient authorities (cf. Strabo III, 1, 8), and known to-day as Arzila.

[35] Cf. *Fragm. Hist. Rom.*, 106 ff.

[36] Appian, *Iber.* 69.

[37] *Id.*, 75.

[38] See *C.I.L.* II, 684 (Turgalium), 791 (Caurium), 2435 (Bracara), for examples.

[39] Appian, *Iber.* 71–3 ; Livy, *Epit.* LV.

[40] Excellent maps of the main scene of the Celtiberian war are to be found in Schulten, *Numantia*, I (Karte III), and in the same author's *Geschichte von Numantia* (Munich, 1933) (Map II).

[41] The most detailed ancient account of the Celtiberian war is that of Appian (*Iber.* 45 ff., 76 ff.), much of whose vivid detail is derived from sections of Polybius which are now lost : Polybius was, of course, the contemporary and companion of Scipio Aemilianus, and his authority therefore (even when borrowed) great. Evidence of a more incidental nature is to be found in Polybius, bk. XXXV ; Livy, *Epitomae* ; Dio Cassius, bks. XXII–XXIII (fragments) ; Florus, bk. I ; Velleius, bk. II ; Valerius Maximus, bk. II. Of the modern accounts, Schulten's *Numantia*, vols. I–IV (Munich, 1914–31) is fundamental and exhaustive, though its scope is too wide for the ordinary student : it is to some extent an encyclopaedic study of the history and archaeology of Iberians and Celts in Spain. The same author's *Geschichte von Numantia*, cited above, provides an excellent summary of his great treatise : reference may be made also to F. Behn, *Numantia und seine Funde* (Mainz, 1931)

and to *Historia de España*, cit., where Schulten's evidence and maps are given.

[42] See Schulten, *Geschichte von Numantia*, p. 38 f., with map VI thereto.

[43] *Id.*, p. 39 f.; *Historia de España*, cit., pp. 99 ff.

[44] See Schulten, *Geschichte von Numantia*, pp. 41 ff., with maps III and V thereto; and the same writer's *Numantia*, I, pp. 342 ff.

[45] It is just possible that the Arevaci based their attitude on something in the nature of a tribal federation, unified in their support, if the famous 'Arekratoks' bronze tablet found at Luzaga (*M.L.I.*, p. 171, no. XXXV; figured in *Historia de España*, cit., p. 96) is to be assigned to this period. 'Arekratoks' should refer to the Celtiberian town Aregrada (mod. Agreda, east of Numantia), and among nine other apparent town-names listed on the bronze is that of Lutia, which attempted to assist Numantia during the Scipionic siege (Appian, *Iber.* 94). But the tablet (which is written in Iberian characters) cannot be dated with certainty; and *Historia de España*, cit., p. 96, may be correct in assigning it to the last period of Arevacan resistance *c.* 98 B.C.

[46] The Scipionic 'legend' is strongly marked in Polybius' fragmentary bk. XXXV.

[47] See Schulten, *Geschichte von Numantia*, maps III and VII; *Historia de España*, cit., fig. 114.

[48] Perhaps commemorated in *C.I.L.* II, 3426.

[49] Appian, *Iber.* 80. The Numantine forces were no more than 8000 at the outbreak of war (*id.*, 76).

[50] A good aerial view of Numantia is to be found in *Historia de España*, cit., fig. 142. The relative maps are available in Schulten, *Numantia*, I (Karte V), and *Geschichte von Numantia*, maps III, IV, VII, VIII.

[51] Appian, *Iber.* 97.

[52] The number to which the defenders had dwindled during the siege: see Livy, *Epit.* LV.

[53] Cf. Schulten in *C.A.H.* VIII, p. 322 f.

CHAPTER V

[1] Compare the subsequent activities of Didius in Citerior: Appian, *Iber.* 100.

[2] See Schulten, *Geschichte von Numantia*, pp. 153 ff.; and *J.R.S.* XXI (1931), p. 156 f.

[3] See Albertini, op. cit., pp. 17 ff.

[4] Appian (*Iber.* 100) records, for what the statement is worth, the continued presence of the senatorial commission during the governorship of Didius. The conquest of the Balearic Isles in 122 B.C. by Metellus would also have called for provincial adjustment.

[5] The only narrative of a continuous nature is that of Appian, *Iber.* 99 ff., with isolated references elsewhere.

[6] Cf. Schulten, *Geschichte von Numantia*, cit., p. 151. Bosch Gimpera and Bleye (*Historia de España*, cit., p. 96) incline to the view that the 'Arekratoks' bronze tablet of Luzaga (see ch. IV, note 45) should be attributed to the period of this final Arevacan revolt. Lacking a certain interpretation of the inscription, we can regard it only as evidence (of undoubted importance and interest) for tribal federation falling somewhere between *c.* 140 and 90 B.C.

[7] See Plutarch, *Sertorius*; Appian, *Bell. Civ.*, I; Velleius, bk. II; Florus, bk. II; Livy, *Epit.* XC ff., and *Fragments*, 19–20. The fullest modern account is Schulten, *Sertorius* (Leipzig, 1926): R. Gardner, in *C.A.H.* IX, pp. 318 ff., provides a useful summary, with a warm appreciation of Sertorius.

[8] Sertorius was in fact sent out to Spain as governor of Citerior, but undue emphasis on this fact would obscure the significance of his 'mission'.

[9] He had himself been obliged to bribe the tribesmen around the Pyrenees in order to secure his own safe passage. It is possible that unrest in southern and south-west Gaul had never effectively subsided since the time of the invasion of the Cimbri: see below, note 16.

[10] For the archaeological evidence concerning Castra Caecilia see Schulten, *Sertorius*, cit., pp. 66 ff.

[11] See Plutarch, *Sertorius*, 27.

[12] The adherence of Valentia—a Roman veteran settlement—to Sertorius' cause is worth attention and speculation.

[13] Pompey's first campaign bears some resemblance to the opening campaigns of the two Scipios in and after 217 B.C.

[14] See Schulten, *Sertorius*, cit., p. 121, for the attribution of two of the group of camps at Renieblas to the Celtiberian campaigns of Pompey.

[15] Calagurris . . . ' in fame nihil non experta ' : Florus II, 10.

[16] For Pompey's trophy see Pliny, *N.H.* III, 18 ; VII, 96, and Sallust III, 89. The foundation of Pompaelo (Pamplona) north of the upper Ebro suggests Pompey's extension of regular Roman control during the ' mopping-up ' operations which followed the Sertorian war. It should be realized also that considerable Iberian elements in southern Gaul had necessarily to be dealt with, especially among the Volcae Arecomici of the south-west (see Grenier in *E.S.A.R.* III, pp. 415 ff.). These Iberian influences centred at the modern Montlaurès (two and a half miles north-west of Narbonne), the site inhabited by the ancient ' Neronenses ', whose coinage was the most numerous of the Iberian-inscribed class of Gaul. Archaeology suggests that the occupation of Montlaurès ceased suddenly sometime during the generation after the foundation of Narbo (118 B.C.), and it has been suggested by Hill, *On the Coins of Narbonensis with Iberian Inscriptions* (American Numismatic Society's *Notes and Monographs*, no. 44, 1930), p. 5 f., that this happened during Pompey's general reorganization of Iberian affairs after the Sertorian war.

[17] See R. Gardner in *C.A.H..*, loc. cit.

[18] Cf. Plutarch, *Sertorius*, 6.

[19] *Id.*, 6, 14.

[20] *Id.*, 23 ; cf. Appian, *Mithr.*, 68.

[21] Schulten, *Sertorius*, cit., p. 156.

[22] See *C.I.L.* II, 16 (Myrtilis), 254 (Olisipo), 3744 (possibly recording a descendant) and 3752 (both of Valentia), 3786 (Liria).

[23] Of the favours conferred by Pompey on Spain (see Caesar, *B.C.* II, 18) we know nothing explicit. Possibly they concerned only the areas in which true Roman *nuclei* existed : almost

certainly they were confined mainly to the more romanized districts of the east and south coasts.

[24] Plutarch, *Sertorius*, 6.

[25] Even so, the case of Italica shows that the smaller Roman towns were not sufficiently protected against oppression in times of civil war : cf. Dio Cassius XLII, 15, 16 ; Hirtius, *Bell. Alex.* 48, 64 ; and (for Corduba) Livy, *Epit.* CXI.

[26] See G. H. Stevenson in *C.A.H.* IX, p. 449.

[27] *Historia de España*, cit., pp. 195 ff.

[28] *C.A.H.* VIII, p. 324.

[29] Thus, of the modern works available, L. C. West, op. cit., by his grouping of all products of the Imperial age in all their imposing volume, might suggest that the economic productivity of the Republic was nearly as high, though this would not be true. On the other hand J. J. van Nostrand in *E.S.A.R.* III, pp. 138 ff., confining himself strictly to the Republican period, furnishes a picture which, chiefly because the sources are scantier, is inevitably thin and misleading. Possibly the historico-chronological method of M. Rostovtzeff's *Social and Economic History of the Roman Empire* (Oxford, 1926) might yield the best results.

[30] Justin XLIV, 1, 5-6.

[31] See especially A. Delgado, *Nuevo Método de Clasificacion de las Medallas Autonomas de España* I-IV (Seville, 1871), wherein there is an instructive series of well-engraved plates.

[32] An excellent résumé of the Spanish fisheries (though treated from the Imperial standpoint) is that of M. P. Charlesworth in his *Trade Routes of the Roman Empire* (Cambridge, 1926), p. 157.

[33] Cf. West, op. cit., p. 36.

[34] Delgado, op. cit., I, p. 89.

[35] *C.I.L.* VI, 9677.

[36] Strabo III, 2, 6.

[37] See Delgado, op. cit., I, p. 21 ; II, pp. 131, 254, 261, 308.

[38] See West, op. cit., p. 14 f. ; *J.R.S.* XXI (1931), p. 157 f. Republican references to olive culture occur in *Bell. Hisp.* XXVII, 1 and 3 ; and the coinage of Ulia (Delgado, op. cit., II, p. 322 f.) shows the olive as a constant reverse type.

[39] Diodorus V, 34.

[40] For textiles see West, op. cit., pp. 59 ff. ; *E.S.A.R.* III, p. 141. Tarraco supplies an interesting bilingual inscription (*C.I.L.* II, 4318a=*M.L.I.* vi) ending with the words FVLVIA LINTEARIA.

[41] The question of 'foreign' communities in Spain under the Empire is discussed by E. Albertini, 'Les étrangers residant en Espagne à l'époque romaine', in *Mélanges Cagnat* (Paris, 1912), pp. 297 ff.

[42] T. A. Rickard, 'The Mining of the Romans in Spain', in *J.R.S.* XVIII (1928), pp. 129 ff. ; O. Davies, *Roman Mines in Europe* (Oxford, 1935) ; West, op. cit., pp. 40 ff. ; *E.S.A.R.* III, pp. 150 ff. ; M. Besnier, 'Le commerce du plomb à l'époque romaine', in *Rev. arch.* XII, XIII, XIV (1920–1).

[43] Pliny, *N. H.* XXXIII, 78.

[44] Diodorus V, 36.

[45] Strabo III, 2, 10.

[46] Tacitus, *Ann.* VI, 19.

[47] Strabo, loc. cit.

[48] The references are collected in *E.S.A.R.* III, p. 140.

[49] *Ann. épigr.* 1907, no. 135 ; *C.I.L.* II, p. 323 ; X, 3964.

[50] Cf. Diodorus, loc. cit.

[51] See West, op. cit., pp. 8 ff. ; *E.S.A.R.* III, pp. 141 ff.

[52] Cf. Strabo III, 2, 5.

[53] Cf. Schulten, *Geschichte von Numantia*, Karte II.

[54] III, 39.

[55] *Bell. Hisp.* XXXIII, 1.

[56] Caesar, *B.C.* I, 40.

[57] *C.I.L.* II, 4924–5.

[58] *C.I.L.* II, 4956.

[59] See Hill, op. cit.

[60] See Delgado, op. cit.

[61] Hill, op. cit., p. 122.

[62] Cf. *M.L.I.*, p. 6.

[63] For the bilingual issues of Osicerda see Hübner, *M.L.I.*, p. 42, and Hill, op. cit., p. 99 f.,—an attribution vainly disputed by Vives.

[64] The bilingual coins of Ulterior are discussed at length in *M.L.I.*, pp. 117–36.

[65] *Id.*, p. 73.

[66] Hübner (*M.L.I.*, p. 23) denies the existence of any such reading : but it may be taken as being completely confirmed by Hill, op. cit., p. 36.

CHAPTER VI

[1] See *M.L.I.*, nos. vi, vii ; Hill, op. cit., pp. 39 ff.

[2] See *M.L.I.*, no. xxxia ; Hill, op. cit., pp. 111 ff. ; cf. Pliny, *N.H.* III, 20.

[3] *C.I.L.* II, 3733 (late), 3745, and pp. 500–1.

[4] Pliny, *N.H.* III, 25.

[5] Pliny, loc. cit. (cf. *C.I.L.* II, p. 440) ; *M.L.I.*, no. xlv (cf. no. xliv).

[6] Strabo III, 5, 3.

[7] Cf. *C.I.L.* II, p. 73.

[8] Hübner (*C.I.L.* II, p. 463) emphasizes the 'antiqua simplicitas' of the inscriptions of Carthago Nova.

[9] See, for example, T. Rice Holmes, *The Roman Republic*, III (Oxford, 1923), chapters xvi and xxiv ; *Historia de España*, cit., pp. 243 ff.

[10] Suetonius, *Div. Iul.* 7.

[11] *Id.*, 18.

[12] See Plutarch, *Caesar*, 12.

[13] Cf. Appian, *Iber.* 102 ; Livy, *Epit.* CIII ; Suetonius, *Div. Iul.* 18.

[14] Velleius II, 48, 1 ; Plutarch, *Pompey*, 53.

[15] Caesar, *B.C.* II, 18.

[16] See the reasons propounded by Hübner in *C.I.L.* II, p. 306.

[17] Caesar, *B.C.* I, 86–7 ; II, 21 ; cf. Dio Cassius XLIII, 39.

[18] Cf. Livy, *Epit.* CX ; Dio Cassius XLI, 24 ; Cicero, *pro Balbo*, 19.

[19] See *C.A.H.* IX, p. 707.

[20] Pliny, *N.H.* IV, 117.

[21] See Hübner in *C.I.L.* II, pp. 35, 81 f.

[22] See Hübner, op. cit., p. 112.

[23] Pliny, *N.H.* IV, 117; see also *C.I.L.* II, p. 9, and *Suppl.*, p. 804.

[24] Pliny, loc. cit.

[25] Pliny, loc. cit., and cf. III, 10. Ebora appears as a *municipium* in *C.I.L.* II, 114—of uncertain date.

[26] Caesar, *B.C.* II, 21.

[27] It is sometimes supposed that Augustus' triple division of Spain, i.e. the carving out of the separate province of Lusitania, was no more than the end of a process actually begun by Caesar. But the passage upon which this theory is based (Caesar, *B.C.* I, 38, 1–2) is, as has been remarked by Albertini, op. cit., p. 22 f., not capable of bearing this interpretation. The temporary command of Caesar's three *legati* over separate armies was a strategic and not an administrative circumstance : indeed, the moment that saw the tripartite division under Augustus saw the automatic reduction in the number of ' military ' governors from three to two, as a corollary of the subdivision. The creation of Lusitania is studied by E. Kornemann, ' Die Entstehung der Provinz Lusitanien ', in *Festschrift zu Otto Hirschfelds sechzigstem Geburtstage* (Berlin, 1903), pp. 221 ff.

[28] Suetonius, *Div. Iul.* 42.

[29] See *C.I.L.* II, pp. 152, 191 (and Suppl., 851), 210, 213 ; Hübner suggests the modern Baëna as the site of Itucci.

[30] See *C.I.L.* II, pp. 125, 131, 166, 176. The status of Italica in Caesar's time is uncertain : the use of the word ' municeps ' by the unknown author of the *Bellum Alexandrinum* (52, 4) cannot be used as good evidence for municipal status, as ' municeps ' can be used loosely to mean ' fellow townsman '. Coins prove that Italica was a *municipium* under Augustus.

[31] For the text, and photographs, of the Lex Ursonensis see *Historia de España*, cit., after p. 416 ; and, for discussion, E. G. Hardy, *Three Spanish Charters* (Oxford, 1912), pp. 7 ff.

[32] Cf. Hill, op. cit., pp. 78–9.

[33] Cf. Hill, op. cit., p. 74 f. : the coins show the steps by which Dertosa was promoted. The name of Barcino has been omitted from the list of Caesar's colonies and municipalities, for, though its full title was later *Colonia Faventia Julia Augusta Pia* (*Barcino*) (see *C.I.L.* II, p. 599), it is impossible to analyse the successive stages of privilege which this complex title suggests.

[34] Pliny, *N.H.* III, 25.

[35] The opposing arguments are well summarized by Rice Holmes, op. cit., III, pp. 553 ff. See also E. G. Hardy, *Six Roman Laws* (Oxford, 1911), pp. 136 ff.

CHAPTER VII

[1] See Strabo III, 3, 7; 4, 18, for the existence of matriarchy and primitive systems of barter in the N. and N.W.; and, for brigandage, Florus II, 33.

[2] See especially R. Syme in *American Journal of Philology*, 1934, pp. 293–317, where the principal sources of antiquity (Florus II, 33; Orosius VI, 21, 1–11; Dio Cassius LIII–LVI) are acutely criticized, and the views of D. Magie, in *Classical Philology*, 1920, pp. 323–39, are modified: Syme's theories are summarized in *C.A.H.* X, p. 343 f.

[3] Whatever was the precise date of Augustus' ceding of Baetica to the Senate (see p. 137), there seems to be no reason to doubt that in 26 B.C. there were two armies in Spain, corresponding to the original two provinces, and probably each composed of three legions; cf. Syme in *J.R.S.* XXIII (1933), p. 22 f., and in *American Journal of Philology*, loc. cit.

[4] The sources for the campaign record the activities of Antistius' army only. But as Syme, *American Journal of Philology*, loc. cit., has shown, two armies must have converged and co-operated in the conquest of so large an area as Callaecia–Asturia. The annals of the campaign of 26 B.C. recorded in Florus and Orosius, and derived from Livy's Epitome, were possibly drawn originally from Augustus' own *De Vita Sua* which, as Suetonius tells us (*Divus Augustus*, 85), went no further than the Cantabrian war, i.e. 26 B.C. The poverty of detail in Florus and Orosius for the Asturian war of 25 B.C. is thus natural.

[5] Orosius VI, 21, 7.

[6] See Dio Cassius, LIII, 26, 1. The founding of Emerita is to be associated with P. Carisius. In virtue of his command over a field-army Carisius struck a series of coins, in silver and copper, on which the new foundation is clearly attested; see

H. A. Grueber, *Coins of the Roman Republic in the British Museum*, II, pp. 394 ff. ; III, Plate CII.

[7] Dio Cassius, LIII, 29, 1–2 ; LIV, 5, 1–3 ; 11, 2–7.

[8] Velleius II, 90, 4.

[9] Florus II, 33.

[10] This reconstruction has received admirable treatment at the hands of E. Albertini, *Les divisions administratives de l'Espagne romaine* (Paris, 1923) ; see especially pp. 25–41 therein. It should be noted that the use of the words *in . . . utraque Hispania* in the *Res Gestae Divi Augusti*, V, 28, has led to the opinion (once supported by Mommsen) that the tripartite division of Spain came about, not under Augustus, but in Tiberius' reign. But this, as has been pointed out, is merely a survival of traditional phraseology, invested with a new meaning ('imperial and senatorial Spain ') after the transference of Baetica to senatorial control.

Further useful material bearing on the subject is to be found in J. J. van Nostrand, *The Reorganization of Spain by Augustus*, in the University of California Publications on History, 1916. See also Pliny, *N.H.* IV, 118.

[11] LIII, 12.

[12] Cf. Albertini, op. cit., pp. 25 ff.

[13] This change is attested by Pliny's description of the Spanish provinces in *N.H.* IV, 112–13, as compared with the information, derived from Agrippa's map, which occurs in *N.H.* IV, 118.

[14] By inference from the material contained in Pliny, *N.H.* III, 8–9, 16–17.

[15] The dates of these boundary modifications, both those affecting Callaecia–Asturia and those involving the eastern limit of Baetica, are controversial. For the change in the north, Albertini (op. cit., p. 34) inclines to the years 3–2 B.C. on the strength of an inscription (*Ephemeris Epigraphica* viii, 280) attesting the presence of a *consular* legate, Paullus Fabius Maximus, at Bracara at that time ; this view, of course, implies the assumption that under Augustus the legate of Lusitania was invariably of praetorian rank. Syme (*American Journal of Philology*, 1934, p. 300 f.) suggests the year A.D. 9, when the number of legions in Spain was reduced ; it might be held, against this date, that reduction of military strength was more

likely to happen after a few years of consolidation had elapsed. Albertini's dating receives indirect support from the probable date of the changes in the south : a year not after 2 B.C. is suggested by milestones (*C.I.L.* II, 4701, 4703) and upheld by an inscription (*C.I.L.* VI, 31267) set up by Baetica to Augustus as *Pater Patriae* ‘quod beneficio eius et perpetua cura provincia pacata est.’ That ‘pacata’ refers to nothing more than peaceful settlement of the eastern boundary (previously liable to banditry) is perhaps to be inferred from the analogy of the coins struck in 16 B.C. in Rome in honour of Augustus ‘quod per eum res publica in ampliore atque tranquilliore statu est ’ (H. Mattingly, *Coins of the Roman Empire in the British Museum*, I, p. 17, no. 91); in 16 B.C., and for years before it, the state was far from being in jeopardy.

[16] *C.I.L.* II, 2029.

[17] *C.I.L.* II, 3270.

[18] *C.I.L.* II, 3271 (suspected by Hirschfeld and apparently by Dessau, who did not include it in his *Inscriptiones Latinae Selectae*).

[19] *N.H.* III, 19.

[20] Cf. Albertini, op. cit., p. 40.

[21] Suetonius, *Divus Iulius*, 7.

[22] Pliny, *N.H.* III, 7 (for Baetica) ; III, 18 (for Tarraconensis); IV, 117 (for Lusitania).

[23] Strabo III, 4, 20.

[24] For analysis of the accounts of Pliny and Strabo see Albertini, op. cit., pp. 43–81. The military areas of northern Spain, and the transitional area of central Spain, are there called *dioiceseis*. Although there is no particular virtue in this name (which, indeed, is found in its proper Greek form as an equivalent of the Latin *conventus* : cf. Cicero, *ad Fam.* 13, 53, 67), the nomenclature may be preserved as long as it helps to signify a territorial subdivision essentially different from that of the *conventus*.

[25] Cf. *C.I.L.* II, 2634.

[26] For the importance of this official in Tarraconensis, cf. *C.I.L.* II, 2477 (of A.D. 79) and Hübner ad loc.

[27] Cf. *C.I.L.* II, 2643. This connection of Asturia with Callaecia for financial purposes tends to confirm the modification of Strabo's account of N.W. Spain adopted above (p. 143).—

The procurator in Asturia-Callaecia would be in charge of the collection of taxes and of the conduct of the mines in that district, besides supervising (see Strabo, loc. cit.) the payment of the legionaries stationed there.

[28] Tacitus, *Annals* III, 13 (Piso, under Tiberius); IV, 13 (Vibius Serenus, under Tiberius); Pliny, *Epp.* III, 4, 2, etc. (Classicus, under Trajan).

[29] Cf. G. H. Stevenson in *C.A.H.* X, p. 192 f. The extension of this system to Spain is reflected in the elder Pliny's use of material derived from Agrippa's returns.

[30] *Portoria* of 2 per cent in Spain are attested by *C.I.L.* II, 5064.

[31] The various forms of taxation to which Spanish provincials were in theory liable are summarized by M. Torres in *Historia de España*, cit., p. 394.

[32] *Res Gestae Divi Augusti*, II, 8. Stevenson, *C.A.H.* X, pp. 206 ff., reminds us that Augustus' policy was bound to be affected by his obligation to settle in colonies the soldiers demobilized after the Civil War.

[33] Cf. Pliny, *N.H.* III, 7, 18; IV, 117 (material derived from Agrippa's returns).

[34] Synoecism is attested in the case of Curiga by *C.I.L.* II, 1041 (perhaps post-Augustan). A comparison of Pliny's figures (*N.H.*, loc. cit.) with those of Ptolemy (*Geographia*, II) indicates a decrease in the number of rural communes.

[35] For Augustan colonies in Spain, cf. Hübner, *La Arqueología de España*, pp. 174 ff. For Emerita, see J. R. Mélida, *Arqueología Española*, cit., *passim*; E. S. Bouchier, *Spain under the Roman Empire* (Oxford, 1914), pp. 132 ff.

[36] Early Bracara–Asturica road: *C.I.L.* II, 4775–6 (imperial title curious, but probably early Augustan). Southern parallel route: *id.*, 6215 (2 B.C.). Road north from Bracara: *id.*, 4868 (A.D. 11–12). Celsa–Ilerda road: *id.*, 4920–3 (8–7 B.C.). N. Spain–Aquitania road: *id.*, 6344 (A.D. 13). Carthago Nova roads: *id.*, 4936–8 (7 B.C.), 4946. Castulo roads: *id.*, 4931 (8–7 B.C.). Via Augusta: *id.*, 4701 (2 B.C.), 4703–11. There appears also to have been Augustan road-work at Nertobriga in A.D. 8 (*id.*, 4686), doubtless the beginning of a Caesaraugusta–Emerita route.

[37] For the legions in Spain, cf. R. Syme, ' Some Notes on the

16

Legions under Augustus,' in *J.R.S.* XXIII (1933), pp. 14 ff., and
Hübner in *C.I.L.* II, Supplement, pp. lxxxiv ff. IV *Macedonica*
in Cantabria: *C.I.L.* II, 2916 (Burgos). VI *Victrix* in Asturia-
Callaecia: *C.I.L.* XI, 395. Detachments (*vexillationes*) at
Caesaraugusta, Carthago Nova and Italica: see the coins of
these mints in Vives, op. cit. *Praefectus orae maritimae*: cf.
C.I.L. II, 4138, 4217, 4224–6, 4239, 4264, 4266.

CHAPTER VIII

[1] *Annals* I, 2.

[2] Much of the material contained in this chapter is taken
from the present writer's summary in *J.R.S.* XXIV (1934),
pp. 31–42.

[3] Cf. Vives, op. cit., IV, p. 131, no. 10. This has been (quite
unnecessarily) construed as a sign of fulsomeness with an eye
to Tiberius' favour: see Hill, *Ancient Coinage of Hispania Citerior*
(American Numismatic Society's *Notes and Monographs*, no. 50),
p. 49 f.

[4] That the altar at Tarraco was built during Augustus' reign
is shown by Quintilian VI, 3, 77. For Tiberius' permission to
erect a temple to Augustus at Tarraco (A.D. 15), cf. Tacitus,
Annals I, 78. The altar at Emerita is attested only on posthumous
coin-types: cf. Vives, op. cit., IV, p. 64, nos. 39 ff.

[5] Convenient summaries of the material concerning the pro-
vincial assemblies will be found in E. G. Hardy, ' The Provincial
Concilia from Augustus to Diocletian,' in *Studies in Roman
History* (First Series), second edition, and F. F. Abbott and
A. C. Johnson, *Municipal Administration in the Roman Empire*
(Princeton, 1926), pp. 162 ff. For Emperor-worship in general,
see Lily R. Taylor, *The Divinity of the Roman Emperor* (Connecticut,
1931).

[6] *C.I.L.* II, 3271, recording a *curator* of Titus who was
'Flamen Augustalis in Baetica primus,' implies (if it is accepted)
that a regular Baetican *concilium* was only set up under the
Flavians. See above, p. 195 f.

[7] For accusations conveyed by means of *concilia*, cf. Pliny,
Epp. VII, 33, 4 (against Baebius Massa, procurator in Baetica);
III, 9 (against Caecilius Classicus, proconsul of Baetica). For

the later connection between Emperor and *concilia*, cf. *C.I.L.* II, 4201 (Hadrian), 4055 (Antonine), and *Digest*, XLVII, 14, 1 (Hadrian).

[8] *C.I.L.* II, 114-15 (Ebora) ; 742 (Norba,—A.D. 219).

[9] Cf. *C.I.L.* II, 339 (Collippo).

[10] Priest of *Divus Augustus* : *C.I.L.* II, 473 (Emerita), cf. 3620 (Saetabis). Cult of dead and living emperors : *id.*, 1133 (Italica), 3709 (Mago). Cult of dead Emperor and Roma : *id.*, 2782 (Clunia), cf. 2426 (Bracara).

[11] See the present writer in *J.R.S.*, XXIV (1934), pp. 31 ff.

[12] For the origin and development of the Augustal Sevirate, see A. M. Duff, *Freedmen in the Early Roman Empire* (Oxford, 1928), and Lily R. Taylor, ' Augustales, Seviri Augustales and Seviri : a Chronological Study,' in *Transactions of the American Philological Association*, XLV (1914), pp. 231 ff.

[13] For Anticaria, see *C.I.L.* II, 2038 (A.D. 14-29) ; for Olisipo, *id.*, 194 ; for Urgavo, *id.*, 2105.

[14] *C.I.L.* II, 2107.

[15] Tiberius, *C.I.L.* II, 6080, 5930, 1113 ; Gaius and Lucius Caesar, *id.*, (?)2422, 2109 (2 B.C.), 5093. Ulia, *id.*, 1525-9.

[16] For dynastic propaganda by means of the Spanish coinage, see the present writer in *J.R.S.* XXIV (1934), pp. 31 ff.

[17] Material for studying the distribution of native and Roman cults in Spain is contained in the indexes of *C.I.L.* II, supplemented by additional references in *Ephemeris Epigraphica* ; a convenient summary of the relative inscriptions may be found in ch. ix (' La Religión Anterior al Christianismo ') of *Historia de España*, cit. ; see also G. Heuten, in *Revue Belge de Philologie et d'Histoire*, XII (1933), pp. 549 ff., XIV (1935), pp. 709 ff., and in *L'Antiquité Classique* III (1934), p. 281 f.

[18] Seneca, *Apocolocyntosis*, 3.

[19] The ' Altar ' issues struck at Lugdunum, perhaps under the authority of the Gallic *concilium* (see H. Mattingly, *Coins of the Roman Empire in the British Museum*, I, p. cxii f.) are not a parallel instance ; this series was purely federal in character, and proceeded from a single central mint, while the Spanish issues were struck locally, at a large number of towns, and could only have been rarely connected with the activities of the *concilia*.

[20] Cf. *J.R.S.* XXIV (1934), p. 36.

[21] *Ibid.*, p. 38.

[22] Hübner, *M.L.I.* xlix ; cf. Tacitus, *Annals*, IV, 45.

[23] For a fuller discussion of this question, see *J.R.S.* XXIV (1934), pp. 39 ff.

[24] *C.I.L.* II, 2422.

[25] Cf. *C.I.L.* II, 432, 5238.

[26] *Id.*, 2633 (A.D. 27), 5762–3 (2 B.C.), 5792 (A.D. 40), 2958 (A.D. 57).

[27] *Id.*, 1343 (A.D. 5).

[28] *Id.*, 760.

[29] See *C.I.L.* II, 172 (Aritium Vetus).

[30] *C.I.L.* XI, 395.

[31] See, e.g., those of Capera in Lusitania : *C.I.L.* II, pp. 100 ff.

[32] Tacitus, *Annals*, I, 11.

CHAPTER IX

[1] For Roman methods of road-construction see J. R. Mélida, *Arqueología Española* (Barcelona, 1929), p. 263 f. ; and the same author in pp. 571 ff. of *Historia de España*, cit. Reference should also be made to C. E. van Sickle, ' The Repair of Roads in Spain under the Roman Empire', *Classical Philology* XXIV (1929), pp. 77 ff.

[2] *C.I.L.* II, 4651.

[3] *Id.*, 4712, 4715 (A.D. 35–6), 4713–4.

[4] *Id.*, 4749, 4773–4, 4777–8.

[5] *Id.*, 4904–5 ; for Augustus, cf. 6344.

[6] *Id.*, 4883 ; *Ephemeris Epigraphica* viii, 210a, 219, 295.

[7] *C.I.L.* II, 4935 ; cf. Tacitus, *Annals*, VI, 19.

[8] *C.I.L.* II, 4945 (A.D. 33), 4947.

[9] *Id.*, 6233–4 (A.D. 40).

[10] *Id.*, 4639–40 (A.D. 40).

[11] *Id.*, 4716 ; 6208 (A.D. 39).

[12] *Id.*, 6199 (? A.D. 47).

[13] *Id.*, 4644–5 (A.D. 46–50).

[14] *Id.*, 4750; 4770–1; 6217.

[15] *Id.*, 4875 (A.D. 44–5).

[16] *Id.*, 4901.

[17] *Id.*, 6324 (A.D. 44–5).

[18] *Id.*, 4954, 6242, 6324a (?)

[19] *Id.*, 4652, 4657.

[20] *Id.*, 4683.

[21] *Id.*, 4719–20, 4734.

[22] *Id.*, 6236.

[23] *Id.*, 4888.

[24] Strabo III, 4, 20.

[25] Cf. M. P. Charlesworth, op. cit., p. 153.

[26] See H. Mattingly, *Coins of the Roman Empire in the British Museum*, I, p. xviii.

[27] *Id.*, pp. cxliii f., cl. The ' Agrippa '-type *asses* have been assigned to the reign of Tiberius (*id.* p. cxl) and also to that of Claudius (see H. Willers, *Geschichte der römischen Kupferprägung* (Leipzig, 1909)), but in the opinion of the present writer they belong most naturally to the time of Gaius.

[28] Vives, op. cit., IV, p. 14, has professed to recognize the portrait of Claudius on an autonomous issue of Ebusus, but this attribution must be regarded with great caution, as imperial portraiture on the coins of Spain is notoriously unsatisfactory.

[29] Hübner, *C.I.L.* II, p. 267, assigned the municipal promotion of Abdera to the reign of Tiberius, but there is no good evidence, numismatic or otherwise, for this view.

[30] A. Momigliano, *Claudius : the Emperor and his Achievement* (Oxford, 1934), p. 64 f.

[31] For Baelo Claudia, cf. *Itinerarium Antoninianum*, ed. Cuntz, Leipzig, 1929, p. 62. It has been argued by Albertini, op. cit., p. 61 f., that the feminine adjective *Claudia*, attached to the name Baelo, presupposes the ellipse of a feminine noun, namely, *colonia*. But it might be answered that the very frequency of the feminine termination in its relation to colonies may well have resulted in its occasional extension to the names of non-colonial communities. Albertini's theory is not recognized by Momigliano, loc. cit. For Claudionerium, cf. Ptolemy, *Geographia*, II, 6, 21.

[32] Occasional grants of *civitas* may have been conferred *viritim*, i.e. individually, as happened under Claudius at Ammaia : cf. *C.I.L.* II, 159.

[33] For analysis and dating of Pliny's material, see Albertini, op. cit., pp. 49 ff., and especially pp. 59 ff. In connection with the African reform of Mauretania, note the one-time dependence of Zilis, in Tingitana, upon Baetica : cf. Pliny, *N.H.*, V, 2.

[34] Vives, op. cit., IV, p. 56, nos. 17–19. One of the coins described by Vives appears to have Seianus' name erased.

[35] *C.I.L.* II, 3269.

[36] *Id.*, 1569.

[37] *Id.*, 3114.

[38] *Id.*, 1302.

[39] *Id.*, 1518.

[40] *Id.*, 1281, 1392.

[41] See, for the Astures, *C.I.L.* XI, 395 ; for the Balearic Isles, *id.*, 1331 (a *praefectus pro legato*).

[42] Cf. Suetonius, *Galba*, 9. For the isolation of VI *Victrix* in Spain cf. Josephus, *Bellum Iudaicum* II, 16, 4, with Tacitus, *Histories* V, 16.

[43] Cf. Suetonius, *Otho*, 3.

[44] *Histories* I, 78.

[45] A certain correction for the 'Hispaniensibus' of the Codex Mediceus.

[46] The 'Lingonibus' of the MSS. is clearly wrong, and the word 'universis' following upon the mention of Hispalis and Emerita perhaps suggests the enfranchisement of a district (rather than a town) on a wide scale : hence Lipsius' reading 'Lusonibus' is preferable.

[47] Progress in the economic and commercial life of imperial Roman Spain is reviewed in ch. XI.

CHAPTER X

[1] Much of the material for this chapter is derived from the brilliant paper by R. Knox McElderry, 'Vespasian's Reconstruction of Spain', in *J.R.S.* VIII (1918), pp. 53 ff. ; IX (1919),

pp. 86 ff. (cited as ' Addenda ')—a basic work to which every student of this subject must be deeply indebted.

[2] See McElderry, op. cit., p. 54, n. 3.

[3] E. Darquenne and others, ' Les Gouverneurs de la Lusitanie et leur administration ', *Latomus*, 1938, pp. 261, 276.

[4] The promulgation in the first instance of an imperial edict may be deduced from the *Lex Salpensana*, ch. 23.

[5] *N.H.* III, 30,—*iactatum* meaning ' much criticized.'

[6] *Contra Apionem* II, 4, 40.

[7] *Caesares* IX, 8.

[8] Published with a full analytical commentary in E. G. Hardy, *Three Spanish Charters* (Oxford, 1912), and more briefly in F. F. Abbott and A. C. Johnson, op. cit., pp. 369 ff. The texts are also available as *C.I.L.* II, 1963 (=*I.L.S.* 6088) and 1964 (=*I.L.S.* 6089), photographic facsimiles being provided in *Historia de España*, cit., after p. 416.

[9] McElderry, op. cit., p. 65, argues against the view, held by Mommsen, that *Latium minus* was in the case of Spain specially restricted to the *duumviri* alone, the *aediles* being excluded from advantage; and rightly calls attention to *C.I.L.* II, 1610 (=*I.L.S.* 1981; cf. Abbott and Johnson, op. cit., p. 364), wherein an aedile of Igabrum (Cabra) acts as the spokesman of his municipality in returning thanks to Vespasian for the favours conferred.

[10] Cf. *Lex Salpens.*, ch. 21; *C.I.L.* II, 1610 (' municipes . . . c<ivitatem> R<omanam> c<onsecuti> cum suis . . .'); McElderry, op. cit., p. 65, n. 6.

[11] See Abbott and Johnson, op. cit., pp. 5 ff.

[12] See McElderry, op. cit., p. 76.

[13] To each newly created ' Latin ' community was assigned, for the membership of its privileged inhabitants, one of the regular Roman tribes; all ' Latins ' enfranchised in any one town were therefore added to the same tribe. It was not until Claudius' reign that the imperial tribe was thus employed, uniformly over the whole Empire; by the time of Vespasian the practice was absolutely regular.

[14] We may compare Gellius' quotation (XVI, 13) of Hadrian's speech about Italica : ' mirari se ostendit, quod et ipsi Italicenses, et quaedam item alia municipia antiqua . . . , cum suis moribus

legibusque uti possent, in ius coloniarum mutari gestiverint.'
Clearly a value came to be set upon incorporation as the Principate grew older : for a *municipium* to seek colonial status was in
its way as remarkable as for a free town to seek municipal
status.

[15] See Hübner, *C.I.L.* II, Suppl., p. 876, on *C.I.L.* II, 1953.

[16] *C.I.L.* II, 1041 (transference of *pagi* from Contributa
Iulia ; cf. McElderry, op. cit., p. 80, n. 3) ; Ipsca now becomes
' municipium contributum ' (cf. Hübner on *C.I.L.* II, 1572).

[17] *C.I.L.* II, 1423 (*I.L.S.* 6092 ; Abbott and Johnson, op.
cit., p. 365).

[18] *C.I.L.* II, 2322 ; cf. Pliny, *N.H.* III, 10, for its former
status.

[19] The references are summarized by McElderry, op. cit.,
p. 81, n. 7.

[20] Sisapo, Mirobriga, Vettonia ; cf. McElderry, op. cit.,
p. 85, and ' Addenda ', pp. 92 ff.

[21] Cf. *C.I.L.* II, 1052 (Munigua).

[22] See n. 20 above.

[23] There is no evidence to prove that *tributum capitis* was
imposed on Spain ; but such negative evidence cannot be overlooked : see too McElderry, op. cit., p. 92 f.

[24] Tacitus, *Hist.* IV, 8.

[25] Cf. McElderry, op. cit., pp. 55 ff. ; U. P. Boissevain,
De Re Militari Provinciarum Hispaniarum aetate imperatoria
(Amsterdam, 1879), pp. 31 ff.

[26] This view receives support from Rostovtzeff, op. cit., p. 201.

[27] McElderry, op. cit., p. 63, n. 4.

[28] *Div. Vesp.* 16.

[29] See McElderry, op. cit., p. 87, and cf. J. B. Mispoulet,
' Transformations de l'Espagne durant les trois premiers siècles
de l'empire romain ' in *Revue de Philologie* XXXV (1910), pp.
301 ff.

[30] McElderry, op. cit., pp. 59 ff., and ' Addenda ', pp. 89 ff.

[31] McElderry, op. cit., pp. 82, 89 ; cf. T. Frank, *Economic
History of Rome*[2] (London, 1927), p. 461, n. 24.

[32] *C.I.L.* II, 3271 : suspect by O. Hirschfeld, *Kaiserliche
Verwaltungsbeamten*,[2] p. 6, n. 2 ; and omitted by Dessau from

his *I.L.S.* See in general K. Scott, *The Imperial Cult under the Flavians* (Stuttgart, 1936).

[33] Tacitus, *Annals* IV, 37.

[34] e.g. the prosecutions of Massa and Classicus : Pliny, *Epp.* VII, 33, 4 ; III, 9, 4.

[35] It is unnecessary for present purposes to examine fully the controversy aroused by the interpretation of *C.I.L.* II, 2477, by Hirschfeld, op. cit., p. 377. This inscription from Aquae Flaviae, recording the names of ten neighbouring communities in some unspecified enterprise or act of gratitude (see above, p. 195), bears also the names of L. Arruntius Maximus, *procurator Augusti* ; of Vespasian and his sons ; of the legate of Citerior ; and of the commander of Legio VII. Hirschfeld's theory that Arruntius was governor of Asturia-Callaecia as a province within a province scarcely seems acceptable : such a rank would not justify, by itself, the primary position of Arruntius' name on the inscription : the imperial names, or at any rate that of the governor of Citerior, would in any case have taken precedence if precedence was a question involved ; and there are examples of the time of Nerva and Trajan for procurators of Asturia-Callaecia, whose duties can hardly have extended beyond local finance or jurisdiction (*C.I.L.* XII, 1855 ; V, 534 ; cf. McElderry, op. cit., p. 86). Moreover, as McElderry has pointed out, the milestones of Asturia-Callaecia bear the name of the governor of Citerior at this period (op. cit., p. 86), not that of a quasi-independent procurator. The administration of Asturia-Callaecia had long been, and was still to be, a difficult problem : not until a much later period was an independently organized system set up (cf. Mispoulet, op. cit.). Finally, we know in fact that Vespasian appointed subordinate *praefecti* (for whose authority cf. C. Baebius in Moesia under Tiberius, *I.L.S.* 1349) for Asturia and Callaecia : *C.I.L.* II, 3271 (cf. the later 4616) ; these officers were probably forerunners of the later and regular procurators of whom Arruntius may be regarded as an example.

[36] See the preceding note.

[37] *C.I.L.* II, 4814 ; cf. 4838, 4854, 6224.

[38] *N.H.* XXXIII, 78.

[39] For the flow of Roman gold to India, see references collected by H. Mattingly, *Coins of the Roman Empire in the British Museum*, I, p. xxii, n. 3.

[40] *C.I.L.* II, 5181 (*I.L.S.* 6891) ; text and facsimile in *Historia de España*, cit., after p. 336 ; a translation, from which quotations are here used, appears in *E.S.A.R.* III, pp. 167 ff.

[41] See the preceding note.

[42] See *E.S.A.R.* III, p. 173, as against Rostovtzeff, op. cit., p. 294.

[43] This circumstance explains the growing importance of officials such as the *procurator metallorum* at Vipasca, who, over a century later, has acquired wide authority in both judicial and financial affairs, being styled *iustissimus* and *rationalium vicarius* : see L. Wickert, *Bericht über eine zweite Reise zur Vorbereitung von C.I.L.* II, Suppl. 2 (Berlin, 1931), pp. 9 ff.

[44] Other examples of imperial procurators supervising Spanish mining-communities come from the Rio Tinto mines (*C.I.L.* II, 956—Nerva, A.D. 97), the Montes Mariani (*id.*, 1179–? Antonine period), and the Callaecian *metallum Albocolense* (*id.*, 2598).

CHAPTER XI

[1] The subject of imperial propaganda has recently been fully discussed : see M. P. Charlesworth, ' The Virtues of a Roman Emperor : Propaganda and the Creation of Belief ' (London, 1937) ; H. Mattingly, 'The Roman Virtues,' in *Harvard Theological Review* XXX (1937), pp. 103 ff. ; and, for the early second century after Christ, the same author's *Coins of the Roman Empire in the British Museum*, III (London, 1936). Of the second-century panegyrics on the ' Golden Age,' the most famous is that of Aelius Aristides, εἰς Ῥώμην.

[2] For a detailed account of the Empire at large see Rostovtzeff, op. cit., pp. 180 ff., and Tenney Frank, *Economic History of Rome* [2] (London, 1927), pp. 347 ff., 442 ff.

[3] *C.I.L.* II, 4751 (?), 4781–2 (A.D. 104), 4796 (A.D. 104), 4797, 4855, 5560 (A.D. 104), 6214, around Bracara.

[4] *C.I.L.* II, 4667, 4672–3, 4677–80, 4684–5 (A.D. 98), 6203 (?), 6206 (A.D. 98–9) (Emerita–Salmantica) ; 4890–1, 4893, 4898–4900 (Emerita–Caesaraugusta) ; *Ephemeris Epigraphica* ix, 412 (Emerita–Metellinum) ; *C.I.L.* II, 4933–4 (A.D. 98–9) (Castulo–

Iliberris) ; 4725 (Via Augusta) ; *Ephemeris Epigraphica* viii, 253 (Hispalis).

⁵ *C.I.L.* II, 760–1, of A.D. 105–6 (Trajan's permission had first to be obtained).

⁶ *C.I.L.* II, 2478 (A.D. 104).

⁷ See note 2 above : add *C.A.H.* XI, pp. 491 ff.

⁸ e.g. the indexes to *C.I.L.* II ; West, op. cit.

⁹ The principal excavation-reports available (for Italica, Emerita, Tarraco, Emporium) are listed in *C.A.H.* XI, p. 905. See also G. C. Maxwell in *Archaeological Journal*, LVI (1899), pp. 245 ff.

¹⁰ Cf. *C.I.L.* II, 1640–1 (Iliturgicola, after A.D. 103).

¹¹ Cf. *C.I.L.* II, 5560 (Caldas de Mombuy, A.D. 104), 6003 (Mago, A.D. 98–103).

¹² See Rostovtzeff, op. cit., *passim* ; Frank, op. cit., especially pp. 476 ff. ; and, for the wider issues involved, W. E. Heitland, *The Roman Fate* (Cambridge, 1922) ; *Iterum, etc.* (Cambridge, 1925) ; *Last Words, etc.* (Cambridge, 1928) ; *Repetita, etc.* (Cambridge, 1930), against which should be noted H. M. Last in *C.A.H.* XI, pp. 435 ff. (ch. XI, ' Rome and the Empire.').

¹³ Cf. Heitland, *Iterum, etc.,* cit., p. 17.

¹⁴ Cf. E. Albertini in *C.A.H.* XI, p. 501.

¹⁵ See I. A. Richmond, ' Five Town-walls in Hispania Citerior ', in *J.R.S.* XXI (1931), pp. 86 ff. (Lucusaugusti, Asturica, Legio, Caesaraugusta, Barcino).

¹⁶ See here E. Albertini, ' Les étrangers résidant en Espagne à l'époque romaine ' in *Mélanges Cagnat* (Paris, 1912), pp. 297 ff. Gauls are commonest between Emporium and Saguntum ; Africans at Tarraco and Barcino ; Orientals at Olisipo, Abdera, Malaca (cf. *C.I.L.* II, p. 251). The vast profusion of Greek names is to be attributed to the prevalence of men of servile or libertine stock engaged in trade and industry : cf. A. M. Duff, *Freedmen in the Early Roman Empire*, cit., Ch. I.

¹⁷ Cf. *E.S.A.R.* III, p. 198, for references (where *C.I.L.* II, 323 should read *C.I.L.* II, p. 323). It seems that the shrewd people of Malaca kept the export of fish-sauce in their own hands : cf. *C.I.L.* VI, 9677.

¹⁸ See T. Frank, ' Notes on Roman Commerce ', in *J.R.S.* XXVII (1937), pp. 72 ff. ; cf. *C.I.L.* II, 2029 ; VI, 1625b, 1935, 29722.

[19] See the Ostia mosaic, *Bullettino della Comm. arch. comunale*, 1912, pp. 103 ff.; and, in general, *E.S.A.R.* III, pp. 175 ff.

[20] See West, op. cit., pp. 85 ff.; *E.S.A.R.* III, p. 185.

[21] *C.A.H.* VIII, p. 325.

[22] Tacitus, *Ann.* I, 2.

[23] See J. Gagé, 'Saeculum Novum, etc.' in *Transactions of the International Numismatic Congress, 1936* (London, 1938), pp. 179 ff.

[24] Cf. Heitland, *Last Words, etc.*, cit., p. 23.

[25] See H. M. Last, *C.A.H.* XI, p. 472 f.

[26] Cf. *Lex Malacitana*, ch. 51; and Pliny, *Epp.* X, 113.

[27] Rostovtzeff, op. cit., p. 140 f.; cf. Lex Ursonensis, chh. 71 f., and Pliny, *Epp.* I, 19, X, 113.

[28] There seems to be no need to postulate the town-*versus*-peasantry feud for which Heitland has argued. A silent and discontented rural population would surely have shown itself before long as a rebellious one. In Italy, at least, the peasantry were fast losing in initiative themselves: see Pliny, *Epp.* III, 19.

[29] *C.I.L.* II, 1122 (Italica) is possibly Trajanic. Titus' *curator* (above, p. 193) was probably, as we have seen, an officer appointed specially to deal with business caused by the Flavian reform. Other and later examples of *curatores* in Spain are given by *C.I.L.* II, 1673, 4112, 6283: cf. *C.I.L.* II, p. 251.

[30] Heitland, *Iterum, etc.*, cit., has rightly emphasized the demoralizing effect of periodic municipal benefactions. Local benefactions in Spain do not appear to have been prompted by shortage in the local *annonae* until a later period (cf. *C.I.L.* II, 53, 1532 (?), 1573, 2782, 3586, 4468: though note that Cartima is in debt about the Flavian period, *C.I.L.* II, 1956–7), and the recorded benefactions (summarized in *E.S.A.R.* III, p. 148; and *C.I.L.* II, 21, 183, 1305, 1614, 3240, 3364, 5489, 6102,—including water-supply, baths, theatres, games) fall similarly in mainly subsequent times.

[31] See here *Historia de España*, cit., pp. 525 ff., 565 ff.; Bouchier, op. cit., pp. 93 ff., 153 ff.

[32] H. M. Last, in *C.A.H.* XI, p. 475.

INDEX

KEY TO THE PLATES (I–IV) OF COINS

PLATE I. GREEKS AND IBERIANS

1. Silver *drachma* imitated from those of Rhode. *Obv.*, POΔHT[ων]; female head. *Rev.*, rose.

2. Emporion. Silver *drachma*. *Obv.*, female head with dolphins. *Rev.*, [EM]ΠOPITΩN; pegasus.

3. Roman Republic. Silver *denarius*. *Obv.*, OSCA; male head of Celtiberian type (consciously copying that of no. 4, following). *Rev.*, DOM · COS · ITER · IMP ·; pontifical emblems. Struck by Cn. Domitius Calvinus *c.* 39–37 B.C., perhaps at Osca, during his Spanish campaign among the Cerretani.

4. The Oscans. Silver *denarius*. *Obv.*, in Iberian characters, *Hol*; male head. *Rev.*, in Iberian characters, *Holscan*; horseman with lance. (Presumably the prototype of Livy's *argentum Oscense.*)

5. Cese (Cesse). Silver *denarius*. *Obv.*, male head. *Rev.*, in Iberian characters, *Cese*; horseman with palm and led horse.

6. ? The Arevaci. Silver *denarius*. *Obv.*, male head. *Rev.*, in Iberian characters, *Areqraq*[*s*] (?=Aregrada); horseman with lance.

7. The Segobriges. Silver *denarius*. *Obv.*, M (=S); male head. *Rev.*, in Iberian characters, *Seqbriges*; horseman with lance.

8. The Segobriges. Bronze *as*. *Obv.*, M; male head, with palm and dolphin. *Rev.*, legend and type as no. 7.

9. The Ilergetes. Bronze *as*. *Obv.*, male head. *Rev.*, in Iberian characters, *Iltrd*[*a*] (=Ilerda); wolf.

PLATE II. ROMANIZATION IN THE CENTRE AND EAST

1. Arse (=Saguntum). Bronze *as*. *Obv.*, in Iberian characters, *Valcacaldo* (? magistrate's name); 'Roma'-head. *Rev.*, in Iberian characters, *Arse*; prow.

2. **Valentia.** Bronze *as.* *Obv.*, T · AHI[us] · T[iti] · F[ilius] · L[ucius] · TRINI[us] · L[uci] · F[ilius] · Q[uaestores] · ; 'Roma'-head. *Rev.*, VALENIA ; cornucopiae across thunderbolt.

3. **Clunia.** Bronze *as.* *Obv.*, II ; male head with dolphin· *Rev.*, CLOVNIOQ[om] ; horseman with lance. Note the retention of the traditional Iberian *rev.* type on this coin and on nos. 4–6.

4. **Segovia.** Bronze *as.* *Obv.*, C L (? magistrate's initials) ; male head. *Rev.*, SEGOVIA ; horseman with lance.

5. **Bilbilis.** Bronze *as.* *Rev.*, BILBILIS ; horseman with lance. (*Obv.*, with head and name of Augustus, not shown.)

6. **Osca.** Bronze *as.* *Obv.*, AVGVSTVS DIVI F[ilius]. ; head of Augustus. *Rev.*, V[rbs] V[ictrix] OSCA ; horseman with lance.

7. **Osicerda.** Bronze *as.* *Obv.*, in Iberian characters, *Usecrth* ; elephant trampling serpent. *Rev.*, OSI[cerda] ; figure of Victory. (The *obv.* type is imitated from *denarii* struck by Caesar in Gaul, 50–49 B.C.)

PLATE III. AGRICULTURE AND INDUSTRIES, ETC.

1. **Acinipo.** Bronze *semis.* *Obv.*, bunch of grapes and star. *Rev.*, ACINIPO ; ears of corn.

2. **Ilipense.** Bronze *as.* *Obv.*, ear of corn. (*Rev.* not shown.)

3. **Castulo.** Bronze *as.* *Obv.*, male head and hand. *Rev.*, in local alphabet, *Castulo* ; sphinx.

4. **Gades.** Bronze *as.* *Obv.*, Herakles-head. *Rev.*, inscriptions in Phœnician characters ; two tunny-fish.

5. **Ulia.** Bronze *as.* *Obv.*, female head, with crescent and palm. *Rev.*, VLIA ; olive branches and berries.

6. **Ilercavonia (Dertosa).** Bronze *as.* *Obv.*, MVN · HIBERA · IVLIA · ; ocean-going merchant ship. *Rev.*, ILER-CAVONIA ; light river-boat.

7. **Ebora.** Bronze *as.* *Obv.*, PERM[isu] · CAES[aris] · AVG-[usti] · P[ontificis] · M[aximi] · ; head of Augustus. *Rev.*, LIBERALITATIS IVLIAE EBOR[ac] in wreath.

8. **Carteia.** Bronze *semis.* *Obv.*, CARTEIA ; turreted female head. *Rev.*, D[ecreto] D[ecurionum] ; seated fisherman.

PLATE IV. COLONIES UNDER THE EMPIRE

1. Emerita. Silver *denarius*. *Obv.*, IMP[erator] · CAESAR · AVGVST[us] ; head of Augustus. *Rev.*, P · CARISIVS · LEG[atus] · PRO PR[aetore] · ; trophy of arms. Struck by P. Carisius, on behalf of Augustus, at Emerita.

2. Emerita. Bronze *semis*. *Obv.*, PERM[isu] · CAES[aris] · AVG[usti] · ; head of Augustus. *Rev.*, C[olonia] A[ugusta] E[merita] LE[giones] V, X ; 'eagle' and two standards.

3. Emerita. Silver *denarius*. *Obv.*, as No. 1. *Rev.*, P · CARISIVS · LEG · PRO PR. (see no. 1) ; gate and wall of the city, inscribed EMERITA. Struck by P. Carisius, on behalf of Augustus, at Emerita.

4. Emerita. Bronze *as*. *Rev.*, AVGVSTA EMERITA ; yoke of oxen marking boundaries. (*Obv.* not shown.)

5. Celsa. Bronze *as*. *Obv.*, COL[onia] · VIC[trix] · IVL[ia] · LEP[ida] · ; bust of Victory. *Rev.*, PR[aefecti] · QVIN-[quennales] · M · FVL[vius] · C · OTAC[ilius] · ; type as on no. 4.

6. Celsa. Bronze *as*. *Obv.*, C[olonia] · V[ictrix] · I[ulia]· CELS[a] · AVGVS[tus] ; head of Augustus : all in wreath. *Rev.*, L · COR[nelius] · TERR[enus] · M · IVN[ius] · HISP-[anus] · II VIR[i] ; bull.

7. Tarraco. Bronze *as*. *Rev.*, C[aius] · L[ucius] · CAES[ares] · AVG[usti] · F[ilii] · C[olonia] · V[ictrix] · T[riumphalis] · ; Busts of C. and L. Caesar. (*Obv.* not shown.)

8. Tarraco. Bronze *semis*. *Rev.*, C[olonia] · V[ictrix] · T[riumphalis] · T[arraco] · ; altar, surmounted by palm. (*Obv.* not shown.)

9. Caesaraugusta. Bronze *dupondius*. *Obv.*, TI[berius] · CAESAR · DIVI AVG[usti] · F[ilius] · AVG[ustus] · PONT-[ifex] · MAX[imus] · TR[ibunicia] · POT[estate] · XXXIII ; seated figure of Tiberius. *Rev.*, C[olonia] C[aesar] A[ugusta] LEG[io] IV LEG VI LEG X M · CATO L · VETTIAC-[us] II VIR[i] ; *vexillum* between two standards.

Note.—Of the coins illustrated below, the following are in the British Museum : Pl. I, 8, 9 ; Pl. II, 2 ; Pl. III, 1, 5, 7 ; Pl. IV, 5, 6, 7, 8, 9. Pl. II, 1 and 7, are in the collection of Mr.

E. T. Newell, President of the American Numismatic Society:
Pl. ii, 6, and Pl. iii, 6, are in the Cabinet of the Kaiser-Friedrich-
Museum, Berlin; the remainder are in the Ashmolean Museum,
Oxford. The author's sincere thanks are due for the casts
from which the plates were photographed.

The Mayflower Press, Plymouth. William Brendon & Son, Ltd.

PLATE I

COINS OF SPAIN
Greeks and Iberians
(See Key)

PLATE II

COINS OF SPAIN
Romanization in the Centre and East
(See Key)

PLATE III

COINS OF SPAIN
Agriculture and Industries
(See Key)

PLATE II

COINS OF SPAIN
Romanization in the Centre and East
(See Key)

PLATE III

COINS OF SPAIN
Agriculture and Industries
(See Key)

PLATE IV

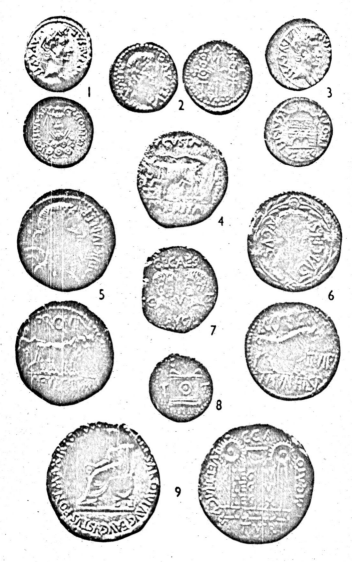

COINS OF SPAIN
Imperial Colonies
(See Key)

PLATE V

THE LADY OF ELCHE
(Louvre)
Greco-Iberian work of the late fifth or fourth century B.C.

PLATE VI

TARTESSIAN (TURDETANIAN) WARRIORS
(Louvre)
Relief from Urso (modern Osuna) of about the third century B.C.

PLATE VII

LUSITANIAN WARRIOR
(Museu Etnologico, Lisbon)
Probably of the second century B.C., and a type of Viriathus'
troops

PLATE VIII

NUMANTIA FROM THE SOUTH

PLATE IX

ROMAN AQUEDUCT AT TARRAGONA
Built in the early Imperial period

PLATE X

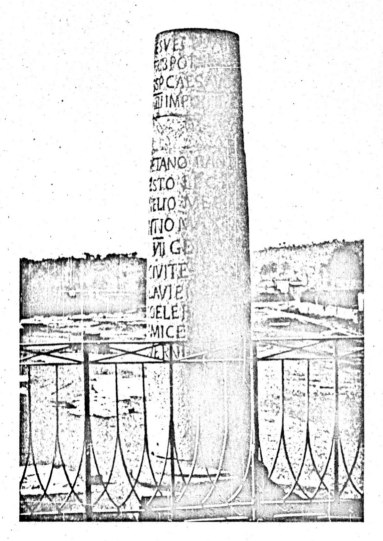

ROMAN INSCRIPTION AT AQUAE FLAVIAE
(CHAVES)
Set up under Vespasian (see *C.I.L.* II, 2477), this records
a joint enterprise undertaken by neighbouring communities

PLATE XI

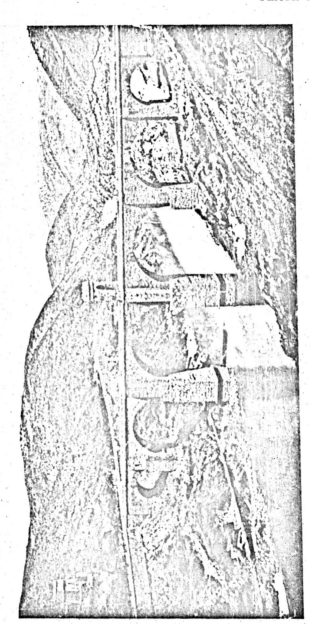

ALCANTARA : THE ROMAN BRIDGE OVER THE TAGUS
(prov. Cáceres)

PLATE XII

BRONZE BOAR

(Scale about one-quarter)

Found in a Roman slag-heap, in the Huelva–Seville district
of Spain, with a hoard of Roman coins buried about the
middle of the first century B.C. Probably Spanish work of
the period 100–50 B.C.

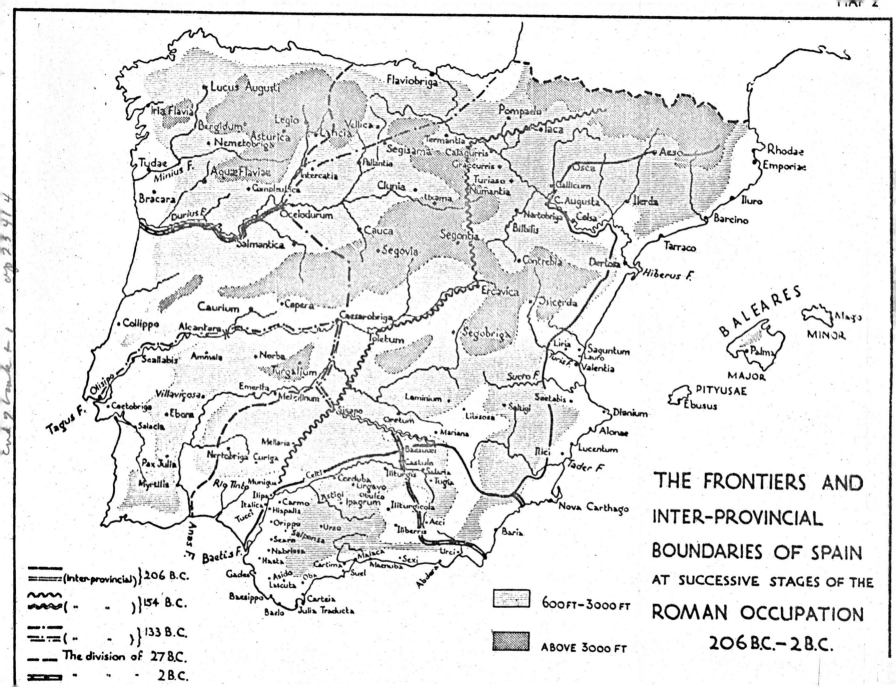

THE FRONTIERS AND
INTER-PROVINCIAL
BOUNDARIES OF SPAIN
AT SUCCESSIVE STAGES OF THE
ROMAN OCCUPATION
206 B.C.–2 B.C.

(Inter-provincial) 206 B.C.
(" ") 154 B.C.
(" ") 133 B.C.
The division of 27 B.C.
" " 2 B.C.

600 FT–3000 FT

ABOVE 3000 FT

MAP 3

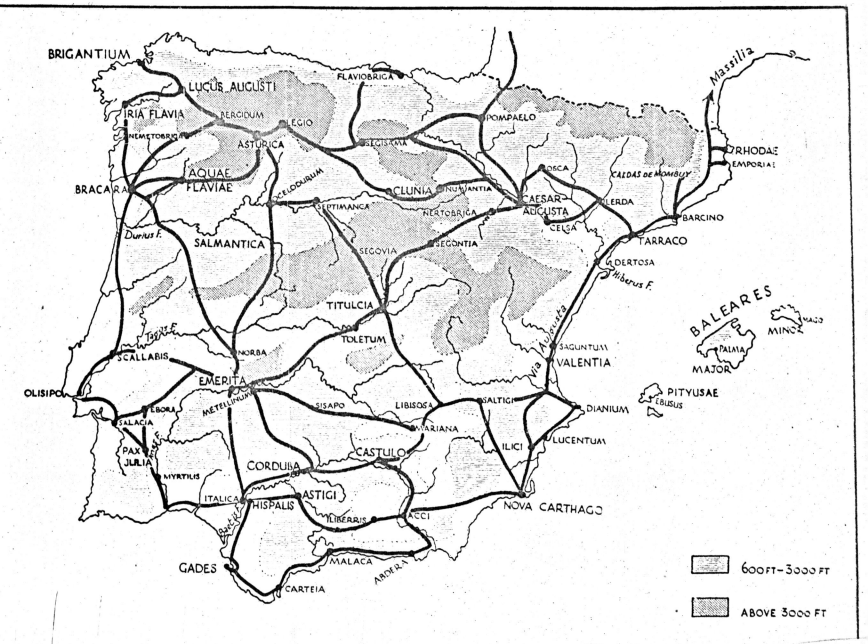

THE PRINCIPAL ROMAN ROADS OF SPAIN